THE MUSIC
WE MAKE

THE MUSIC
WE MAKE

Michelle Rene DeBellis

Paradise Publishing

Paradise Publishing

paradisepublishinginc.com

Second Edition Printed June 2022
ISBN 9798986167206 (hardcover) ISBN 9798986167213 (paperback)
ISBN 9798986167220 (ebook)
Book design by Michelle Rene DeBellis and Paradise Publishing

Paradise Publishing

For my husband,
Domenico DeBellis,
whose own sacred song inspired this story.

Contents

Part 1: Santiago DeAngelo

Part 2: New Perspectives

Part 3: Who Do You Love?

Part 4: Sober

Part 1
Santiago DeAngelo

CHAPTER 1

Pain Introduces Itself

D AD WALTZES MOM about the ballroom of our family's annual New Year's ball. Her sequined dress is a fire of flashes as they move in perfect sync around the piano where I play. All eyes are on Mom. She has the kind of beauty that lasts forever. I play the final notes of the song and Dad dips her with a flourish for the crowd. He gives me an approving nod and she joins me on the piano bench.

"You sounded great, son."

"You think I still got it?"

"Absolutely."

Around us the party continues. When the DJ fires up the dance music again I nudge Mom and stand. "I'm gonna head out now."

"I wish you wouldn't go." She grabs my hand and meets my eye. "I only have you for a few more days, *Vita Mia.*"

"Mom, in 6 months I'll graduate with my big degree,

and be back in Redlands for good."

We join arms and head out of the room towards the front entry way.

"Where's the party again?" she asks.

"Not far. It's at Abby Wilson's parent's place in the canyon."

"Oh, Abby. No wonder you're leaving us, you've had your eye on that dangerous blonde for years now."

"Exactly." I wink and she chuckles. "Besides, you've got two more of your kids here tonight. We wouldn't want to confirm their suspicions that I'm your favorite."

She smiles, but it fades as she touches my arm. "I don't like this feeling I have, Santiago."

"What feeling?"

"Like there's something you're not telling me."

My stomach clenches. "We'll talk about it tomorrow."

"Okay, but promise me you won't drive if you have too much to drink tonight."

"I'll Uber home if I do."

"No, call me. I'd love to escape the party for half an hour and put the top down on the Lexus."

"You're nuts. You're the only one I know that drives with the top down in the middle of winter."

"Its Southern California! Besides, it's the only cure for my hot flashes. And I'll let you pick the music." Her face is playful once again and she hugs me, squeezing me three times like she's done for the last twenty-two years.

"Not sure I'm gonna call. But I love you, Mom."

THE THING IS, I do call. Well before midnight. I guess the party didn't hold my appeal after a group of Abby's friends told me she's engaged.

Abby finds me out by the turquoise lit swimming pool contemplating my escape. She has a hot-pink New Year's feather boa around her neck. Her blue eyes glow in the light of the pool.

"I'm sorry, Santi, I should have told you sooner I was engaged, but we're still friends, right?"

"That's all we ever managed to be."

"Any New Year's resolutions?"

"Don't need any. I'm right on track."

"But what about your music? You don't know how much I miss hearing you sing."

"Yeah, me too." I'm about to tell her more when the sliding glass door opens and a drunken hoard of former high school buddies head to the beer keg shouting my name.

"Happy New Year, Abby. I gotta go. Say goodbye to the guys for me." I give her a quick kiss on the cheek and walk away.

FIFTEEN MINUTES LATER, Mom pulls up to the curb in her black Lexus convertible. She's got a scarf wrapped around her head and tucked into the collar of Dad's topcoat. "Your father will be so glad you're coming home. He's been bragging about you apprenticing for lead architect all night."

"I bet," I say, as I climb into the car.

Mom pulls away from the curb and I choose my song, Rachmaninov's piano concerto no 2. I crank it up loud and rest my arm on the center console beside hers. We drive along the forested canyon road for a few minutes before she turns the sound down.

"You don't really want to go to work for your dad, do you?"

"Mom, the road!"

She turns her eyes back to the road and slows for a tight turn. I look out the open top. The crescent moon is as thin as my desire to admit the truth.

"Is it because you'd rather work for another firm? I know how your father can be."

"I don't know that I want to be an architect at all."

Her face expresses shock as it moves back and forth between me and the road. "But you're four and a half years into a five-year degree. Don't you think you're just exhausted from your finals?"

"That's not it. Can we just turn the music back on?" I reach for the knob, and she swats my hand away.

"I always knew you'd regret choosing your father's plans over your music."

"He made me feel like that was a long shot and it seemed like you agreed with him."

"You know I only went along with things because you seemed so sure."

"It was the only way for Dad to see me."

She slaps the steering wheel. "It's not too late for you to change your mind, but you have to graduate!"

She takes a turn a little too fast and I lean into her.

"I will graduate. I get that much."

"After that, we'll just figure it out. I'll help you do whatever it takes."

She grabs my hand in confirmation of the promise. We both glance at our hands and in that moment an SUV squeals around the bend. Its headlights are blinding as it swerves into our lane. Mom screams. I grab the wheel and jerk us hard to the right. It isn't enough. The speeding SUV strikes her corner of the car.

Pain introduces itself.

Our convertible crumples into the SUV.

Air bags explode.

I smell the sweet scent of antifreeze mixed with the pungent odor of brake pads.

Both horns blare making it impossible to think.

A fire erupts in the SUV, creating a kaleidoscope of color in the crushed windshield of our car.

I scramble out the open top to escape. But mom isn't moving. I run to her side of the vehicle and find her leaning into the buckled frame of the car. When I touch her head, I feel the warmth of blood that's soaking through her scarf.

Adrenaline floods my limbs but doesn't offer the strength I need to open the damaged door. The fire is spreading and sharpens my thoughts.

I reach over the door to move her seat back and make space, but a partially inflated airbag blocks my way. I pry a broken piece off the frame and use its jagged edge to rip the thick bag. My guts feel like they're being torn open as I hinge my weight over the door to move the seat. It slides back and her head lulls forward. When I try and lift her, I notice the hump of broken bone in my right forearm and release a roar of pain as I wrench her over the door. Mom's limp in my arms. I pivot and her gown catches on the wreckage. We both go down. Her head hits the asphalt with a sickening crack. It's all I can do to move her weight off me, but I have to get us further from the two flaming cars. I drag us both along the cold road until whooping sirens close in and a man runs towards us.

"You're a Goddamn hero, kid."

With that, I surrender to my pain.

CHAPTER 2

My Pain is All I Have to Offer

PAIN WAKES ME. I twitch and jerk. A chemical smell permeates my senses. Little pinpricks of light: orange, blue, and red stand out against the shadows of the dark hospital room. I focus on my breath. This is the third surgery I've woken from since my arrival. According to hazy recollections, they've just installed titanium plates and screws in my right forearm to reassemble the broken bones. In the first surgery, to repair the internal bleeding in my guts, I'd awoken to my own shrieking—my body reeking of iodine and anesthesia. The second surgery, to repair my broken nose and jaw, I'd woken from screaming again. That's when a kind nurse taught me to breathe and settle myself, so that waking from the third surgery, I breathe to a count and accept the pain. I close my eyes and recall the light leaving my mother's. My eyes snap open. My right arm throbs above me, strung to a pole.

Will you still be able to play the piano? I ask myself.

My guts feel like the surgeon took a chain saw to them. I focus on the clock above the door. The little hand just above the 4. The big hand on the 5. I have to think about what that means, and *when* it means they'll bring another pain pill. Two more hours. Fuck, I can't wait more than one.

A shape passes the open door in the hallway. "Santi, oh Santi, you're awake." The voice, full of tears, reaches me like sunshine at the mouth of a cave.

"Lucy?" I'm shocked by the gravel in my voice. "Where's Mom?"

My little sister's brown eyes well with tears. Her petite form approaches. All five foot two of her. Her short cinnamon brown hair is cut longer in the front and hangs in an uncharacteristic greasy curl around her chin.

"Oh, Santi it isn't good." Lucy drops her tiny face into her tiny hands and sobs.

I twist the sheets in a tight fist. "Is she alive, Luce?"

Lucy sucks back tears and tells me Mom's in the ICU at a nearby hospital that's home to a team of renowned neural surgeons. She's in a coma, has been for the last four days. But there's zero brain activity.

I bolt up along-side pain and fear. "It's my fault, isn't it?"

"No—the other driver—"

"I mean, Mom wouldn't have been in the car."

"That's what Dad keeps saying, and the doctor said, something . . . about the way you moved her?" She looks down at her hands.

The sickening crack I heard when Mom's head hit the asphalt plays over and over in my mind as the pain from my surgical incisions are set on fire like the vehicles we escaped from. I peer over at the poster of pain to the right of my bed. It shows escalating facial expressions of physical distress 1 through 10. None exist for the anguish of guilt. And yet, I fear the pain Dad is in somehow surpasses my own.

"How's Dad?"

Lucy looks up. "It's hard to tell, he's been camped out at the hospital. Everyone's there since they're not sure how long she has." Lucy chokes up again. "If you're okay, I kind of want to go back."

"Yeah, you should totally go. But, Luce—" my voice catches "—has anyone come to see me?"

She smears her tears across her face. "Mariano and Uncle Carl were here while you were in the first round of surgery. They wanted to stay but the doctors induced a coma to help you heal."

"What about Dad?"

"It's just that Mom's situation is so serious. I know he would have come if it wasn't for that."

But we both know she's wrong. That I've slipped into that place where Dad doesn't see you. A place I've worked like hell to avoid.

Of course you have, after what you did to his wife.

My mother. His wife. Who Dad called—*Vita Mia*—my life. Though Mom called *me* that. Not him.

Thing is, I'm Dad's third son, and most of my life he thought he already had what he needed in my two older brothers: two sons to take over DeAngelo and Sons Architectural Firm. A company that defines him. Really, I think he gave me up to me to Mom at birth. (And she'd accepted me greedily.) But that never stopped me from wanting to be a part of their club, or spending the last four years ensuring a way in.

I'M RELEASED FROM Loma Linda University hospital on

the seventh day and Lucy drives me to Arrowhead Regional in Colton. My fear of seeing Mom and the family ignites my pain. Lucy looks tiny in the driver's seat of Dad's BMW sedan. She has a matted knot of hair at the back of her head and smells like a day-old sandwich. We slip into exhausted silence as I clutch my bag full of pain meds.

MOM'S HOSPITAL ROOM is fronted in glass and covered with a beige curtain that Lucy zips back. We enter the open sliding glass door. Mom's body is upright, powered by a multitude of tubes in a state-of-the-art hospital bed in the left corner of a large grey room. I see Mom, and I can't breathe. My ears ring. Her head is swollen hideously, the right side of it shaved. And the smell—I gag on undertones of rotting flesh. My nose says she's gone so the steady rise and fall of her chest trips me out.

"Lucy, will you leave me with her a while?"

She wheels me to the bedside. I'd wanted to walk into the hospital, but the moment I'd climbed out of the car in the parking lot I'd known I couldn't trust my strength to stay standing. Lucy had gone for a wheelchair, and I know now that was the right choice. I grasp one of Mom's bloated hands, resting my forehead against it long enough to lose time.

A while later, Dad joins me. His suit is crumpled but his posture is erect, cologne attempts to mask his ripe odor. My wounds scream that it is time to take another Norco, but my pain is all I have to offer Mom.

Dad glares at me. "I'd like to be alone with my wife."

"Dad?"

He stares at Mom.

"Dad?"

He traces her face.

I stand, wobble, and throw my arms around him. Dad's arms shoot up to keep from hugging me back, but I bury my face in his neck. "It's my fault. I'm sorry."

He lays a death grip on my triceps and shoves me back. "I'm not ready to forgive you," he says.

I stagger into my wheelchair and attempt to escape from the room, but my right arm is gimp in a cast and the chair wheels in a circle.

"Lucy, come and help your brother."

She steps out from behind the curtain.

I drop my head as my sister pushes me out. "You gotta get me outta here, Luce, I can't breathe."

I DON'T SLEEP that night, just sit awake in my old bedroom at my parent's house imagining my father awake at her bedside.

Shouldn't we be there together?

NEXT MORNING, LUCY wheels me to the family waiting room. Decision time. Life support or a natural death. The room is a battlefield between hope and despair. Doctors brainwash my family in groups. By the end of the day, I'm the only holdout in hope's camp. Dad's only let the charade go on this long because he can't bear to make the decision he knows is his to make.

At 11:23 p.m., my father asks my Uncle Carl to perform the sacrament of the Last Rites. Six of us join hands in a circle during the prayers. My uncle—my mother's older brother and the Monsignor at our church—anoints my mother's forehead with the holy chrism oil. It fills the room with the fragrance of balsam. He then says a prayer and offers the blessed host to each of us in turn. First my father, then my brother Mariano. When it's my turn, I clamp my mouth shut and shake my head. My uncle stands before me, his fit form a close match to my own. He pleads silently with his eyes—eyes too tired with grief for their usual smile to make an appearance. The lines in his pale face are deeper than I've seen them before. When I won't give in, he makes the sign of the cross over me. At the end of the line, he calls for God to receive his servant, Ana DeAngelo. The family prays the rosary. I merely move my lips while I envision strangling the chief neurologist with a blood pressure hose for his effort in convincing my family a natural death was the best choice. We needed more time and his hard facts and statistics pressured us before we were ready. With his approval a nurse powers off the life support. Moments later, Mom's body ceases. The nurse checks her watch and scribbles something on a chart. Chills spread over my arms. I look at Lucy's where the hair also stands on end. Her eyes get huge when they meet mine, *did you feel that too*? they say.

Dad asks to be alone with her body. The others amble out. I leave with them but hang back in the hall. Dad zips the curtain closed. I stand just outside the closed curtain, unable to peel my eyes off his shadow behind it.

Dad's breathing gets ragged, and he collapses in a bawling heap on the floor. He'd had to stay so strong for the family. But now his strength gives out. My throat constricts. I step closer and grip the corner of the curtain. He wails in ugly spurts. I'm ready to rip it away and lie down beside him until I remember his words, *I'm not ready to forgive you.*

I leave him where he lays.

AT HOME, IN my old bedroom, I slump into the faded brown recliner my mother stuffed in here when grandpa died. It's worn leather still smells like Pop's vanilla tobacco. I avoid the mirror on my left. The itch of my hairy face and the pressure around my eyes tell me what I'd find there. I skip the next dosage of Norco and antibiotics.

Pain doubles its power. I curl into the recliner, as if it were the lap of my grandfather himself, until I'm delirious enough to call out to Mom like she's in the next room.

"What the hell's going on in here?" Lucy throws open the bedroom door.

"Get out of here."

"Why are you sweating like that?"

"Leave me alone."

"I'll never leave you alone, Santi."

The timer on my phone sounds. Lucy picks it up. It reads PILL TIME. She shakes the bottle. It's only half empty.

"Have you been taking these? Why aren't you taking these? You've had three major surgeries. You need to take these."

"I want . . ."

Lucy—Norco bottle in hand—closes the distance between us and kneels at the foot of the recliner. "What do you want, Santi?" The look in her face says she'll do anything to help me.

But how to explain the desire to let your physical pain equal your emotional agony.

"I just have to suffer. What else can I do?"

"No, no. Even I know that's not true. Mom wouldn't want that." She twists the cap off the bottle and hands me a pill. I put up two fingers. She passes another with a glass of water that I drain. "I'm going to take care of you, Santiago."

"It's not your job."

"I'm gonna take care of all of us," Lucy says.

When pain is dethroned, the sense of relief—coupled with Lucy's assurance—activates a new longing for the pills. Physical pain feels repugnant to me, and the bliss each pill holds becomes my purpose.

Time feels strange to me. Sometimes it stretches into endless waking hours and sometimes it's swallowed up by whole days of sleep.

Awake, I detect my father outside my bedroom door and hold my breath. Dad moves on down the hall. My face burns.

Next day, I pop like a coiled spring when Lucy hits me with a book. I glance at the title and read the word GRIEVING in a cursive font. I look away. Lucy sets it on the TV tray beside my recliner and takes the empty bowl. She holds the book again. "If you're not gonna read it, fine. If you don't want to get up, fine. But you can't cry all the time. You're keeping me up nights."

"I cry?"

"I wake up at night to the sound, and then *I* start to cry." She wipes her eyes with the back of her hand. "I'm making you a sandwich."

"I won't eat it." The pills have zeroed out my desire for food. My appetite only returns when I let the time between doses stretch a little.

Her head shakes softly. "I'll get you a glass of water."

I gulp down the water with some extra Norco and two Ambien.

I set the half empty glass on the nightstand and wait for the sleeping pills to weave their magic. But a trippy thing's happening lately, the opiate buzz wires me up, so I'm still awake in the Ambien's hypnotic hold. Thirsty, I guzzle what remains in the large green glass. At the bottom I find a pond Lucy and I used to swim in at our grandparent's house. I imagine us as kids emerged in green water with sunshine streaming through in golden drafts. But despair floods the vision and leaves me at the bottom of the grey water alone. I hold my breath until there's a burning in my chest that feels like it could kill me.

Do you want to die?

Yes, but not like this. I need a real plan. Help me, Mom!

That's when tiny bubbles tickle my feet on their way to the surface of my illusion. What is that? Laughter?

No.

Music?

Yes!

Faint, original music. The melody of a song bursts to life. I suck down a huge breath and clutch four musical notes as I emerge from the depths. My arms are plastered with goose bumps. My thoughts spin out of control.

The music is my salve in the days that follow. I transpose the sound I heard so many times I lose track of the original. Were the notes filled with love? Or was the tone a somber demonstration of my pain? My eyelids weigh more than these questions.

All I know is this, the notes didn't come from me. Mom sent them. She sent them to keep me alive.

CHAPTER 3

A Calendar of Daily Self-Loving Affirmations

2017 IN SHORT

FOR OVER A month I bide my time in bed, healing and gaining my strength while I wait for the cast to be removed from my right arm. Mom's music in my mind manifests my revival and I can't wait to get at the piano when I'm alone in the house to make sense of the music.

One morning, when I hear Dad and Lucy leave for their day at school and work, I fold back the blankets and creep from my room. The walk to the piano in the ballroom zaps my energy, and I slump at the keys. When I press them with my right-hand, pain shoots from my wrist to my elbow. I suck air through my teeth and rub my forearm.

I try again. This time, I tune into the ethereal notes and it eases the physical pain. I picture the notes as iridescent bubbles, but each key I play bursts the bubble I was reaching for.

I can't do this, Mom.

My heart rate jumps.

I take a deep breath and play scales. The routine calms me. *I can still play.* But my right arm aches so badly I decide that's enough for the day.

Back in bed, let down by the difficulty of transforming the intangible, I obsess on the *ifs* surrounding the accident. *If* I hadn't called her that night from the party. *If* I hadn't left home at all that night. *If* I'd seen the oncoming car sooner and pulled harder to the right. *If* I hadn't dropped Mom when I wrenched her from the car.

The guilt is a stone that rests heavy on my chest. To temper its weight, I take a Norco to ease my pain and a Valium to take the edge off the opiate high so I can lie still and enjoy the bliss that dances through my limbs.

The next morning must be the weekend because neither Dad nor Lucy have left the house by their usual time. Lucy comes in and pulls the shades.

"Let's get you out of here today," she says.

I groan at the brightness and pull a pillow over my face. She moves the pillow away and smiles down at me.

"How do you do it, Luce? Don't you miss her?"

She sits down beside me on the bed. "I didn't even know what it meant to miss someone until now. But Mom always said, 'If you need love, be love.'"

My eyes well. *Why can't I be more like Lucy?*

Dad strides down the hall.

Lucy calls out to him. "Dad, will you come in here a minute?"

I tense, but he doesn't break his stride. "I'm late for a client meeting."

Since I've been home from the hospital my

conversations with Dad have been limited and uncomfortable for us both. Lucy has been attempting to alleviate that discomfort to little end.

I put the pillow back over my head and whimper into it. She lays her hand on my back.

"People make bad choices when they lose the people they love," she says.

I move the pillow aside. "It's like Dad is trying to punish me for taking her from us."

"I think that's what people do when they don't forgive each other."

"Can you blame him, Luce? I can't forgive me either."

"If you don't, you'll never heal."

DAYS LATER, LUCY places a calendar of daily self-loving affirmations on the nightstand beside my bed. She's ripped the pages away to the current date. I stare at the message February 9, 2017, holds—*I am worthy of love*. With Mom's love I always felt worthy. I want to feel worthy again.

BY MARCH 8—*I am authentic, true, and expressive*—I've made it to the piano at least a dozen times. The Norco boosts my energy now, like it was a caffeine pill, and its effect on me is morphing. Instead of a gauzy happiness I could face my emotions with, there's an angry edge waiting in each pill's high that bullies my weaker emotions aside. Especially when Dad walks down the hall without so much as pausing at my door. By the time his car is down the driveway each day I'm on my way to the piano.

BY APRIL 10—*I honor my own life path*—the song is taking shape beside my eagerness for living. The daylight has stretched so much longer I forget to retreat to my room before Dad is home from work. I feel him watching me at the piano and the hair rises on the back of my neck.

"Is this what you're doing with your life now?" he says.

I swivel atop the piano bench to face him where he stands, ten feet away, in the wide entry to the room. "I think so." Inside, I'm torn between the anger I feel that this is how he begins our first real conversation, and my gratitude he's begun it at all.

"I'm writing a song for Mom." I spin back around and play the intro while twisting my neck to watch his face for approval.

Dad walks towards me. "Lucy tells me, you think your mother sent you the notes."

I nod with enthusiasm ready to share the miracle while I play some of the prettiest parts of the melody. But as he gets closer, he crosses his arms and I read in his face that he isn't amused. My heart drops.

"You plan on getting back to school any time soon?"

"I need more time," I tell him as he stops near the bench and looks down on me.

"Time is our most important resource. I'd hate to see you waste it in here."

"I'm finding myself in here."

I honor my own life path.

"We can't let what's happened derail our future."

"It already has, Dad."

"That's why you should get back to school as soon as possible."

The dynamic that has emerged between us has me questioning my motivations to go back to school at all.

I plunk middle C over and over while I consider things.

Was I ever becoming an architect for myself? Or just to gain his approval?

I still want his approval. I'm just not sure I can trust myself to decide what my true-life path is under the influence of both my pain and my pain killers. But he's not the kind of guy you explain something like that to.

Mom would have understood, and her love was unconditional. I wish Dad's was. But now we've both lost her love and are struggling to overcome our anger in its void.

"Stop that!" Dad says and swats my hand to halt the incessant plunking of middle C.

I rub my face with both hands. "I just need more time, Dad."

"I hear that, but getting back to work has been the best thing—"

"This is my work right now." I spent too much of my youth deflecting his disapproval of my music to have patience for it now.

"I didn't come in here for a fight, son."

"What did you come in here for?" I say as I stand to meet his height with a more abrasive tone then I'd meant to employ.

He balls his fist in an automatic reaction to my tone. I stare into his eyes, and I don't know who's angrier.

"If you're going to stay under my roof, Santiago, you need a plan to get your life back on track. You only have two quarters of school left before you'd earn your degree."

"What are you going to do throw me out?"

He grabs me by the shirt and pulls my face close to his.

"How would that make me look?"

"Like an asshole."

He releases me with a shove, and I stumble back into the piano bench but remain standing.

"How much time do you need?"

I shrug. "I don't know, a year I guess."

He turns and walks away. "Next January then," he says as he goes.

The pages of my calendar are all the time I have left.

I won't waste them.

APRIL 20—*My success is defined by my willingness to keep going*—I play through the powerful, bass-rich chorus of Mom's song. It sounds like a pop music ballad, sentimental with a few stanzas all sung to the same melody. Except I don't have the words and I've applied too much technical understanding of the way songs are pieced together to feel any authenticity towards it from the notes Mom originally sent me.

Each day at the piano the feeling of a mental block to Mom's song becomes more apparent. I try to struggle over, but the block is a wall with no footholds.

Is it the pills? They cloud my brain.

You just need more of them, my addiction assures me.

I start chewing my opiates to change their impact and to chase the euphoria they still occasionally provide. I need to use that feeling to float over the wall.

MAY 12—*My life is a celebration of my accomplishments*—Today, I have a fourth surgery to remove the titanium plates in my right arm. With the surgery—and my exaggerated complaints of physical pain—I achieve a new prescription for

Norco, Valium and Ambien. With three refills each!

JUNE 10—*My every step is one of courage*—I open a mountain of mail. There are so many cards from friends and family that could have been a boost to me if I'd faced them when they were first sent. As I've ignored those friends and family their calls and texts have dwindled down to nearly nothing. I place the get-well-cards around my bedroom to keep my spirits up as I tear through the huge pile of letters from lawyers who want to represent me for a personal injury suit. Their claims of what is due to me are intense. I begin to feel entitled to the dollars my pain and suffering represent. I finally select the female attorney whose sales pitch makes the path to a fair settlement seem easiest. I don't want a fight like Dad does. He has no intention of settling his own lawsuit.

JULY 15—*I engage in activities that empower me*—Each day at the piano there emerges this blank space in my mind where the *real* song should be, and it makes my time there more and more of a chore. The black and white of the piano keys blur together. My body aches. The thought of even another minute of this activity that feels so unempowering drains me. I need to get away. To drive.

I CLIMB INTO the old VW Jetta my parents bought for my brother and handed down to me in high school. It feels good to roll down the windows and let the warm wind whip around me as I meander the outer streets of Redlands. Before long, I randomly find myself at the Redlands Municipal Airport. Most of the planes I see parked here are the small single prop size that guys own themselves and either fly in, or wrench on, every weekend. There's a wooden sign with the words FLIGHT SCHOOL in red painted letters. In the distance a small plane lifts off the runway and seems to float into the sky. The same floating sensation I aim for with every opiate. I get out of the car and walk towards the office.

I hear Mom's voice in my head, *That's too dangerous, Vita Mia.*

I nod. "Yeah," I say aloud. "That's what I like about it, Mom." And then I realize what's happening, how Mom isn't beside me where I can talk to her. She's just a memory. Those words are simply what she might have said. I crouch down and hang my head in my hands on the sidewalk just fifteen feet from the flight school door. I cry just long enough to ease the ache in my throat, then spit in the dirt to the right of the sidewalk. As I stand, a large military looking dude in his fifties with a blonde buzzcut opens the glass door to the office and heads towards me with a clipboard in hand.

"You're late, kid."

"Excuse me?" I look around for the guy he's mistaken me for.

"You should have been here fifteen minutes ago. I like to keep my test flights on a tight schedule. You chickening out?"

"No, sir."

"Then let's get you in the air."

I engage in activities that empower me.

Flying thrills me, and I commit myself to its thrills on a daily basis. Not only does it replace the aggravation of finding Mom's true song, it provides an outlet to achieve a new and difficult skill. That empowers me again, at first. The danger feels like a bonus. My flight instructor is impressed by my lack of fear. What he doesn't get is, if I die, my pain will cease to exist. As I form that understanding, I also recognize that my time away from writing the song, alongside my daily opiate high, has turned my eagerness for life into a disregard for death.

OCTOBER 5—*My choices enrich me*—I settle my lawsuit early for much less than I might have gotten if I'd waited.

Let the retail therapy begin! I take Lucy with me to test-drive a brand-new royal blue Chevy Camaro convertible. When she realizes I'm serious about buying the car that day, Lucy pulls me aside to lecture me about spending my money this way.

"You don't have to try and wear Mom's shoes all the time, Luce. Don't you think we both deserve to have a little fun?"

At sixteen that's all the logic she needs. Lucy loves cruising with the top down as much as Mom did, though she's a stickler for safe driving. If she's in the car I am too. Soon after, I buy an airplane of my own.

NOVEMBER 10—*I create a private sanctuary*—Escrow closes on a newly renovated bungalow built in 1936 in a chic part of downtown Redlands. The house is only 998 square feet. It has refinished hard wood floors, two bedrooms, one bath, a big room for both the living and dining area and a black-and-white kitchen that Lucy calls adorable.

I know I can create a better life for myself here. I just want to try to be happy again. I'll buy that piano I have my eyes on and start playing again every day. I can even picture myself bringing dates here, cooking for them and watching movies together. Until now, dating felt like something I couldn't face.

Dad didn't know about the purchase of the house until I was ready to move in. When he comes to see the place for himself, he can't hide his anger.

"You're supposed to be living back in the dorms at Cal Poly in a few months."

High as hell on opiates, I say, "Chill out, Dad. A posh little bungalow in the heart of down-town Redlands, the jewel of the Inland Empire, in glorious Southern California, will be a great long-term investment. And I can rent it out for a profit when I make it back to school."

Dad hangs his head. If my brothers had just stuck to getting their own degrees in architecture as planned, Dad would leave me to my choices. But just this year, Mariano, whose been handling the invoices and the sales calls for the firm, finally confessed he has no intention of finishing his degree. He'd started it years ago on a part time basis but gave up when his daughter, Ava, was born. My brother Rudi dropped out of the school he was attending in New York, lured by the wealth of Wall Street. Now he works there for Goldman Sachs and hasn't been home since the funeral.

So, it's down to me, and everything that comes between Dad and his precious plans for DeAngelo and Sons Architectural Firm are his personal enemies. He glares at the diamond white Concert Grand piano I force into the tiny space of the dining room. And he can't hide his irritation when I discuss the details of a difficult landing in Catalina over the Sunday dinner, I've prepared us. After a while, we revert to the silence we shared in the months following the accident. At first, I'm relieved, but then it hurts. Ah well, nothing an extra Vicodin can't take care of. Even if I do have to get them from a friend/dealer since my doctors won't write the prescriptions anymore.

DECEMBER 25—I haven't torn the pages from my calendar in weeks. Who knows what it says? In the days of December, the bungalow has been a bunker of refuge from Christmas cheer. It was Mom's favorite holiday, and I can't face it without her. But on Christmas day, Lucy insists I attend the traditional family dinner my aunt is cooking at Mom's house in her honor. I arrive in my sweats, unshowered, unshaven, unpleasant in general. Lucy meets me at the front door beside Dad. They're both agape. Behind them are the aunts, uncles, cousins, and friends I can't bear to face because I haven't seen them since the hospital and I'm sure they still think Mom's death is my fault.

And Dad won't let me face them, not looking the way I do. He walks me down the driveway.

"Son, go home and get cleaned up. I'll have your aunt hold dinner until you're back."

My heart swells. He's gonna wait for me. But I can't help but test him—my pills make me testy these days. "If I leave, I'm probably not coming back."

He puts his arms around me, and I think it's about to happen. A Christmas miracle! I rush into its promise like a fool. Squeezing him tightly I say, "I'm sorry, Dad. I'm sorry for everything."

His arms tense. He pulls out of the hug. It's as if my apology has reminded him that I'm responsible for Mom's death. His words at the hospital are always with me.

I'm not ready to forgive you.

The vacant look in his eyes tells me they're still true. He presses me back a step.

"Christmas is harder than I thought it would be. I

understand if you don't make it back."

I don't.

CHAPTER 4

Back on Track

I TEAR THROUGH my bungalow on a cleaning mission. I gather crushed cans of Red Bull floating atop a sea of balled paper, failed renditions of the words for Mom's song. But I'm writing again! New Year's 2018 resolutions: play every day, find Mom's song, make peace with Dad. This morning he called to say he'd like to come over this evening and have a talk.

I shake open a trash bag and fill it with the crumpled paper to reveal the wood floor. I check my phone. Dad will be here in forty-three minutes. I eye the mess in the tiny living room beside the piano crowded dining room. Nothing to it but to do it! I swing into action. I find an empty bottle of vodka, and a half empty bottle of brand name Vicodin whose resting spot surprises even me. But that's what happens when you binge on enough pills and alcohol to wipe an entire couple days off the calendar. I just couldn't face the anniversary of the accident sober or even conscious. Now, I swear I'll never drink again, and I'll only take enough pills to prevent withdrawals. By March I'll be drug free. I got this!

A bolt of pain rips down my right wrist. A year later, I don't know if it's the addiction that manifests the pain, or the countless hours at the piano I've re-instated.

I twist the cap on the Vicodin bottle and crunch an oval shaped opiate. In the bathroom I flick on the light against the coming dusk and jam the pill bottle back in the mirrored medicine cabinet. When I slam it shut, I'm taken aback by the resemblance of my face to Dad's. Like for a second, he'd arrived early to find the illicit pills and judge my dependence on them. I study my face in the mirror and compare it to his. Same arch of wild black eyebrows, roman-curved nose, cleft chin, and black eyes. Though mine are heavy-lidded like Mom's. Dreamy eyes, she called them.

I smell my armpits, wince, and throw off the t-shirt I've worn for a couple days. I examine my thinning physique. Thin is good. Tall and thin. Sort of—I'm just shy of six foot. I flex what remains of my six pack until the muscles cramp so bad I have to lean over the counter to recover. I tongue the Vicodin grit from my molars and think on Dad's imagined judgment. "Just until the song's finished, I only need the pills until then," I say aloud.

The opiates merge with my blood stream and bolt me back to action. I stride down the short hall and survey the cleaned casa with a sense of pride. It was the right thing buying this place. Especially since the down payment kept me from blowing too much more of the rest of the cash. Dad's putting what remained of the money in trust, ensured its safety for good. But now the problem is maintaining my access to that money. Dad's deal with me is simple, as trustee, he will pay my mortgage and living expenses from the trust as long as I remain in accordance with his plans for me. The conditionality of his support is frustrating, but at least it's one way I know he still cares.

I haven't forgotten that it's January and he's expecting me to return to school. My only hope is to gauge what currency I have with him and use it to buy myself some more time.

I don't know if it's the drugs that make it feel impossible to return to the rigorous demands of my previous life or my lack of will to comply with his goals for my life in lieu of my own. I think these things over as I polish my piano to a shine.

I check the time again. Just enough left to dress to impress and still prepare the appetizer Mom always said was Dad's favorite.

DAD'S KNOCK IS as deep as his voice when I swing the front door wide and smile wider.

"You look well, son."

He eyes my clothes, still warm from the iron and smelling of heavy starch. My Adam's apple bobs. The crisp pleat of my jeans is the fine line I'm walking here.

I usher him in. He takes a few steps across the living room into the tiny black-and-white kitchen. There he sits at a small, round, wooden table nestled in the corner against a window. He folds his hands and waits. I set out the caprese salad—thick, soft mozzarella layered with tomato, basil, and a drizzle of garlic infused olive oil—along with a bottle of red wine and two glasses.

Dad says, "I'll just have a glass of water."

Not a good sign. I remove the wine things, get a glass of water for each of us and sit opposite him. Outside, the sky is already as dark as my hopes for this meeting.

Dad says, "We're moving forward with the renovation

of the cathedral. We start next week so we need to talk about your intern hours." A sly grin spreads across his face.

My heart swells. I'd thought he'd open with a demand to return to school next week. The renovation of the cathedral is something I'm actually interested in.

Mom loved that church. Over the years, some of Dad's and my best conversations were about this project. If it were ever to be endorsed by the diocese.

"That project was finally approved?" I ask.

He nods.

Is this fates way of guiding me back to the life Dad planned for me?

My smile encourages Dad. He plows on with enthusiasm. "I've spoken with the head of the Comprehensive Intern Development Program. They're going to make an exception for you logging your intern hours before you earn your degree with a promise to return to Cal-Poly in a timely fashion. And as long as you take a few accelerated courses over the summer you can go back in April and earn your degree by the fall."

My gut goes cold. While I'm honored he wants me for the project, mention of going back to school at an increased pace feels impossible.

I slouch at the table while my hopes for my future shrivel in the shadow of his well-defined plans. But, when he explains how he'll list my house with a property management company for rental, I gather my courage and sit up straight.

"Dad . . . your plans for my life can't be more important than my own."

His energy shifts. "If you had a plan, it would be different. But you don't! You've exhausted all your time between playing that thing"—he turns a quarter turn in his seat and gestures to the piano "—and becoming a pilot." He turns back to me and rubs his furrowed brow, muttering beneath his breath, "I should have stopped you from buying that stupid plane."

I seize the tangent. "I'm a good pilot, Dad."

Pride distorts the set of his face for a mere moment. "Being good at too many things will be your downfall, Santiago. Success is about focus."

"You've never even asked me why I fly."

"I think I've indulged you long enough."

My chin shakes. "I do it to be closer to Mom."

Dad's eyes dart to the funeral flier and get glassy. "She's not up in the clouds where you can reach her."

"No, but I could hit the ground pretty hard from that height."

He rolls his eyes. "Then what's stopping you?"

My throat gets too tight to talk. He dismisses my mention of suicide as hyperbole, but he shouldn't. The unstable ache to die is often closer than I've dared to admit. I gulp some water. When I no longer fear my voice breaking, I change the subject. "I'm super close to making a breakthrough with the song—"

"Enough!" He leans towards me and pounds the table. "I'm tired of hearing about this magical song your mother supposedly sent you." The water in our glasses trembles like my insides as our anger arrives to help us say the things we really want to say. Dad's on a roll.

"I'm this close to getting your life back on track, and you want to screw it up with this age-old, tortured musician's melodrama? Why can't you trust me to know what's best for you?"

"Because you don't! I gave up music before college

because you made me believe I couldn't hack it, and that your goals were more achievable. But there's been a hole in my life ever since. I was just too busy to figure out what it was."

Dad leans back in his chair and folds his arms.

"Besides, you never really wanted me for this, Dad. It's only because Mariano and Rudy weren't up to it that you're even here."

His head jerks back. And then he leans forward over the table again. "Rudy lacked discipline. Mariano the brains. You've got both. And you're an artist, like me." The veins pulse on his forehead.

"Exactly. Just let me finish the song first."

"Why this prolonged obsession with the song? People write songs in an afternoon."

"This is bigger than that. It's how I stay close to Mom."

His mouth turns down. "It's taking you too long. To me, it's case in point. You've got just enough talent to think you can make a life for yourself in music."

Beneath the table, I dig my nails into my palms to keep my cool. "Is that right?"

"Listen, I've spent my adult life creating a company in which my art can earn a stable living."

"*Your* art, Dad, not mine?"

"I get it, what you do with the piano may be more expressive, maybe even more elegant, but it won't build you a house made of bricks."

"I can't just give it up. When Mom died it changed my priorities."

"If you want me to keep paying the bills around here, then first, you log your intern hours, then you go back to school next quarter. I'm sure you can write the song between time if it's so important to you. Let that be your hobby."

I hang my head in defeat.

Dad finally reaches for a piece of mozzarella and puts the entire piece in his mouth. We both chew on things.

Given my progress with the song—it really does feel like my music will only ever be my hobby. But at least I'm committed to it again, whereas before the accident I'd given it up entirely. And if I'm honest with myself I am eager to do some of the work we've discussed over the years on the church project together. Things that were important to Mom. Dad's and my relationship being one of the things that was most important to Mom.

Dad licks the olive oil from his lips, he has a tiny piece of basil stuck between his front teeth that makes me chuckle to myself. That little laugh shifts my mood—and my high—ever so slightly to the positive.

Maybe, with the right drug ratio, I can prove to Dad that I can do both! Then, he'd really be proud of me.

I lift my chin, ready to give myself to the new plan. "You're right, Dad, that's exactly what I should do."

"Good, I knew I could help you see the sense in things. Now, let's have some of that wine with these. They're really good. Just like your mother used to make."

He points to the bottle on the counter then puts another piece of cheese in his mouth. I get up and begin uncorking the bottle of Cabernet, grateful for his praise of the appetizer. I pry the cork from the bottle, pour two glasses and hand Dad his. He swirls it, sniffs it, glances at its legs, then takes a sip and nods his head approvingly.

I take a long sip as I sit back down.

Dad says, "On the project, I'm going to make you the liaison to the church's expense committee."

I set my glass down hard. Too hard. "What! No! You know I wanna work on the acoustical engineering. We've talked about this for years. I've gotten perfect grades in those courses."

Dad sets his wine down gently. "We won't even be able to consider unique architectural acoustics if the church's budget isn't addressed first."

I groan and stare up at the ceiling.

"Look, I'm not just foisting this off on you. I think you have the right skills for it. And—" he raises his eyebrows playfully "—there's a girl on the committee you should meet."

I can't' remember the last time Dad was playful with me. It feels so good, that along with my curiosity about the girl—and my desire to remain in his financial good graces while I mount the strength to make something of myself—I agree to meet the committee next Tuesday.

WHEN HE'S GONE, I text Lucy to tell her what's transpired. She wants to meet. Our special place, a tree house our Uncle Carl built for us on the church grounds, where he lives and the project will soon begin. I decide to walk the mile and a half through downtown to clear my head and give Lucy time to drive downtown from Dad's house up in the hills.

I step into the crisp January night air. Streetlights display the style of the neighborhood against the backdrop of the night. Bungalows, Craftsmen, and Victorians nestle together and whisper to me my love of architecture. Half the homes on this block have been renovated by Dad's firm in the last ten years. One after the other. His reputation is sound. He's right. I should be grateful for the opportunity.

I comb through my Spotify play lists for some upbeat pop music to maintain my optimism about the juggling act I'm already beginning to fear.

I ARRIVE AT the cathedral and give a sentimental wave to the adobe structure which will soon be torn down. I continue down narrow sidewalks lined with ferns and flowers into a grassy square of mature trees. A silver-dollar eucalyptus in the center supports the tree house Uncle Carl built years ago for me and Lucy. I climb a rope ladder through the trap door and into the wooden room that is approximately five foot by seven.

My sister is waiting for me. She wears a brown knit beanie with a bear's face and ears. Her short bob sticks out under the hat and rims her tiny face which is illuminated by a small battery-operated LED lantern.

Lucy drapes a blanket around herself and hands me another. I put it on and sit down. Lucy's face twists with emotion that spill out in tears. "I miss Mom so much. Ever since New Year's Eve, I've been going over every detail of that horrible week in the hospital last year. Is that sick? I can't help it."

"I couldn't help it either," I tell her, leaving out how I finally blotted out those memories in a drunken opiate stupor.

"I tried to call, but you never answered."

"I needed to be alone."

She nods. "Did we make the wrong choice?" She refers to our decision to end the life support.

"Just me, Luce, when I put her in that car."

Lucy diverts course, which trips me out every time. "Stop. It's not your fault. God called her home."

I stop listening. I can't handle her nonsensical blabbering about fate. I shut her up with a tight hug I never want to end.

When it does, Lucy hesitates. "How's the . . .?"

I take a seat. "The what?"

"You know, the song."

"Let's not talk about the song right now."

"Maybe if you spent less time flying."

I roll my eyes. "Look, Luce, getting my pilot's license has kept me sane."

"Mom sent you the song to keep you sane. You're just so far from the love the song embodies."

"The song's not about love, Luce."

"Yes, it is, Santi, I've heard it."

"Well, I'm writing it! And I'm telling you it's about pain."

"Don't you get it? The song isn't even about the song. It's about you figuring out about you so you can actually write it."

"What's that supposed to mean?"

"I think you're in danger of never getting over it, because you won't forgive yourself."

My lips twitch and I lean in with a loaded pointer finger.

But Lucy's eyes close and she begins to chant something in what I can only assume is Sanskrit. Two words are being repeated—no—sung, over and over, "*Ahem prema, ahem prema, ahem prema.*" This goes on for a while and I catch myself internalizing the chant before she opens her eyes.

"What was that?"

"A mantra I use to change the mood. It means *I am love*, wanna try it?"

"No." I snicker.

"That's okay it's already worked. You're laughing. Hey, I have an idea. Let's sneak into the church and you play—"

"I don't want to play the song, Luce."

"Not Mom's song, stupid. That one . . ." She begins to snap her fingers above her head to will the lost name out of her memory. "You know the one you shocked the shit out of Dad with at that piano competition in D.C." She continues snapping her fingers. "Fantasy something."

"Chopin's Fantaisie-Impromptu in C minor. Ya know, I thought when I won that prize, Dad would finally be proud of me and accept me as a musician. But he told me tonight I only have just enough talent to think I have a chance." My jaw sets.

"This thing between you and Dad has gone on too long."

"He just makes me so angry."

"Maybe anger is a healthy response to the injustice you've suffered."

Her words deliver validation I want more of. We lock eyes. "What injustice?"

She takes a breath. "It isn't fair that Mom died the way she did. It isn't fair that Dad blames you. And it isn't fair that Dad needs you to be what he wants you to be before he'll have a relationship with you."

I revel in her words. "Still, my anger doesn't feel healthy," I tell her.

Probably because it's driven by the pills I can't seem to stop taking.

Don't say that out loud.

Lucy says, "Because you're stuck in your anger. And there are no shortcuts out."

"My song for Mom used to feel like a way out."

"You're trying too hard. You need to connect to the

music that's less fraught with difficult emotions." She stands and pulls me by the arm. "Come on, come play Fantasie on the Steinway."

Lucy knows better than anyone that I have gotten serious about classical music again in the last year to stay tuned into the piano when writing Mom's song felt too hard. I feel dizzy. I've been fiddling with Chopin's Fantasie, but it's just so hard to get right again.

Lucy's flashes a smile at me. "You know you can do it." It's the same smile Mom would flash to keep me playing a tough piece.

"Alright, let's go."

INSIDE THE CATHEDRAL, I smell the incense used at the Saturday evening mass which ended over an hour ago. My eyes adjust to the limited light that streams in through the stained-glass windows as I walk over to the piano. It is a rare Centennial Steinway that unfolded its musical secrets to me through my piano instructor, Barbara Holladay. Sitting here is like coming home.

"Do you want me to get the lights?" Lucy says.

I hesitate, without the sheet music I'm in the dark either way. Lucy flips the lights on and I'm grateful. This piano is so stunning it deserves full light. They reflect gold from the oiled wood finish. I crack my knuckles, find middle C, and play scales and arpeggios to get reacquainted with this old friend. My fingertips tingle as I touch the ivory keys. Bone absorbs the oil of the fingers, so they never slide, and that alone is priceless. Maybe this piano is the secret to Mom's song?

Why didn't you think of it sooner?

The first time through Fantasie is awkward. I stumble over whole sections of the song. I pound open palms against my forehead. Lucy remains silent. Her peace reminds me of my former instructor Mrs. Holladay. I hear her voice in my head.

Straighten your back, Santiago. Trust yourself. You know the music. You're one of the special ones. Again!

"Again" was her favorite command. I played this song hundreds of times with Mrs. Holladay standing right where Lucy is now.

I retrieve the song slowly, bit by bit. My passion rejoins me. A bead of sweat rolls off the tip of my nose onto my moving fingers. Having an audience forces me to focus in ways I wouldn't alone. I surrender to the intensity of Chopin's masterpiece. When I pause to catch my breath, I hear the applause of more than just my sister.

I look up and see a girl about my age, twenty-two maybe twenty-three, walking towards me. She draws closer and my mouth falls open. It's her eyes—not just the silvery-grey color—but their almond shape and their perfect distance apart, like the all-important space between musical notes. Her left cheek dimples in a smile and when she speaks, I notice a tiny gap between her front teeth that makes her beauty even more unique.

She says, "I remember you. You sang in church a while back. Why'd you stop?"

"I left for college."

"I remember your voice, it always made getting up for the early mass easy. Your Chopin needs work though." She turns away.

Lucy covers a grin with her hand and her eyes get huge with excitement.

She tilts her head towards the girl and mouths, "Go!"

"Wait, what's your name?" I rush over to her.

She chuckles. "Sophia."

With my heart pounding in my ears, my singing voice rides a euphoric wave onto a questionable shore. "So-phi-a, I've just met a girl named Sophia."

She rolls her eyes and bites back a smile. "You're out of control."

Behind us Lucy laughs, the kind of laugh that assures me I'm on the right track.

Sophia shakes her head. Lucy is still giggling.

I quit singing and shuffle my feet. "I take it you don't like *West Side Story*, Sophia?" We make eye contact when I say her name. Her pupils widen then she looks away nervously.

"Musicals aren't my thing." From the front pew she picks up a basket of collected items left behind after mass.

I gesture to carry it for her, she blushes, then she steps around me towards the Sacristy. "Thanks, but I've got this."

"What is your thing?"

Sophia carries the basket into the room behind the alter.

Lucy rushes to my side and whispers, "Oh my God, she's so beautiful! Follow her you idiot!" She pushes me towards the sacristy. But before I've taken a few steps Sophia rejoins us.

She says, "I like Chopin. Truth is, one more time through and I think you'll have it. I was cleaning up in the back when I heard someone start playing. I've never heard anyone play like that in person. Will you try it again?"

Lucy says, "You should have heard him play it at the National Competition in Washington D.C. He won!"

"That was a long time ago," I tell Sophia and give Lucy a glare.

Lucy says, "What? You did win, Santi."

"That's pretty cool," Sophia says. Her long, wavy, chestnut hair shimmers gold from the stage lights. She brushes it back from her face. "Would you play it one more time?" she asks.

I walk directly to the Steinway. She follows and I play Chopin's Fantasie like it were my own. Lucy stands behind me. Sophia leans over the end of the piano and each time I look up at her we make deep eye contact again. Her glittering eyes confirm my success with the piece.

Lucy cheers enthusiastically when I'm finished. Sophia nods her head in admiration.

The feeling of being loved by this audience is so overwhelming that, before I know it, I launch into the ballad I'm composing for Mom. The angst that often accompanies playing this song is gone amidst their appreciation for my talent. I'd forgotten how important that was. I play my own piece with new confidence.

The music I write is nothing like the classical pieces that taught me what the piano was capable of. Still, my classical training textures my approach to pop music in the same way it was the foundation for legends like Elton John and Alicia Keys.

Mom's song has a bass rich chorus with big chords. On the Steinway, which has a legendary lower register, the bass heavy emotion of the song thunders back to me from the acoustics of the Cathedral. It gives me a new impression of the song's power.

Lucy's grip on my shoulder tells me she feels that too. And I know Sophia must feel it. Her lips part. She concentrates on what she's hearing. Her head moves in time with the music. I get this crazy gut-feeling she's perceiving the missing lyrics.

Sophia's response tells me more about the song than I knew before. So much more, that—when I reach the chasm of missing notes that should be the bridge I've struggled through for months—eight new notes inspire me from its depths.

They are subtly different from the rest. And altogether the perfect bridge to join the chorus to the stanza—and my life, to my will to keep writing it. As I consider putting this to her, her eyes leave mine to study the Steinway. Like she's seeing the piano for the first time.

"I have to go," she says.

I don't protest. What she's left in her wake is just as beautiful.

CHAPTER 5

Ready or Not Here I Come

READY OR NOT, here I come. The Fugees song in my head propels me towards the committee meeting. The old lyrics bolster my courage but dredge up memories of teenage Mariano. He'd been on a quest to inform his five-year-old brother that classical piano music wasn't all the world had to offer. His love of pop music had begun my obsession with it too. When Barbara heard me singing those songs my voice had intrigued her even more than my passion for the piano. My brother was always coming up with new songs he wanted me to try singing. His music united us through our eight-year age gap. Mom's death separated us again.

I set my files down at the head of the long oval conference table. I'm the first one here, but committee members aren't far behind. Sophia is among them. My heart races.

Is she the girl Dad was talking about?

She carries a laden grey backpack with a University of Redlands logo that thuds the tabletop when she swings it off her shoulder. She's selected a seat about midway down the right side of the table. The room's only window is behind her, and the morning sun crowns her. I give her a little wave as the other's find their seats. Her eyes light up and she waves back.

I'm glad I prepared as well as I did. Sophia seems impressed by my grasp on the financial challenges that have plagued the project. But the quibbling over mind numbing details forces me to paste a smile over my indifference. My eyes dart over the room; oak paneled and only slightly larger than the fourteen-foot-long oak conference table. There are twelve seats, and each is taken. I slip my cell phone from my pocket and attempt to download a game of Fruit Samurai beneath the table. But the Internet connection is weak, and the download wheel spins fruitlessly. I glance over at Sophia, who scribbles meticulous notes. I slip the phone in my pocket to manage my boredom more pro-actively. I begin writing down the names of committee members from their name tags.

Alice Cole, who heads the meeting from the opposite end of the table says, "I have a family who wants to commission the baptismal font, but they are in dispute of your firm's estimate of seventy thousand dollars." Alice has hair as white and airy as fallen snow, styled in a short bouffant. Her bright blue eyes are shrewd. I flip through my notes and confirm the quote. Alice continues, "The Chua family would like to bring their own contractor in to build the font, they have an estimate of thirty-five thousand dollars."

I find the page I need, scan it while holding up a single finger, then look up at her. "That won't be possible Mrs. Cole, their estimate doesn't take into consideration the plumbing factors that my firm used to arrive at the figure."

Rodger, a well-groomed man in his fifties says, "It can't possibly be a thirty-five-thousand-dollar plumbing problem, can it?"

The room buzzes for and against my father's estimate. Knowing my father, the price is well justified. I remember something about this in my notes and sweat as I read faster. This morning my dad made it clear how diplomatically I was to handle these scenarios. There were things they just didn't understand about permitted construction; he'd explained. Eureka. The price discrepancy is based on the location the committee chose. I open my mouth to speak, but before I can, Sophia stands and addresses the group.

"I may have an answer to the financial shortcomings of our plans," she says as she adjusts the jewel on her necklace, a large rose quartz that matches her suit. Beneath it, her white blouse is buttoned up to the neck, but I can see fingers of red nerves crawling past the neckline to her face. I try to think of an actress she reminds me of. Audrey Hepburn? God she's beautiful.

The committee focuses their rapt attention on her words.

She lifts her chin. "The Centennial Steinway is our answer."

I jump to my feet and my rolling chair shoots out behind me. I hear it crash into the wall. "The Steinway is not an option."

She's taken aback.

Did she think I'd be pleased?

"I know you have a connection to it," Sophia says, "but the cathedral doesn't need a piano of such high value. My research suggests it could bring over two hundred thousand at the right auction."

Patrick, the lectern who sings the Psalm each Sunday, finds his voice. "The music department is very proud of the

Steinway."

Is that all he's got?

"'When pride comes, then comes disgrace, but with the humble is wisdom.' Proverbs 11:2," Sophia says.

Patrick looks down.

I crack my knuckles and clutch for something to save the Steinway. "The piano doesn't belong to the church."

Sophia's head jerks back. "Of course, it does! It's been here since I was a girl."

"On donation to the music department from Barbara Holladay." My eyes blink rapidly.

She folds her arms across her chest. Heads swing from me to her. "If the donation was finalized then it's the church's property."

I dig my fingernails into the back of my neck. "It will have contingencies." *It must!* "Barbara Holladay didn't donate the Steinway so that the church could sell it to buy pews made of fancier wood."

Sophia raps her well organized hand out. "These embellishments are for posterity."

I address the group. "I'm curious, who's pride is in question here?" My comment is met with nervous laughter around the table.

Alice interjects. "Barbara is a friend of mine. She wants that piano to stay with the music department. I vote against the proposal."

Rodger joins the dispute. "It does seem like a prudent option." Murmurs of support follow.

Sophia sits down and taps her lower lip while staring at the empty center of the table. "I'd like to speak to Mrs. Holladay on the matter."

"That's not an option," I say.

"When her husband died," Alice says, "it went very hard on her. Her dementia has grown steadily worse. Barbara didn't even recognize me the last time I saw her."

"Where is she now?" Sophia asks Alice.

"Her son took her home to live with him in Brentwood."

"Isn't he the music guy?" Rodger asks.

"He owns Holladay Records," Alice says. "They weren't very close. It surprised me."

I take a Vicodin from my pocket and slip it in my mouth. I was saving this pill to keep my energy up midday. My addiction requires them as an energy source. But mention of Barbara and loneliness grabs hold of me. I miss our dynamic. I could use her help on the song. With Mrs. Holladay gone, I need the Steinway more than ever. I crunch the pill and re-emerge in the group's chatter about Holladay Records, a successful company with the power to make trends. The talk devolves into reports of its infamous CEO, Dirk Holladay.

"He has more money than God."

"Because he cheats every artist he represents."

Barbara always warned me away from her son. The wariness returns as acid reflux.

When the gossip dies down Sophia says, "I'll ask Monsignor Carl to get me up to speed on the legal parameters of the Holladay's donation."

I bite my nails. I can just hear Sophia convincing my uncle to auction the piano and relieve the churches financial burdens with the proceeds. I'd get to him first if I had the balls, but he's one of the people I've evaded for the last year. Our grieving tactics don't quite line up.

Maybe if I had Barbara Holladay on my side that would rally several members to my cause. I know she'll remember me. She has to! I remember visiting her with my mom before she'd gone to Brentwood. She'd recognized me then. But not my mother. It was weird.

I jot down the names I think I can count on. My pen taps on the paper as I scan the name tags at the table. The meeting breaks up and Sophia's advocates surround her with whispers.

I engage Alice. "Thank you for your support."

"See what you can do about reducing the cost of the font." She crosses her arms and taps her fingers against them.

I approach Sophia, struggling for the finesse to take our dispute down a notch. On the table her notebook exposes her notes. An elderly committee member invites Sophia to coffee, but she tells her she has class. Hence the crammed backpack. I scan her handwriting in the little time my guilty glance allows.

Plays with so much power, His energy transformed, scribble, scribble, *an Angel with dark hair.*

I work to keep a smile off my face. Sophia looks at me out of the corner of her eye and closes the notebook.

The elderly woman pats Sophia's shoulder. "I think it's a brilliant option, dear."

The opiates stream through the hot current of my blood as the pill I chewed takes effect. Each one I eat is like spinning a wheel on a game show.

What do we have for him Johnny? Soothing bliss or the state of the irate?

A vein twitches in my neck and I know the chilled out, fancy free high I was hoping for will be overridden by the short-tempered backlash prolonged dependence on opiates *actually* equals.

"When did this brilliant stroke of genius come to you?

Because I'm thinking it was Saturday night. It's no wonder you got the hell out of there."

Really? That's your idea of finesse.

I wish now, I hadn't taken that last pill. When I'm alone it's easier to surrender to any hope of enjoyment a pill might offer. But dealing with people while high can be a real buzz kill.

She scoffs with a little shake of her head at my temper tantrum.

I rub the back of my neck and pull myself together. "I'm sorry, it's just the piano is really special to me. And I wasn't expecting that."

A patient smile replaces her disappointment. The last of the group departs, and she shrugs. "I get it. But selling the piano makes sense. When I heard you play it Saturday night it hit me that it was the answer to our money problems. So, thank you for that."

But I'd felt like the Steinway was the answer to my song problem, and I don't want to lose it now. I don't want to lose her either. I puff my cheeks and blow out. "That song I played Saturday night. Not the Chopin but the other one . . ."

Our eyes lock. "I remember," she says.

"You do?"

"It was powerful." Her eyes glitter. "I can't remember hearing anything so beautifully sad."

Everything slows down and the euphoria I chase crashes into me.

She bites her lip and breaks our eye contact. "I'm late." She stuffs the notebook into her backpack, and without zipping it first, swings it onto one shoulder as she turns towards the door. A book falls to the floor. She notices and turns as I pick it up: *Pride and Prejudice.*

"You have bewitched me." I tell her, quoting Darcy and handing her the book.

Her cheeks light on fire. "You've read it?" She reaches for the classic.

"It's one of my mom's favorites. Since she died, I've been reading all her favorites."

She takes the book from my light grasp. "I heard about your mother's death. I'm sorry."

"Sophia, I need the Steinway to finish that song. I'm writing it for my mom."

She chuckles. "The magic didn't come from the piano, silly. It came from you. You don't need a talisman; you just need to *focus!* You play like no one I've heard before. Just keep playing, and don't let anything stop you."

"Okay. But I am gonna try and stop you from selling the Steinway."

"And I'm going to try and sell it to the highest bidder."

"All's fair in love and war," I say.

"Which is this?" Her brows bounce.

"I guess we'll find out."

We both work hard to bite back smiles.

ALONE IN ONE of the church admin offices Dad arranged for me to have onsite during the renovation, I type the alphanumeric letters for CARL and Uncle Carl's number pops up. All I need to do is select his number and hit send. But my teeth clench and I set the phone down on my wooden desk. My tiny office is stale. A small room with brick walls painted Navajo white. From the wall, a faded poster of the sacred heart of Jesus questions my reluctance to speak to my uncle.

What makes him think forgiveness is the answer to

everything?

I use the phone on my desk to reach the human resources extension. The receiver is bulky with one of those funky old pieces from the 1980s that make it easier to hold the phone with your shoulder and multi-task. When Norma takes my call, she tells me that the only information on file for Barbara Holladay is her former Redlands address and the phone number which is no longer current. She has no information for the son, Dirk Holladay. So, onto the next best thing. A Google search gives me the contact number for Holladay Records. But little luck there when a sophisticated operator informs me that Mr. Holladay can't be reached by phone without an appointment and that if I were to leave a detailed message, he may respond within fourteen business days. I start to leave a message, then just hang up.

Meanwhile, I imagine Sophia and Uncle Carl in cahoots to auction my piano and laugh aloud. The game we've set in motion compels me to win. I'll secure the piano—not just for me, *for Barbara*—and I'll find a way to negotiate Sophia's embellishments into the budget. That will impress Dad too. A total win-win. The elation is still with me. I got this!

The buzzing of my old-school desk phone makes me jump. It's Norma again.

"Santiago, I checked one other place, we had an emergency card on file for Mrs. Holladay and the son had a cell phone number listed."

I feel so triumphant it doesn't even occur to me to plan the call. I just dial.

"Holladay here." His voice is smooth and confident.

"Uh, Mr. Holladay, I'm a friend and former student of your mother's."

"She can't come to the phone, please don't call this number again." He hangs up.

I call back but am sent to voicemail. I lick my lips while I listen to his professional message prompt then nip loose skin on my lip until I taste blood. "This is about the Steinway piano. I'm calling from Holy Angels Catholic Church, please call me."

I toss the phone down, there must be other church administrative personnel besides my uncle who would know about the donation. I dial Norma back; besides Monsignor Carl, she isn't sure who I should talk to. I'll have to suck it up and call him. Then my cell phone rings, a 323 number, like the one I just dialed. I answer.

A woman's voice. "You called my husband about the Steinway piano, who is this?"

"Santiago DeAngelo, I was a student of his mother's. Whom do I have the pleasure of speaking with?"

"Katherine Holladay, his wife. Are you calling on your own? My husband says you are calling on behalf of the church."

"I'd like to speak to Barbara. I have some questions about her intentions in the donation, any contingencies that she may have . . ." I stop talking. It took me a moment to register the clipped tone.

She continues. "If you're asking about the contingencies, it's because you don't have the document in your possession. Is that because it doesn't exist?"

"It's not in front of me," I say, aware of how quickly this call is going against me.

"Mr. DeAngelo, we are not in receipt of the legal documents executing the endowment of the property to your organization and hereby challenge the assumption of the donation in their absence."

"What does that mean?" I'm overwhelmed by her legal vernacular and my own absurd assumptions about the direction this call would take.

"It means we are coming to collect our property."

"We have the paperwork."

"And we have ours. My late father-in-law was gifted the Steinway from the Cole Porter estate. We'll see whose paperwork the piano movers are more convinced by. You have one week to produce the legal documents." She hangs up.

Part 2
New Perspectives

CHAPTER 6

KITTY HOLLADAY

Your Best Work

KITTY, I JUST got a call about the Steinway. Call this number back. I'm going to text it to you," Dirk says over the phone.

"I'm busy, Dirk, have your assistant call."

"Kitty, this is the Steinway we're talking about. I need you to handle this. I'm swamped."

"Your mother donated it, what are you expecting?"

"What if I never received the final paperwork? Let's work it from that angle. I can get it back."

"Dirk, I'm working on some songs right now."

"You know what this means to me, Kitty. Make the call. You're good on the phone."

I throw myself back in my plush office chair with a groan. "Text me the number, I'll call this afternoon."

"Good, but call right now, and then text me the details," Dirk says.

I picture him pumping his fist towards the vaulted ceilings of his glamorous office of clear glass and black leather on the twentieth floor of Holladay Records Headquarters. I growl. "Fine! I'll tell you how it goes."

My own home office is a simple space painted a tranquil sage green—a color my therapist recommended for its soothing qualities. To my right is the white door to my studio. But I promised myself I wouldn't open it until at least one of the seven songs I'm currently composing is ready to be sung by its fated artist. It won't be long now. And I know which song it will be. My mind moves in music. When the words and measures sync into songs, I submit to them. Manifesting them takes focus, and only some songs survive. This one is more than a miracle. It towers over the others. I want to use it to escape my dependence on Holladay Records and my husband.

On the wall in front of my desk is a cork message board framed in a coordinated shade of green. Its papers, pinned in perfect columns, mark my progress and communications for the song.

I yank my headphones off and drop them on the desk. I wish I hadn't answered Dirk's call. It's a constant debate, phone on—phone off. The colored waves of the music pulse on the screen of my laptop. Without sound they look like the etchings of a Richter graph.

I slip the headphones back on and startle to an email chime at full volume. The notification bubble shows the first line of a message I've been waiting for. First word "sorry". I reach for my wireless mouse, and it skitters across the room. By the time I've retrieved the goddamn thing, my heart threatens to escape through my throat.

Sorry Kitty, there's not a spot on the album for your song after all. Keep sending them though. –Jerry

I hit reply and type:

"Fuck You Jerrrrrrrrrrrrrrrrrrrrrrrrrrrrrrrrrrrrrrrrrrrrrrrrrrr," letting the r fill half of the screen before I delete the message and pick up the phone.

"Look Kitty," Jerry answers, "you know I've got no control over—"

"An email, Jer."

"I answered the phone, didn't I? You know how email is, I've got proof I let you know by the deadline—"

"Of today. It's a great song, Jerry. It was perfect for your girl."

"Then it's her loss, right? It's going to be perfect for someone else."

"I needed this. This song could be a hit and Halsey would make it one, she's hot right now."

"Hot shit, and you know how that makes 'em. Look, I know Holladay Records has taken a hit with—"

"This isn't about Holladay—this is about me. I don't need Dirk to be a success!"

"Okay, okay, I got it. But the song might be good enough to make a star out of anyone. I'm doing you a favor here. This song is your best work, Kitty. Just use some of that Holladay influence."

I groan in disgust.

"You sound a little high-strung. Can I recommend something?"

"No!"

"Jesus, okay, I was just going to suggest a Xanax. Gotta go Kit, chin up."

My heart is thrumming, my eyes blur. I close them and see the negative image of my hands behind my lids. Minutes pass and my heartbeat still reminds me of a lead guitarist strumming away in a do-or-die strum off. Maybe the Xanax *is* the right thing. The morning is shot no matter how you look at it.

But you hate mixing your highs.

Dirk's text comes through with the number he wants me to call. God, I wish I hadn't read Jerry's email. Maybe I can pretend as though I didn't—as though I don't know, yet, that my goal for the month was just dashed.

I'll make Dirk's fucking call and then I'll deal with my new plan. First, I lift a small scoop of cocaine to my nose and inhale. Dopamine flares like solar hot spots in my brain.

I dial. It sounds like a boy on the other end of the phone. His name sounds familiar.

Barbara's protégé? I think so. She wanted him to have that piano. How interesting.

He doesn't know the tiger he's caught, and a few whacks with my claws retracted do cheer me. Next time I'll extend my claws. Dirk won't let it end there.

When I roll my chair back and stand, my vision goes dark. I put my hands down on the desk for support and wait for the empty feeling to pass. When was the last time I ate?

You don't need food, get the Xanax.

I rack my brain: bottle in my purse, purse in the kitchen.

I leave the serenity of my private space. The backyard is bright with Southern California sunshine that my dark glasses do little to combat. I pass the pool house and the oval pool surrounded by Greek columns and comfortable lounge chairs. Its heated water beckons. But the Xanax call is louder.

The sliding door glides smoothly, and I enter the marble vault that is our home. I prop my dark glasses on my head. Everything is oval and arched, ivory or taupe. The cream-colored sofas have dove-grey throws that pretend at comfort but have never once been used. The floors are heated at my insistence and feel as warm as the sunbaked travertine outside. I run across them and pass under an arch that leads to the kitchen.

My spring-green Kate Spade bag looks small in this massive space. It's right where I expect it to be on the light-grey granite island, which alone is twice the size of the kitchen I grew up with.

I paw through my purse, but the orange bottle isn't here. Someone's been touching my things again!

Dirk's mother shuffles towards the peanut butter sandwich I set out for her earlier. The smell nauseates me, but I take a moment to kiss her on the forehead and encourage her to eat it before I run to the entryway. I grab the cold, black, wrought iron banister of the grand double staircase and fly up its left steps to my master bedroom. My sunglasses fall off my head on the way and I hear them bounce down a few marble steps.

In my room the shades are drawn. Much of the light is absorbed by the dark wood floors. The maids have spread my Tiffany blue bedspread. There's even a fire in the double fireplace between the sitting area and bedroom space.

After this perusal of order, I enter the earth toned master bath, and consider running a bath in the oval-shaped tub staged on a raised platform against a window. Instead, I throw open the medicine cabinet and pick through various bottles. All the good shit is gone. Dirk in action. *Unsympathetic asshole.* I slam the cabinet then pound it with my fist. It shatters. I strike again and pieces keel onto the brown marble counter.

I gape at my split reflections in the mess of mirror. A dozen broken Katherines, one for each long-curved fragment of glass. Time to clean up. I could call for a maid, but I don't want to. I made this mess.

I find a small waste basket liner in the cabinet beneath the sink. I transfer the broken mirror to the bag while I obsess on the conversation with Jerry.

It's just a setback, but I'm sick of setbacks.

I seize a giant, glittering shard of glass and squeeze. It sears my palm with hot pain. I unfurl my hand and let the blood run into the bag amongst the other jagged pieces. My teeth chatter. I squeeze again, blood drips like juice from pressed fruit. Smaller chards begin to float in the sanguine pool that collects in the bag. Dark spots float across my vision. There we go. If it weren't for the coke, I'd already be out. I wring tighter as air whistles between my teeth. The spots grow. I'm fading. Oh, thank God, the only relief I know, unconsciousness.

I come to—babbling my horoscope like a mantra. *It's a good year to be Sagittarius, with respect and admiration on its way to you. Trust your sound and critical judgment.*

"Kitty," Dirk says in the living world. He snaps his fingers, but I ignore the sound.

Your emotional judgment is strong especially in February.

"Kitty, open your eyes."

I obey.

"Kitty what the fuck?" Dirk asks.

I'm woozy, the kind of tired I can use as an excuse to stay in bed and do nothing. My eyes rove over the room. My own room. Good. The hospital ruins it. The shades and curtains have been closed and I can't make out what time it is. I hope the day is over. I huddle on my right side. My hand is bandaged to numbness. I see Dirk and Jess, Barbara's in-home nurse, standing over the bed. I know what happened. Jess found me, bandaged me, called Dirk, and put me to bed.

Outside, motorized gardening tools break the quiet. Dirk peeks out the window and the sunlight that pours in tells me little time past.

I look at my husband and feel my face shine up at him. "You came home for me, D." I reach out to him.

Jess turns on an overhead light.

Dirk shakes his head at me and tsks his tongue. I lower my reaching hand, bite my lip, and give him the girlish smile that matches the childish voice I save only for him.

He rolls his eyes—but teasingly—then grins at me, and in a matching tone (that embarrasses Jess to hear him use) he says, "You're a mess kitty-cat. This is the last place I need to be right now."

"But you're here." I scoot back towards the headboard, reach for him and he exhales his remaining irritation before sitting on the bed. He takes my bandaged hand and kisses it.

"What happened with the Steinway? Did you make the call?" he asks.

"What?"

It takes a minute before I remember the call he asked me to make. He stares expectantly. The numbness in my hand spreads and I pull it away from his. "Yes, I made your stupid call." I look away.

He takes my hand again and changes his tone back to the tender shade I long for from him. He wears a crooked little grin on his thin lips. "You should eat something," he says. "We could have lunch together in here."

"No, I'm not hungry. I want to sleep." I rub my head against him like a cat.

He caresses my forehead. "My little kitty-cat." He puts his thumb and fore finger around my wrist, they overlap. Dirk shakes his head at me. "Kitty, when was the last time you ate?" His tone is serious now.

"I'm not a child, Dirk," I say, risking the moment I crave between us.

He also seems to sense what we might lose and reverts his attitude. "But you're my baby."

Sitting beside me on the bed, he scoops me into his arms and pulls me onto his lap. At six feet, I'm tall, but he is taller and bigger than I am. He's always made me feel so feminine with his size.

"What happened?" he asks.

He probably means with the Steinway, but I refer to the call with Jerry. "They didn't want my song."

He strokes my hair. "They'd take you more seriously with a Holladay agent."

"Why do I need *you* for them to take me seriously?"

"We can't keep doing this, Katherine. Let me call them."

I hold my breath. I don't want to let this moment go. But the truth I conceal gets away from me. "I don't trust you."

Dirk rolls me onto the bed.

My hand throbs. My heart throbs. My belly throbs. "I'm sorry."

From the doorway, he says, "Good luck, Katherine," before flicking the room into darkness. He trudges down the steps and I hear keys scrape the glass table in the center of the entryway. The door thuds behind him.

CHAPTER 7

SANTIAGO DEANGELO

Alone in Our Grief

I LOSE TIME staring at the phone. *I can't lose the Steinway to that woman.*

I stride through the parish gardens to my uncle's quarters, but the closer I get the slower my feet move. I pause at the tree house out front. The bark of the eucalyptus is peeling away, like the feeling I marched here with. I move away from the door. But really, it's the forgiveness—of myself and my father which Uncle Carl encourages—that I shy from.

I search my pocket for another Vicodin. I find one and crunch it down. As I'm walking away, the door squeaks open.

Through the metal security-screen my uncle says, "Santiago, you've been avoiding me."

I reel around, and shrug. No point in denying the obvious. The screen screeches on rusty metal hinges and he opens his home to me. He's wearing a black dress shirt with his white, Roman priest's collar. His face adopts his practically permanent smile. It's hard not to smile back, but I manage. I step in. Sophia is sitting on the sofa holding a cup of tea in her lap. My heart drums. In my anger, and fear of losing the piano for us both, I want to blame Sophia for what's happening. Blame is easier than guilt, but it offers no way out. Just ask my dad.

I pull myself together. "I'm glad you're here," I tell her. I really am.

Sophia sips her steaming tea and flashes a coy smile. "Me too, because Monsignor assures me, there are no contingencies in Barbara Holladay's bequest."

"Well, that won't matter much since her son is contesting the donation. His wife claims it was never even finalized."

My uncle motions towards the sofa. "Santiago, why don't you sit down. I'll make you a nice cup of chamomile to calm your nerves."

"I am calm! Do you have the paperwork? They're threatening to collect the piano."

"What!" Hot tea splashes onto Sophia's hand and she startles, blowing on the burn.

I want to kiss the burn.

"Santi, please just sit and I'll find the paperwork that assaults your peace." Again, he gestures at the sofa.

I take a seat beside Sophia. "Is your hand okay?"

She stares straight ahead and nods.

"I'm sorry. I was just trying to get in touch with Barbara, and this *woman* called me back. Next thing I know she's—"

My uncle returns. His voice stops me short.

"Truth is, I always feared Barbara's son would contest

the donation." He flips the pages of the document in his hands, and he seats himself in the armchair caddy corner to Sophia's side of the couch. "I told Barbara as much when we wrote it." He looks at me, "But Barbara always wanted you to have access to the piano, Santiago. She swore you had a special bond to your talent through it."

My face twists to fight back tears. Sophia sets her tea on the rectangular wooden coffee-table in front of her and scoots towards me. I stare ahead at the tree house through the window. She puts a hand on my forearm. "I couldn't have known that."

I squeeze her hand then let go of it to wipe my nose on my sleeve. I couldn't speak if I tried. I need to get away from her until this horrible blend of anger and embarrassment, intensified by the pill, passes. In the beginning, the opiates would soothe my nerves and emotions. But now the addiction only *promises* me they will, while the opposite result of riling them sets in.

I can't live like this anymore.

I stand, move around the coffee-table, and turn to Sophia. "I'm gonna fix this."

"Is this my fault?" she says.

"No."

"It'll work itself out," Uncle Carl says. "The donation is legally sound."

He hands me the paperwork and follows my haste towards the door. As I lay my hand on the cold brass doorknob, he puts his on my shoulder. I pause but don't turn.

"You needn't stay away so long, Santi. We both miss her, and we don't have to be alone in our grief."

Loneliness joins the melee of emotions and makes it more unbearable. For a split second I imagine turning my face into my uncle's chest and sobbing these emotions out of me. But not with Sophia watching. I pull the door open and leave his offer behind.

I SEND THE Holladays a copy of the legal paperwork with every certified send receipt known to man and the U.S. Postal Service. Still, I worry. I try to untangle the Steinway from my convictions, and my pride, so it can just be the property of the church. But Uncle Carl's comment was too much.

She swore you had a special bond to your talent through it. And his mention of being alone with my grief has brought on a desperate loneliness.

It's 9:48 pm and I sit on my bed propped with pillows against the headboard, a video game controller in my hands, and a brutal game of death on the flat TV screen affixed to the wall. As if blasting holes in the core of animated soldiers could ease the hole in mine. In two-hours of gameplay not a single text to past conquests has been returned. I wonder if the game allows you to turn the gun on yourself. I try, but it doesn't. My avatar is shot down. He bleeds out and the color drains from his flesh. The opponent that destroyed me stands over my corpse, then looks out at the screen. I see my father's face in its, startle, and throw the controller at the wall. Then I click the screen to darkness and clutch my chest.

I curl into a ball on my bed.

I hear Uncle Carl's words again, *We don't have to be alone in our grief,* and I wonder how much different things could have been if I had thrown the curtain aside and lay down with my father on the cold hospital floor. We shouldn't have been alone when we were both right there.

A tear falls onto my arm. Its warmth is Sophia's

fingertips, the moment she'd said, *I couldn't have known*, with the compassion I'd been longing for. It Would have been nice to enjoy it in the moment.

If I hadn't been high, I think I could've.

You know you still need me, my addiction chides.

I bury myself beneath the covers.

An old pop song my mother loved and sang like crazy in the car, comes to mind.

"Back 2 Good" by Matchbox 20.

I've got to get it back to good.

Not knowing how, I pop an Ambien instead.

IN THE MORNING, I surrender my angst and text Lucy.

"Just PLAY!!" Lucy texts.

"What??????????"

"The Steinway, you idiot."

Lucy's right, of course. Playing the Steinway in the cathedral is a sensory high that clears my mind like a forearm across a messy desk. I need this after the week I've had. I play Beethoven's Piano Trio in B-flat major, op. 97. Hours pass.

Just as I'm lowering the fall board to cover the piano keys, a woman's voice surprises me from behind. I face her.

She says, "I was happy when I heard that last."

She has a faraway look in her eyes. Her gaze is directed up at the blue and purple stained-glass window. The light that comes through it shades her in melancholy and makes her tall figure even more surreal than it might have been. She's thin. So thin I can see the ball of her shoulders jutting through her sky-blue silk blouse. She continues to stare off and I can't stop staring at her. She has fawn blonde hair that is cut to frame her face and fall below her shoulders. Her skin is fair porcelain, and her features are royal in their polished poise, from the prominent cheekbones and Grecian nose to the well-shaped chin and full lips. She turns her gaze on me and her cerulean blue eyes, dramatized by heavy makeup, cast a spell.

"Then I hope you heard it yesterday," I tell her.

Her eyebrows pike, and she shakes her head with an amused laugh. "Keep playing."

I extend my hand. "I'm—"

"I said, don't stop." Her hands remain at her sides. Her eyes aren't smiling any more.

My head jerks back, the voice is familiar, and not in a good way. "Who are you?"

She closes her eyes and laments. "Please, keep playing."

I spin back to the keys and work to get back in my zone. But now I'm performing, the snap of my wrists is sharper, my back is straighter, and I hold more concern for her experience than my own. The way I would if I were making love to her.

In my periphery, I catch her playing an imaginary violin with her eyes closed. I can almost hear the sweet whine of the instrument that accompanies the song. She mimes it as only a true violinist could. Respect.

Two blue-collar workers enter the cathedral at the far end. The heavy wooden door slams. Our imaginary duet comes to an end. One of the men wheels a professional piano dolly in while the other holds both doors open. She raises her hand. They spot her and move towards us. She makes her hand into a stop sign.

There's a shooting sensation down my legs. "What's happening?"

Her poise falters. "Go and get your legal documents.

I'll act surprised by them and cancel the order."

"You're the bitch on the phone. I sent you the papers."

"My husband is going to contest it. He's already filed a motion to have the legal endowment reversed."

"On what grounds?"

She leans in. "When the donation was made by Barbara, she hadn't inherited the property from her husband yet."

"She was his wife, and he was dying."

She puts her hand on my back and pulls me even closer. I can smell her expensive perfume and feel her height advantage of an inch. "It wasn't her property yet, and if that fails Dirk will contest the fact that her trust was written by the monsignor of the church when she wasn't of sound mind. That he manipulated her for his benefit."

"You could convince them to steal it out from under a church on a fucking technicality that hasn't even seen a courtroom yet?"

She stands up straight. And cocks her head at me. "Possession is nine-tenths of the law."

"Then why stop now?"

She puts her hand her over her forehead, looks to the Steinway, and the hand drops to her cheek along with a deep sigh. "Because it would never be played that way again, and I know Barbara wanted you to have it. She loves you."

I freeze.

Her eyes bore into mine. "Go! Get any papers."

"If you can call it off, then why put on a show?"

"I know how to handle my husband. He's used to getting his way."

With her eyes, she points to the door, and I run to my office where I scramble for random pages for the charade.

Questions whip through my mind about this tactic, about Dirk Holladay whose greed I never considered, and this woman. I carry the stack of papers back to the cathedral with a heartbeat I can't control.

She takes the pages, glances at them, snaps the papers back into my hands and leads the men out. The thudding dampens.

I stand guard over the piano. My fists clenched. The woman returns alone. "She taught you to play that Beethoven trio?"

I release my fists and nod.

"What else did she teach you?"

"To protect what I love."

She guffaws, it echoes through the church, and I see her silver fillings. "And you were ready to take on those men to prove it?"

"If it came to that." I hunker down on the piano bench.

She rests a hand on my shoulders. "Play me something else."

I stare ahead. The skin on my neck prickles.

She tsks. "I take it your repertoire is all tapped out."

I start in on a Liszt etude.

She squeezes my shoulder. "I don't need to hear anything more from dead men today."

"Then you pick."

"All right. Play 'All of Me,' by John Legend. If you can."

I smile because I totally know that one.

As I start in, she says, "Barbara also taught you to sing, didn't she? Sing for me."

She smiles at the parallel the lyrics hold for us. But

wags her finger as if to say I have no right to draw those lines. Then, knowing she has me right where she wants me, she whirls away, and abandons me mid-song.

CHAPTER 8

KITTY HOLLADAY

Overnight Sensation

I ALWAYS ATTEND the quarterly meeting, Dirk. Why would I miss it today?" I ask my husband with one eye on my eyelashes as I coat them with mascara and the other on him, tying his tie in the bathroom mirror.

"I haven't forgiven you for letting the Steinway slip yet." A growl forms in the back of his throat and he undoes the failed knot.

"I've taken my punishment." I wink at him in the mirror where our eyes meet.

"I still don't get it, Katherine." He slides either side of the lavender and grey paisley tie into proper lengths and starts again.

I temper the tremble in my hand. "He had his paperwork in order, the scheme didn't come off." I smear my upper eyelid with the mascara and grope for a Q-tip.

"We don't fumble simple handoffs. We're not

amateurs." Dirk cinches the knot into place.

I blend my eyeshadow to perfection and turn to him. He approaches to caress my face. I smack his hand away. "I don't like your playbook, D."

He rushes me and I hop up onto the countertop behind me.

"But I'm the coach." His head tilts towards me. I can see gold streaks in his hazel eyes. Anger always brightens those veins of gold.

I bat my lashes at him. "Tell me again, coach, how you lost the ball in the first quarter?"

His lip curls. "My dad was dying, we were bringing the company public, and I'd just lost the head of A and R to Sony. So, yeah, it kind of got by me. But don't think my mother didn't plan it that way."

I suck in my cheeks and swallow. I'd helped my mother-in-law with her timing. She wanted the piano for someone she loved more than her son. I wanted to silently punish Dirk for his devious move to ensure I couldn't get pregnant. Though that didn't satisfy me. But the piano coming back into play now fits nicely into my plan. Dirk wants a response.

I whip a quip. "So, you just don't want anyone outsmarting you?"

He drives a fist into his palm. "That piano is a family heirloom, it's my birthright."

"And you don't want legal involved because your maneuvering is questionable. And you know they have an obligation to report every case they handle to the public. Or to the board. I'm not sure which is worse."

He runs his hands through his hair. His face begs for sympathy. "I know you don't agree with the decision to go public."

I clasp his shoulders and stare into his handsome face, indicative of good breeding, smooth, tan, elastic skin with few wrinkles despite his age of fifty-three. Twelve years my senior. His dark blonde hair has hardly receded and still possesses a thickness that makes him look a decade younger. His thick eyebrows are well groomed. I love that about him. I run my thumbs through the short hair above his ears. "You've been getting a little grey in the last few years."

"And you have crow's feet." He strokes my temples with soft fingertips.

I straighten the knot in his tie, and wrap my legs around him, pulling his groin to mine. "But we're still in the game."

IN THE MEETING, we announce missed earnings wide enough to elicit gasps around the conference table. The stock will slide. Quiet moves over the boardroom like the fog behind the sixteen-foot, floor-to-ceiling windows that overlook downtown Los Angeles from twenty stories up.

The conference table is clear glass, and through it, I watch as the board's bodies react to the news. A few men adjust shrinking testicles. There's the blowing of noses, the chipping away at chipped nail polish, and the refusal to make eye contact. The blame hasn't been placed, nor the path to redemption.

Our CFO, a seasoned, white-haired executive that has always reminded me of Perry Mason, sits at the opposite end of the table from Dirk. He folds his hands in front of him and summarizes our issues with one question.

"Why are we losing artists?"

"Sony is utilizing social media in ways we aren't," says a younger man from marketing.

The middle-aged woman from legal leans back in her chair with her yellow pad over her chest. I know she's relieved the lawsuits artists have been filing against us won't be brought to bear as the culprit.

Dirk says, "That social media nonsense is for self-publishers who can't use traditional methods to get their music heard. Why do we have to stoop to that?"

"It's not just for the unlabeled anymore. Every artist needs a YouTube channel, an Instagram account, a Facebook and Twitter page to be relevant," Marketing says. "I've been trying to tell you this."

"That's why I've hired Victoria Thompson as the new VP of Publicity," the CFO says.

"Hired?" Dirk says, "I didn't approve that. The bidding war put her salary well out of range."

Our CFO rubs the edge of his mouth and refolds his hands. "Sony only kept at the bidding to keep Victoria off our team. They have a handle on exploiting social media that we need to leap towards. Her salary will be worth its weight."

Dirk's face reddens. His eyes glow gold. "Exactly, and the exploitation happens to the artists. Look people, we're still in the game because once we have an artist in demand, we keep them relevant. We don't make one-hit wonders here. We make artists that bring in revenue for decades!" He pounds the table with his fist, and I feel the vibration travel through the glass to my seat mid-table.

"Why don't we listen to Victoria Thompson's presentation before we assume she'll do any damage? She has her own reputation to uphold," Marketing says.

The CFO buzzes his secretary. "Is Victoria Thompson here?"

"Coming up the elevator now, sir."

"Wait for my cue to send her in."

"I don't want to use any of these untested methods on the three hopefuls you've groomed," Dirk tells the head of Artists and Repertoire.

I sense my moment. "How about on someone unknown? Someone you haven't already placed a stake on? Someone, we can afford to let fall from the summit of overnight sensation?"

"An overnight sensation would correct this stock dip," the CFO says. He notifies his secretary to send Victoria in.

The head of A and R rubs his salt and pepper goatee. "I'm a team player. If the experiment works, we'll use it again."

Dirk licks his lips. "I can agree to that."

"We need a song, *and* an artist," A and R says.

"I have both in mind," I tell them.

Eyebrows arch. I slide my phone across the table towards the CFO and the approaching figure of Victoria Thompson. She advances towards us with an all-business walk. Her tall designer heels don't slow her down. From what I hear nothing does. Victoria Thompson is petite. No taller than five foot four. But her presence commands attention. She is all poise and polished beauty. She wears a tight fuchsia skirt suit that compliments her figure and her milk-chocolate skin. Her long, sleek black hair is as dark as her eyes. They zero in on the phone. She picks it up as it slides toward the edge of the table and eyes the screen.

"Click play," I say. A simple version of my song plays. I watch Victoria Thompson's face while her head nods to the beat. She has a sensual mouth that parts in a genuine smile as she listens. Everyone looks for approval from A and R. He signals two thumbs up.

"I take it this is one of your songs, Katherine?" Dirk eyes me.

"Yes, and I'll take payment in stock."

That has everyone nodding.

"The song works. Who's gonna sing it?" Victoria asks. We make eye contact. She and I have talked before today. But no one else needs to know that.

I stand up. "Santiago DeAngelo. You don't know him. No one does. Not yet."

"DeAngelo?" Dirk scowls.

Victoria Thompson interjects. "What does he look like? I need a face. Can he sing?" she says while typing on her phone. "His Facebook pic isn't a head shot. I need to see him."

"You won't be disappointed," I tell her.

She grins. "Is he signed?"

"I'll handle that. I want to be his contact point," I tell the CFO directly. He nods.

"If he's not the real deal, he won't hold up under my plan," Victoria says.

"Give us our money's worth. We've got stockholders to impress," Dirk says.

CHAPTER 9

SANTIAGO DEANGELO

New Kind of High

SOPHIA BURSTS INTO my office. "I thought you were going to fix this!" She thrusts a torn envelope at me. Her face is ashen. "The Holladays are contesting the Steinway donation. There's a court date."

I stand and pound the desk with the side of my fist. "What?" I shake my head in confusion. "We can't trust them. I'll handle it."

She drops her arms to her side. "I didn't know what that piano meant to you and I'm sorry."

"I'm sorry too."

Her face twitches into a reluctant smile.

"What's going on in here?" Dad enters. He's clearly pleased to see me and Sophia together.

I grab the folder I'd been working on before Sophia surged. "Dad, I worked out a twenty percent cost reduction on the font."

Both their faces light up.

"Good work," Dad says. He musses my hair. If I had a tail, I'd wag it. Dad departs.

I turn to Sophia, but a shrill ring pierces the moment. I fumble for the desk phone. It's Nora.

"Santiago, there's a woman here to see you, I told her to wait here but she said she'd be at the piano. Didn't give her name."

The receiver slips out of my hands. I picture the piano movers.

"Shit, they're here for the piano again."

"Why? What's happening?" Sophia says, as I make for the door.

"Don't worry, I got this." I bolt for the cathedral.

At the wooden doors, I double over to catch my breath before entering. Inside the church few items remain. The pews, the podium, and the piano, which is being played by Katherine Holladay.

"Get away from there," I say, my breath ragged. I limp towards her with a cramp in my calf. She plays "All of Me" where I left off last time. "Stop it!" I slam the fall board over the keys. Her hands slip out right before it thuds down. I search the cathedral for the moving men. "Where are they?"

"I came alone."

"You're contesting ownership?"

She folds her hands on the piano and shines her eyes up at me. "I told you he would."

"So, it's not over? Don't you get it? Barbara wanted me to have it."

"I know more about that than you ever will. How do you think that made her son feel?"

"I don't give a fuck. We went over everything with a

lawyer, it's all sound."

"Then why are you shaking?"

"It matters to me. Call him off."

She stands and puts her hands on her straight hips. She wears grey slacks and a dark purple cashmere sweater. Her eyes maintain the intensity of her first impression on me.

"You don't win with Dirk that way. He never stops until he gets what he wants."

"But you stood up to him last time."

She takes a folded slip of paper from her back pocket. "Dirk's legal grounds are questionable. Give this to your lawyer."

I scoff. "Like I'm gonna take that."

"Take it. I want you for other reasons."

"Like what?"

"I want your voice for my song, Santiago." She tucks the paper into the front pocket of my dress slacks.

"My voice?" I touch my throat. Katherine smirks and reaches for a soft-sided black leather briefcase at her feet. She hands me sheet music. Its edge slices my finger. I suck on the paper cut as I look at the music.

Song title: "New Kind of High," music and lyrics by Kitty Holladay. Funny to think of her as Kitty.

"I'd have to hear it." I thrust it back at her.

"Here." She offers a pair of earbuds. Black wires dangle from her hands to her cell phone.

I shake my head. "Nah, I'm good."

"Just listen. Please?" She sits down at the piano bench and looks up at me. Her cheek tics with the anxiety all artists feel when they share their art.

I sympathize with that and settle next to her with both of us facing the keys. She sits to my left. I insert one of the ear buds, and hand her the other half. "Let's listen together." I scooch closer until her perfume tickles the back of my throat. She takes the ear bud, and sets the sheet music in the holder, an ornate G clef carved from wood. Her cheek is warm against mine, and I'm glad I shaved this morning. She presses play. The music has a seductive beat. We listen through once. The second time through she squeezes my knee.

"Sing."

I sing, "I got a lust for trusting on a dark night, pushing the boundaries back and hunting for the high. There's no solace in peace, I need relief, but relief keeps slipping, escaping just like time."

She giggles into the piano. The ear bud slips free from my ear. My cheeks ignite. I try to stand, but she presses me down.

"No, Santiago, you're perfect. I'm just happy. Sing the chorus."

My voice cracks in the impossibly high crescendo of the word high. She squeezes my triceps. "It's a high note, tighten your abs so you can hit it clean." I flashback to Barbara using that same exact phrase. She moves the music back and I try it twice more.

When I hit the note, Kitty's eyes flare. "You delight me. Your voice is everything Barbara strove for."

I rub my chin. "I don't get it. This song is amazing, what do you need me for?"

"I want to give you a contract to make this song a hit."

"I don't think so." Acid burns my throat. I swivel around and stand.

She hooks her finger in my belt loop and slides across the bench as I step away. "What do you mean, no? I want to make you a star. This song will take us to the top of the charts, then we attract all the best songwriters for a stellar debut album."

I rub my face. "This doesn't make any sense."

"Don't question fate."

"Shit, when someone says fate, I know they're selling something."

"Okay, you're right. Holladay Records needs to show the world they can compete with an overnight sensation."

I spread my stance and arch my brows. "How?"

"Social media blitz like no-one's-business." She stands up and moves in on me. With heels she towers over me.

"Why me?"

"You want to hear it's your voice and your face." She runs a fingertip along my jawline. Then thrusts her finger in my chest. "In your case, you wouldn't be far off the mark. But truth is, you're expendable. Not many people can take what we have planned. You game?"

I gulp. "What do you mean?"

"Half the business of stardom is the pressure. It either makes diamonds or dust. Can you take it?"

"Do you think I can?"

"Barbara knew you could, but she hid you away. All I know is you play like a mother fucker and your voice is even stronger. That didn't happen by accident. I know first-hand the methods Barbara used with you. So, yeah, I *think* you can take it. But I don't care if you can't."

I stand there with my mouth open. "I'll do it if you drop the claim on the Steinway."

"Not negotiable. Don't you trust me?" She looks down at the corner of paper peeking from my pocket.

My foot taps the marble floor, maybe this is the way into Mom's song. I could share it with the world.

"Could I write a song for the album?"

"I'd have to hear it."

I hold my breath and search the transparent blue of her eyes. They twinkle back at me, and I sit back down at the piano to play Mom's song with my heart in my throat. Kitty listens, taps her lips, and sits again. Our shoulders touch, and she slides me towards the octave she wants.

"Try it like this." And she plays my intro in a transposed key. It tweaks the mood of the song to match what I was searching for.

"How'd you know to do that?"

The apple of her cheeks bob. "That's what I do."

My eyes prickle with tears. I play the song again in the new key.

She stands by. "Your song's not done. Can you finish it while recording nine others? Because no one cares, except you, if it makes the album or not."

"I'll finish it."

"Good, then it's time to sign." She whips the contract from the briefcase while the doors of the church open and my dad leads a team of workers into the church. He waves across the distance.

I bring a shaky hand to my forehead. "Let's go outside." We escape through a side entrance door. I shrink from the bright sunlight.

"What's wrong now?" she asks.

I pull the hair at my brow and weigh things out against this crazy-ass-killer chance. How will this look to Dad or Sophia? Things have been better between me and Dad, but only because I'm doing what he wants.

Shouldn't he love me no matter what?

"I can't do it all!"

Kitty grabs my arm. "Santiago, life never supports our art. Our art supports our spirit and makes life worth living." She releases her grip.

I suck a deep breath in. "Yes, exactly! Give me the papers."

She hands me the contract with a Golden Mont Blanc fountain pen. She turns so I can use her back to sign. I sign *Santiago Lorenzo DeAngelo* in a flowing script I've practiced.

She takes the pen and I turn around so she can use my back to sign in her place. "That'll be your autograph soon enough, kid. I'll make sure you get a copy. Give me your number, I'm gonna have Victoria Thompson, your publicist, call you. You do *everything* she says. Got it?" We exchange numbers.

"This is going to be so fun." Kitty giggles and kisses me full on the lips. It makes me cold all over.

Minutes later my phone rings. "This is Victoria Thompson. I want you to take a selfie and text it to this number." She hangs up.

I take three selfies and freak out over which is best. Eany-meany-miny damn. I send the second one and pace the twenty odd seconds it takes Victoria Thompson to respond by text:

"Nice! We start with headshots. Here's two photographers in your area. Jenna Clauson and Dara Clarke. Google them both. Pick one and send me your appointment info."

I pull up the website for the first chick, Jenna. Her work is mostly headshots, all black and white. I recognize a couple of her clients from TV shows. Then I google Dara Clarke. Her website opens onto a grainy nude shot that reminds me of the Penthouse layouts I used to find at the bottom of my brothers' laundry hamper. I scan the site. The artist works from her historic estate in Redlands. I scroll to the bottom of the page and find an eye-popping shot of the artist herself. I know that face. No . . . holy shit, Dara Clarke is Sophia's mother.

I text Victoria Thompson. "I have an appointment set up with Dara Clarke for 11 a.m. Saturday morning."

CHAPTER 10

SANTIAGO DEANGELO

You're An Addict

I PRESS THE intercom button at the street-level-gate to Sophia's house. Her voice, shrouded in static, answers the call.

"I'm early for my 11 o'clock with Dara Clarke," I say.

Can she tell it's me?

The gate buzzes and moves with a jerk and a screech. I ascend the long tree-lined driveway which wraps around the aging Italian villa built in the 1890s. My dad has been eager to restore this estate for years. So, I couldn't pass up a chance to kill a few birds with one stone—and not be stoned while doing it. I took just enough Vicodin to make it through the morning without a splitting headache. I can't take the chance of acting like a complete asshole in front of her again. Though, I have a few handy in case I need to summon some extra charisma for the photo shoot. Victoria assures me these photos are essential. Which is kind of crazy to think about . . . so I don't.

I park in a round driveway and walk the brick lined path to the front doors. I ring the bell and twirl the bird of paradise I brought Sophia.

Was this a good idea?

When Sophia answers the door, her smile assures me it was, though her face clouds with confusion.

"Did someone drive in ahead of you? I was expecting my mom's client." She peers past me towards the circular drive.

"I am your mom's client."

"What?" Her brows peak.

"I wanted to see what your world was like, meet your mom, win her approval." I extend the bird of paradise. "These were my mother's favorites. I thought you might like them too."

She ignores the flower. "My mom's not going to like this. She's been preparing for the shoot for a couple of days."

"No, the shoot is real. I need the photos, my publicist recommended her."

"Why do you have a publicist?"

"I signed a contract with Holladay records to do a single. The pics are a marketing thing."

"You signed with Holladay? What happened to 'we can't trust them?'"

"It's him we can't trust. But his wife is different, she's going to help us keep the Steinway with the church."

"And you believe that?"

I flinch with the fear she might be right about Kitty and the worry that I misread Sophia's feelings for me. My voice drops. "Is that stupid? Was it a bad idea to come here?" I hold out the cut flower again. Its sapphire petals crown the tangerine head like a bird in a tropical paradise.

She grasps the flower. "No, I'm glad you came. Thank you for this, it's beautiful. We have them growing wild in the yard."

"Will you show them to me?"

"My mom doesn't like to be kept waiting. And I'm expecting my friend soon, we're going for a hike."

That explains the hiking boots and casual workout clothing she wears. But is the friend a girl or a guy?

I check the time on my phone. "It's only 10:51."

She glances upstairs where the high-pitched whine of a hair dryer can be heard coming from the second floor.

"All right, I have a few minutes too. This way," she says and nods towards the hall. She is still holding the bird of paradise in her hands and brings it with her as we walk.

I follow. She looks back as we walk towards the entrance to a library.

"By the way, thanks for all of your efforts on price negotiations for the project. We're going to get a lot done with that money."

"It's nothing," I say, while inwardly rejoicing.

In the library, I pause and scan the shelves. There is a blend of hard backs, paper backs, random novels, classics, and art books. I search for one or two I may have read and discover a section with titles like *Living Sober*, *Blackout*, and *Alcohol Lied to Me Again*. That last one makes me scratch my head.

When have opiates ever told me the truth?

Sophia slides a sliding glass door out to the patio and beckons me out.

Outside, the January air is chill beneath the covered patio. There is a set with interchangeable back drops and professional lighting in place. Beside it is a wicker bar with a clean glass top, several water bottles, a bottle of Don Julio tequila, and two shot glasses.

Sophia rolls her eyes and looks at me. "About my mom. She's not . . . well . . . I'm not like her. You know what? Never mind, she's an amazing photographer."

She motions me into the warm sunlight beyond the patio where a six-foot tall, three-tiered-concrete fountain spews a thin stream of water into an algae-lined basin alive with bright-colored fish.

"I keep koi," Sophia says. She tosses a few pellets from a cannister in for them.

I light up like a kid as I watch them suck the surface of the water for the food. "They're beautiful."

"So is this, come see." We walk towards the top of a staircase that descends the hill her home is built on. The crumbling concrete steps have four separate levels breaking up the path. Each level has its own feature. I stare out at the view of the valley beyond. Bright blue winter sky, green treetops, and the snow-covered mountains in the distance make it one of the best views in the city.

I whistle. "I've always wanted to see this place. My dad would love to get his hands on it."

"It's charming as it is. Don't you think?"

"I'm charmed."

We trot down the first level of steps towards half-a-dozen overgrown bird of paradise bushes with orange heads protruding their unkempt nests. I worry the spontaneous decision to bring the single flower may appear petty amongst this overgrown paradise, but the fact that she's still holding it puts my concern to rest. Nestled between the bird of paradise bushes, beneath a decrepit wooden pergola, is a wall of rock with what seems to be a replica of the *Boca Della Verita*: a famous stone carving in Rome with an open mouth that legend has it will bite the hand of those who lie.

"This is cool!" I approach the carving and run my hand along the edge of the massive mouth.

"My mom made it. Are you superstitious?" she asks.

"It's only a copy. It can't bite my hand off."

"Are you sure?" She flashes her eyes at me.

She must know the movie. I mean it's old, but, with something like this in her yard she's gotta know *Roman Holiday*. And here I am Gregory Peck to her Audrey Hepburn. Her silver blue eyes sparkle at me with a childish amusement so fresh I want to bottle it and distribute it, if only to make the world a place worth living in. Her mirth calls me to the comic. I extend my hand into the hole, then scream and mime the struggle to pull it out.

Sophia laughs out loud.

I fall on the ground clutching my hand and say, "Don't worry, it only got my finger." My right wrist still aches from the accident and the chronic pain makes my portrayal more believable as I slide the tip of my thumb along my hand to perform the illusionary removal-of-my-index-finger trick I learned to awe my niece with.

Sophia goes to her knees laughing, the flower still in her hand. "No one's ever done that," she says with a snort that makes us both laugh even harder.

"You're kidding me, what with the movie and all."

I crawl over to her and we help each other to our feet. I pull her into me. She's still clutching the bird of paradise in her hand. I hold her to me to resist the feeling that I'll float away. She closes her eyes and I tilt my head to kiss her, but stop, because the unbearable lightness is the presence of my mother . . . and I've never felt her like this before.

"What? What is it?" Sophia's eyes widen, as though

she feels Mom, too. I look down and see the hairs on her arms standing on end. Beneath my long-sleeve dress shirt mine do the same. She breathes heavily. I haven't dared take a breath yet.

"What's happening?" Sophia whispers.

"My mom is here. You feel it too, don't you?"

"I feel something. Does this always happen to you?"

"No, never. It's the first time. I think it's because of you."

She shakes her head in confusion. I pull her in for the kiss, but she pulls away. I hear a camera shutter click repeatedly. Sophia moves towards the sound.

"There you are! What are you doing out here?" A woman approaches.

"Mom, this is my friend, Santiago DeAngelo, the one I was telling you about from church. He's also your client today. So crazy, right?"

Sophia's mother descends the stone steps with a sway like an old Hollywood diva. From a distance she's as beautiful as her daughter, but as she nears, I realize she isn't aging well, and given the books on her shelves, I can't help but guess at alcoholism.

"Sophia, Heather is here, she's waiting in the driveway."

Oh, thank God her friend's a girl.

Sophia turns to me and nibbles her lower lip, "It was good to see you." She jogs up a few steps and turns back to her mother. "Mom, why is the bar . . .? Never mind, just be good." Sophia climbs the last few steps then turns and gives me a little wave that makes me feel good all over.

I can make you feel like that.

I know it's a lie. But I still can't stop myself from

putting the pill in my pocket into my mouth. Dara turns to me and introduces herself with a vice-grip handshake that shoots pain through my aching wrist up to my elbow. She gives me the once over. There's an empty feeling in the pit of my stomach.

Dara steps back, holds her hands in a square shaped box and says, "Victoria Thompson has placed a tall order today. I thought we'd set the mood with some refreshments." She points up the steps and guides me towards the bar. I hear a car pulling away from the house as we approach.

"Have you done this kind of photo shoot before, Santiago?"

"I've taken a few pictures, but nothing that would qualify as a photo shoot?"

"Are you nervous?"

I shrug.

"Sure, you are. Everyone is. It can be a difficult thing to warm up to." She moves behind the bar and clutches the tall bottle of Don Julio.

"It's a little early for Tequila, isn't it?"

Dara pours two and slides one to me. "Great shots—for great shots." She gives a flirtatious wink.

Does she think that's sexy?

I clutch the shot glass and consider my options: one—high tail it back to the car and get an appointment with the other lady, two—put on my biggest smile and make the best of it.

I don't want to drink the shot. Not after my vodka binge this New Year's.

Dara holds her glass to her lips in a dramatic pause.

I am here—and I do need to get into the right mood. It'll be fine.

I set my phone and keys on the bar and toss my shot back. Dara shoots hers and sucks a lime wedge. She hands it to me.

I wave it away. "We ready?"

She pours another. "So serious. This is supposed to be fun."

I turn my glass upside down. "I'm good."

"If you were good, you'd be smiling. That's my job. Consider this a short cut."

I pour myself another drink.

She tsks, "Where's the love?" and steals the bottle back.

Doubling-down on that note should register, but it doesn't, and the next thing I know—several shots later—Dara's pointing the camera, while egging me on like we're on the set of a Zoolander remake. We move all over the sprawling yard and back to the professional set with rarely a dull moment as she manipulates a wide variety of expressions with her voice.

"What turns you on more? Pink nipples or red lips?" She asks.

My answer is a raging blush, followed by a snicker and the look she was waiting for as she pounces on it with her camera.

"Santiago, Victoria wants a couple shots al fresco."

"Huh?"

"Take your shirt off, young man."

"I dunno." I walk backwards, this doesn't feel right to me. And besides that, vain as I am, I would have done a routine of pushups and sit ups all week if I would have known. Then Dara's fragrant hair is in my face, camera hanging from around her neck, the scent of tequila strong on her breath as she works on a stiff button.

"I got it." I back up further, still trying to legitimize the request as a normal part of a shoot like this. She shrugs and returns her attention to the previous photos on the back of her digital camera.

It's nothing. It's fun.

I grapple further with a few buttons. Why did I even wear a button up shirt today? Oh yeah, it was to impress Sophia.

She wouldn't be impressed.

I button the buttons back up. I'm beyond thirsty. And I get it—the label on the prescription painkillers, warning you not to drink alcohol while taking them, is not there to keep you from having a good time. A headache sets in.

Retch up the alcohol and take another pill.

"You know what? I think I'm done for the day." I walk over to the bar and grab a water bottle, guzzling it halfway down.

Dara looks up from the back of her camera. I register a glimpse of disappointment, followed by approval. I feel like I just passed the bigger test she was holding for her daughter.

She turns the camera around and shows me a tight headshot. "You have a beautiful smile, but no matter what I said there was still so much sadness in your eyes."

I feel tears welling as I fight off the sadness that is always with me. I gulp more of the water.

Dara's quiet a moment still scanning the screen, I pocket my phone and keys and announce my departure.

Dara looks up from the camera. On her face, I recognize the daring grin an alcohol buzz gives you before you broach the taboo. I brace myself.

She says, "Sophia likes you, Santiago. But you're not

her type."

"Excuse me?"

She frowns and shakes her head. "She's been talking about this great guy who's saving the church project, plays the piano, and reads Jane Austen. And I think—yeah right—sounds too good to be true. Then you show up here, and you're like this." She spreads her hands wide.

"Like what?"

"Like me."

"What is that supposed to mean?"

"You're an addict. Or on your way to becoming one. I saw you eat a pill, and once I convinced you to drink, you had plenty. Don't be embarrassed. I've heard what happened to your mother, and I get it. But I'm here to tell you, you don't have to become some tragic figure to protect your right to be angry and sad."

I rub my face with both hands. "What are you saying?"

She turns the camera around and shows me the image she captured of me and Sophia near the stone carving. "It's the only time your smile made it to your eyes. It's okay to be *that* guy."

"That's who I'm trying to be!" My voice hitches. I sip some more of the water.

She looks back down at the camera and scans through the digital images. "We got a lot of great shots. Victoria can definitely work with these . . ." she mumbles to herself, "and with my logo on every pic she publishes . . ."

"I'm gonna go then."

"I don't think you're okay to drive."

"Yeah, you're right. I'm gonna call an Uber and come back for my car later."

She looks up. "All right. Good luck, and just know, if

you get a chance with my Sophia, and you hurt her . . ." She shakes her head and leaves the rest to my imagination.

CHAPTER 11

KITTY HOLLADAY

One of the Special Ones

TAKE SIX. I restart the track off a count and Santiago pours his voice into the microphone in front of him. But the sound is wrong. "You're not coming in on beat," I tell him through the microphone.

He flinches at my voice in the cans.

"Again."

We're in my home studio. Why can't I get him to sound the way he did in the church two weeks ago? I watch him through the glass that separates us, his forehead sheens, and he uses both hands to wipe the sweat into his dark wavy hair. I can almost smell that clean damp on him again, like I could when we first listened to my song together for the first time. "Santiago, let's take a minute."

His face smarts. "I got this Kitty, roll it again."

"If you miss a note, fine, but if you miss a note and you can't hear that you missed a note. We have a problem."

He drops his head.

"Tell me what's different, right now, from the first time you sang this for me?"

"Just roll it again," he says.

"Close your eyes."

His head rocks back and he sighs up at the ceiling, but he *does* close his eyes.

"Tell me about your surroundings."

"It's pretty amazing here. I've never been in a real studio."

"Keep your eyes closed. Use your other senses."

"There's a chemical smell from the foam in the walls. It's brighter than it needs to be. Uh . . . there's a Yamaha piano that I'd like to try out."

"Take the headphones off and play something for me." I dim the lights.

At the piano, he warms up with scales and arpeggios in the same way Barbara taught me to. I remove my headphones and turn my controls off to let him find his groove on his own. I sink into my chair, pinch the bridge of my nose, and wonder how long it's been since I've really slept. I'll close my eyes for just a second.

I startle awake, unsure of the elapsed measure of sleep. I guess about twenty minutes. Santiago is on the studio floor floating on the surface of his music's movement. He is playing the song he would like to write for the album. It has an intense chorus and beautiful bridge with a lot of emotion being translated through the music. It will turn a lot of heads. Songs that powerful always do. But the words will matter most. I watch him in a sleepy haze until his composition invigorates me again. Then, I float towards that untainted influence to appear at his side and lay a hand on his shoulder.

"May I?"

He slides over and I sit beside him. His body is warm against mine.

"What are the words for your song, Santiago?"

"She hasn't told me yet."

She? I assume he means that the same inspiration that led to the music hasn't provided the words in kind. But I don't ask, preferring to draw his attention back to my own song. I crack my knuckles. "Lyrics are like tits on a woman, Santiago. Some people could take 'em or leave 'em, but most people want to put 'em in their mouth." I watch his Adam's apple bob as he swallows my words. "Ya know, sing along. Take my lyrics for example, those came first for me."

"For me, the music came first."

"You're worried, aren't you? That the lyrics haven't come."

He nods, almost imperceptibly.

"Well don't. Some of the best song writers I know can't write a song top to bottom on their own. They're collaborators. You're a collaborator. You need a connection to the person you're writing with. The music you've written is wonderful, you just need to find your lyricist."

He faces me. "Will you help me?" he asks.

I know this is what he wants from me, but I'm not the one he needs. I stare into his face. He's so young, the plump of his cheeks is an insult to me. For him, time is still on his side. But his youth smacks of something else. Virility.

"You're just a baby," I tell him. Beneath my voice is the hint of a laugh.

He misinterprets the mirth he hears. "I'm no baby." He starts to stand.

I press my palm against his chest and feel the thump of

his heart beneath his collared Polo shirt. "I could teach you things," I say in his ear.

"Why would you if I'm such a baby?" Anger dangles from the edge of his words.

I sing the beginning of my song in a husky voice, "I've got a lust for trusting on a dark night." I hum the next bar and nudge him to pick it up. He follows with the next line.

And then we sing the third together. "You're there now. Let's get the headphones back on."

But, behind me, Dirk says, "Am I interrupting something, Pussy Cat?"

I jump up from the piano. "Dirk, you scared me."

"I see that."

I approach him. "I thought you were in court in San Bernardino?"

"Why aren't you using the company recording studio?"

I stand stock still. "You know I always like to use my own studio."

"But you're working for me now, Katherine."

"I have more control here."

"Is that what I'm witnessing?"

I muster nonchalance and saunter closer. "We're finding our harmony. That's how hits are made." I draw up closer and kiss his lips. Dirk doesn't kiss me back.

"I want him to record at one of the corporate studios." Dirk brushes my hair out of my face and tucks it behind my ear. He searches me.

"I'm clean, I promise."

He nods.

"How did it go today?" I ask him.

Dirk's answer is directed at Santiago. "Your uncle

must think he's awfully clever wearing his priest-collar into the courtroom. I know that's why the judge agreed to dismiss the case. But the Steinway isn't safe yet."

"They dismissed?" My voice cracks. My husband turns his gaze back to me. His green eyes are flecked with gold. I tense. Movement behind him catches my attention. I turn and see his mother at the sound board behind the glass. I often let her sit in with me. Music still lights her up. But today I'd gone out of my way to encourage her to join me. I wanted to see if Santiago's presence would trigger one of her spells of lucidity, she still occasionally experiences. The moments that she comes back are priceless, even though they're brief and exhaust her.

I'd even gone so far as to scour her old photo albums for pictures of her and Santiago together and pointed them out to her while mentioning he would be coming to the studio today. But I never know how much sinks in and the last thing I wanted was for Barbara to see Santiago with Dirk in the room.

"Your mother's in here. Let me call Jess." I reach for my phone, but it's not in my pocket. Barbara calls out to us. I walk over and open the door.

Barbara says, "Bobby, Bobby?" which is what she called her late husband and now calls Dirk half the time in diseased misunderstanding. Barbara creeps out onto the studio floor towards him. Her shoulders stooped, her back humped with age. Santiago gasps and looks away.

"Barbara, you're not allowed in here," Dirk says.

I wish he would just call her *Mom* like a normal person; it would help her confusion. He puts both hands on his mother's shoulders to restrain her, but Barbara ignores him, recognizing Santiago beyond a doubt.

Barbara peeks around her son's body.

"My boy?" she says to Santiago.

Dirk cocks his head at her. "Come on, Barbara, let's get you back to bed."

"I want to talk to my boy. Santiago, are you playing every day?"

He jumps up and walks towards her. "Yes, Mrs. Holladay, every day."

Barbara's nurse joins us and lays a hand on her patient's shoulder. Dirk lifts his off. "Jess, you need to keep a better eye on her than this."

"It won't happen again, Mr. Holladay. Come on, Barbara, I made lunch for you." Barbara straightens her humped back and looks directly at her protégé. "Santiago, you were always one of the special ones."

"Thank you," he says standing just a few feet away, looking like he wants to hug her but unsure if he should.

"Jess," Dirk growls.

The nurse takes Barbara's hand and tugs her. Barbara resumes her stooped posture and shuffles out of the room. I cup my mouth.

"Katherine, a word," Dirk says to me. My heart aches for my husband. If Barbara had only told her son, *he* was one of the special ones, he might be a different man today.

"Santiago, why don't you let yourself out," I tell him.

"Nice to meet you Mr. Holladay," Santiago says with a hint of sarcasm that Dirk ignores.

The kid's got balls. Good to know.

When he's gone, Dirk crosses his arms and narrows his eyes at me. I chew the insides of my cheek while I wait for it to start.

"I don't like what I just saw," he says.

"Let's go upstairs and talk."

"I don't like that boy."

"I'm surprised your mother recognized him," I say, hoping to steer the conversation towards the odd ending and away from the awkward beginning.

"She can't even get my name right and she remembers his?"

Shit, land mines in that direction too. "Let's just go upstairs and talk. You look tired."

"I was up all night with my lawyer forming our case for the judge. Can you believe that asshole dismissed?"

"Just buy your own antique piano. You never even played the Steinway."

"But you did. Shouldn't I have the right to give it to my wife, or my children?"

"You had a vasectomy, Dirk!"

"Barbara didn't know that."

"Neither did I, struggling in vain to get pregnant all those years." I quiver with pent up anger.

"You said you wouldn't bring this up again, Kitty."

"It's no wonder your mom has Alzheimer's. It was the only way to forget how awful you can be."

He takes one step towards me and grabs my wrists. I try to wriggle free. He smirks at the pain he reads on my face, and my way out hits me.

I draw up close to him and rub myself against him like a cat. "I need you," I purr.

"Forget it, Pussy Cat, you can't fuck your way out of this one."

"I need you to punish me for being wrong. I shouldn't have touched him, you're right. You're always right." I rub my hand against the fine wool of the crotch of his pants. He responds as expected. With my free hand I pull down the loose waist of my knit pants and dip a finger inside myself then hold it up to his nose for him to smell. His eyes roll back in his head and I put the finger in his mouth. He squeezes my breast and I walk backwards to the piano bench with my finger still between his lips. He spins me around and hinges me forward. I slip the pants off and kneel on the cushioned piano bench. He thrusts himself, and I welcome the known force. Then I disconnect into my own world of jumbled musical tracks, disjointed, and spread over the whole of my musical career. There's the classical music his mother drove into me, there's the multitude of songs I produced, some that hit the charts, (never number 1 though) there are the jingles I wrote that still pay the bills and there's my new song at the end of that vortex with Santiago singing it. I submit to my husband's cadence, occasionally making an obligatory moan to keep him invested. The rhythm speeds up and then I brace myself for the dead weight he becomes when the spasm ends. I flip around. The gold is gone from his eyes. I run my fingers through his handsome hair.

"Better?"

He gathers me in his arms and kisses my neck with a passion I haven't felt in him in years. Perhaps his jealousy has reminded him what a prize our connection still is.

"You're mine, Kitty."

"Yes D." I want to tell him that I send him out into the world everyday knowing the number of women who compete for his attention. I want to tell him that he can trust me the way I trust him. I do trust him. Infidelity is not his weakness. But all that would be uphill from where we are now.

"We're happy . . . aren't we, Kitty?"

"Sure. Let me take you upstairs and rub these kinks out

to prove it."

After a twenty-minute rub down he wants to make love properly. Afterwards, he lies on his back with his hands folded on his chest, his eyes closed. I trace my finger over his nipple. "Dirk, I have an idea."

He pretends to snore.

I squeeze his nipple hard. "I know you're not sleeping."

He opens one eye.

"I'm worried. Victoria Thompson is about to unleash this massive campaign and I don't think the kid's prepared for it. I mean she's pulling favors at all the radio stations, using contacts at Instagram, and has a team of interns ready to post and respond on Twitter and Facebook."

"So? That was the plan."

"I think I need to keep him out of LA until the smoke clears."

He adjusts the pillow under his head. "I don't really care what happens to the kid, so long as this plan gets the board off my back."

"Well, we can both use him. I just . . . well you know how much making this song fly means to me right?"

He sinks back into his fluffed pillows. "That's one thing you've had *no* problem communicating."

I sit up on my knees and trace my fingers through his thick chest hair. "I need to insulate him from the storm and have him focus on just my song."

"Spit it out, Kitty."

"I want to use your mom's home studio in Redlands. I could..."

He sits up. "Absolutely not."

"What's the point of keeping the place like a museum

if we don't ever take advantage of it?"

"I got you out of the Inland Empire."

"I like it there, Dirk. It's private. It's home."

"What do you need privacy for?"

"To coax my song out of him, Dirk. It's a process. He's never done this before."

"That studio needs upgrades."

"I know, about seventy-five thousand dollars' worth."

"Don't look at me—ask the kid for it." He scoffs on the assumption that's impossible.

I sit up taller, excited he's taken the bait. "What if he did pay for it?"

"What, you think he has money?"

"I had one of your PIs check him out, he has some kind of trust account with money from a settlement."

Dirk lies back down. "Still, how would you get him to pay for it?" he says with an air of challenge.

"Leave that to me. Just tell me you'll let me record there if he does."

He looks at me apprehensively.

I rub his chest. "And I'll be close to the piano in case you finagle something."

He shakes his head.

"Come on, this song is going to take me to the top, and I'm this close." I hold my fingers millimeters apart.

"I just don't like the idea of the two of you spending all that time together alone."

"The music we make together is all that matters."

Dirk puts his arms behind his head and looks thoughtful. "Do we own the masters for anything he writes while he's under contract?"

"Of course, that's standard new artist contract

language."

"Good, I like that song he's written, and I want to use control of it to keep him in line."

CHAPTER 12

SANTIAGO DEANGELO

I'm Gonna Take My Shot

AT HOME, AT the piano, I imagine strangling Dirk for the way he spoke to his mother and his wife. What did he see between Kitty and me? What *happened* between Kitty and me? I tear off my jacket and throw it in the corner of the room.

Even now, I get hard thinking of her. But I shake off the carnal feeling; our purpose is bigger than that. If I master her song, she'll help me master mine. I depress the piano keys in a grating groan that matches my own, then jump up from the bench and make for the bathroom.

I whip the Vicodin bottle from the bathroom counter. It's lighter than I remember.

Only four left.

I check my phone, no texts back from my pill connect Zenon. I rub my knuckles against my teeth.

A text from Lucy pops up:

"Any progress on the song?"

I pocket the phone and pick up the pill bottle again. The Z man always comes through.

I take the last four to the kitchen, crush them on the counter inside a Ziploc bag and pour the powder into a glass with just a little water, then I swirl and gulp the bitter mixture.

I pass the piano by and head for the speed bag on the back porch, punching to a rhythm while I practice explaining my recording contract to Dad. My tempo sputters. My opiate-high hits like the climax of a bad joke.

Instead of the pleasure I'd hoped to float away on, my fears and shortcomings arrive to heckle me in stereo. I head for the couch and pull a blanket over my head. If I wasn't so high, I'd take my plane out for a spin. Flying would offer the perfect escape. The intense concentration, the shift in perspective of a bird's eye view, and the natural rush of adrenaline from a difficult landing. I wish I hadn't taken those pills.

A buddy from high school texts to grab a beer, but people grate on me when I get to this place. I text back. "Not today." Then I wonder how long it will take for him to quit texting like the rest of my friends did after the accident. They don't know how to take what I've become.

What have I become?

I can't keep living like this.

Next morning, my bleary eyes don't want to open, and the left one feels like an ice pick hit it when it does. Still no text back from Zenon for a pill refill. My head pounds and I do the best I can to muddle through with caffeine and ibuprofen. In the shadow of approaching withdrawals and after a night of battling my demons, it's obvious to me, what I need to do. I break out my files on the church project and get to work.

I spend the next few days in meetings doing the kind of negotiating my dad knew I was capable of when he gave me the job.

TUESDAY MORNING, I wake up late. When I realize the time, I leap from bed against the weight of a crushing headache. Zenon never came through. But today I see Sophia and share the progress I made for the church in the last few days. It was rewarding work that I fought for through some of the worst withdrawals I've had yet. And the closure it will bring to the committee's plans should shore things up with Dad before I break the news about my contract with Holladay.

While shaving at a cut-neck pace my phone chimes continuously on the countertop. I resist the urge to check it, switch it to vibrate and hurry to the meeting I'm already late for.

I rush into the conference room, eager to tell the board all the headway I've made.

"You're late," Sophia says. She's seated at the head of the conference table alone with notepads and papers surrounding her workspace. She wears a fitted coral sweater, her hair swept over one shoulder.

I move towards her. "Where is everyone?" I'd hoped to revel in *all* their praise.

"We met earlier to make some tough compromises. They nominated me to pass them on to you. But I don't have much time left."

I drop into a chair to her right and place the file folder and my phone on the table. My phone buzzes noisily on the wooden tabletop. We both look at it, and away, then at each other. Her eyes—her beautiful eyes—smile at me.

"No one likes tough compromises. Maybe this will help." I slide the folder towards her with a smolder that makes her chuckle at me.

"You're too much."

But she opens the folder and begins to read in earnest while my phone buzzes again several times. I ignore it to watch the joy spread across her face as she tallies the sum of my efforts.

I was able to save the church over two hundred thousand dollars with a little creative bargaining. And as Sophia reads, I recall with verve some of my more imaginative efforts.

A portion of that savings came by simply asking for a loyalty discount from the president of the construction firm we habitually hire. While he looked at me with annoyed confusion that the boss's son was screwing up his chance at big profits, I hinted that his rival had submitted a much lower price to put their name on the prestigious project.

When he assured me, any further discounts would put them at a loss, I called his bluff by suggesting they could officially donate some of the expenses to the church organization and receive a tax benefit that would put them back in the black.

In addition, I asked the favor of a prominent interior designer to donate her services. "You're kidding, right?" she'd said. Perhaps it was because she happens to be Jewish, and attends services at the temple down the street, that my request came as a surprise.

But she also happens to know that her career got started on my father's recommendation of her work. Even when she'd admitted that fact, she balked. But I pressed on, explaining that we would etch her name in a stained-glass window with gratitude for her gift. Not only, I dared to say, would she be bridging our faiths, but while a multitude of countless Catholics caught themselves daydreaming during mass of a space as beautifully designed—they would see her name in connection to their reverie.

After that, it was all I could do to convince her we couldn't put her firm's phone number in the stained-glass window as well. But we would include a free advertisement in the church bulletin with reference to her donation for as long as she remained in business.

Once she had taken the bait, several other local firms bidding for smaller jobs fell in line to do the same with plaques throughout the church proving their generosity for generations to come.

Sophia looks up from the file with a wide smile. "You did all this in the last week? That's the money we might have gotten if we'd auctioned the Steinway."

My head pounds and nausea looms in my guts, but her new impression of me tempers the pain.

"Yep. And have you heard? The Steinway case was dismissed."

"Are you serious? I'm so glad for you. I swear I didn't know what it meant to you when I came up with the stupid scheme to sell it."

"I think the piano will be the crown jewel to the renovated church."

"It really will be, won't it? I'm getting excited again. This project has been a real drain on me for the last few weeks."

"Why are you even involved in this?"

"The church is important to me."

"Really? That's it?" I pry.

She sighs. "Don't tell anyone, but I'm using the experience as part of my thesis on group dynamics."

"For a master's in what?" I lean in to ask.

"Psychology."

"You're a psych major?" I say with surprise.

"Double master's program. I'm also pursuing an MFA in poetry. But my mom says to take it from her, an artist needs something to fall back on. So, ya know? Yeah, psychology, because figuring people out . . . the way they think . . . why they do what they do . . . I don't know, it just fascinates me."

"*You* fascinate me," I tell her.

Her cheeks color, and she looks away.

"What are your poems like?" I ask her. "I'm having the hardest time with the lyrics for my song. Maybe you could help me."

My phone vibrates again, nearly dancing off the edge of the table.

"You gonna get that it's been going crazy this whole time. I bet it's about your photos. My mom's phone has been going nuts all morning too."

"What do you mean? I haven't checked it yet."

"The pictures she took were released at midnight. Mom says Holladay Records launched them from their site and they were re-posted on Facebook, Twitter, and Instagram throughout the morning. I guess your publicist has been busy."

"So, you've been following me?" I bounce my brows.

She rolls her eyes. "Oh brother. My mom mentioned it when I asked why the phone wouldn't quit ringing. I don't participate in social media. Mom says you even made the Instagram Hot List, or whatever it's called. And her name is on all the photos, so, it puts her on the hot list too. She needed that."

Sophia picks up the folder I made her, sweeps up the papers spread over her workspace and stuffs them all in her backpack.

"I'll let you check your messages. Thanks for all your hard work." She heads for the door.

"Wait, Sophia."

She turns from the doorway. I don't even know what to say yet. But the further away she gets the heavier I feel.

"Will you look at the pictures with me? I haven't seen them yet."

"I've already seen them, and I *really* gotta go. But there's at least one you'll really like."

I MAKE FOR my office where the wi-fi is best. On the way—my nose buried in the phone—Dad hooks my elbow. "Son, while the committee's on hiatus I need you to crunch some numbers on supply orders."

I slip the phone in my pocket and raise my eyebrows. "Really?"

"You still remember your formulas, right?"

I hold my chin high. "Of course, I do."

He pats me on the shoulder. "Good, then I'll send the info in an email. We need the orders placed by 10 a.m. tomorrow morning."

"I'll handle it, Dad."

I flip on my office light. A dying fluorescent bulb flickers overhead. My headache throbs in response. I switch off the light and hunker down in my chair to spend some quality time with my phone. *Damn the back light feels bright.* I dial it down, take it off vibrate and scan the messages, things like:

"Looking hot!!"

"What the hell bro??"

"Let's reconnect."

And when my phone meows with the downloadable chime I bought for Kitty's messages I read:

"It's happening!!!!!!!!"

I pull up Instagram. And there I am. #santiagodeangelo, in classic black and white. I do a double take—after the circus of that photo shoot, the picture they used was one of the first Dara shot. When I had Sophia in my arms and my mother's spirit was hovering over us. Sophia's cropped out. It's a similar shot on Twitter and Holladay's Facebook page where the hype is hustled by a multitude of responses from me . . . actually, not me. Who the hell is answering for me?

The next couple of hours are sacrificed to the vortex of social media clicking on comments and authenticating responses with my own vibe.

Kitty shoots another text: "I'll be in town tomorrow. I have a surprise for you."

WEDNESDAY MORNING FINDS me searching for formulas through every textbook I have strewn across the living room floor. My breath shortens. What's worse, the headache that started a few days ago, has taken over my entire being. The pounding increases. All light is impossibly bright.

Where the fuck is Z? Dealers do this sometimes. I had actually thought that I might shake it this time, in between praying Z would come through. But I thought, if he didn't . . . and a few days of suffering went by, I'd be done. A couple more days maybe? Fuck that. My hands shake. I find some Tylenol and make another cup of coffee. Neither touch the nausea that had me dry heaving on the kitchen floor with a bowl beside me while the coffee brewed. I need Vicodin. I wretch up a little more bile into the bowl I carried with me to the living room and slam another book shut in failure.

"I don't have time for this shit," I say aloud, and throw the book across the room. I crack open my laptop and work through Dad's supply orders from memory. Good enough. I set the laptop aside and curl up in Grandpa's old recliner in the corner of the living room. I sleep fitfully for a few hours then head out the door with a plan.

AT LUCY'S HIGH school, I stand in the middle of the football field and scan for my sister through the crowd of kids running the track. Practice winds up and I'm about to give up on finding her when a sweaty body knocks me to the ground. Lucy springs up. I lay back on the grass, hiding in the small shadow she makes.

Her hands go to her hips. "You don't look so good, Santi."

I curl into a ball. "Luce, I need you to drive home and get the pills Dad got when he hurt his back, I know he only took a couple of 'em."

Lucy scoffs. "I won't be an enabler."

I put my hands in prayer position. "Please, I need you."

She crouches down to me. "Maybe we can do a mantra for purification."

The sun punishes again. I squeeze my eyes shut behind my dark glasses. "Help me, Sis. I'm in pain."

She bites her lip. "It's been months since your last surgery. I don't get why you still need the pills." Her eyes fix on my quivering pout. "Fine!" she yells and stomps off.

I find a shaded spot in the bleachers and lay down flat

on a bench, hoping to fall asleep but in too much pain to do so. The thirty minutes it takes her to return feels much longer.

"I won't do it again," Lucy says as she slaps me in the gut with her water bottle and hands me the orange prescription bottle before leaving me alone.

I unscrew the lid. My heart leaps. There must be at least twenty-five glorious pills in here, even if they are the godforsaken generics. I crunch two. Never has the bitter powder between my teeth and tongue been sweeter.

My phone meows: "Meet me at this address."

Memory hesitates. Barbara's house? I decide to walk. Decisions made while coming onto opiates tend towards optimistic. I'm dry mouthed but feeling good. My headache dissolves, my nausea evaporates, the cramp in my calf disintegrates, the hitch in my hip unwinds, and the sunshine is a wash of warmth across my shoulders.

I reach the address. Barbara's single story, 1940s Spanish style home is a shamble of its former elegance. I tramp over the overgrown lawn, rife with spoiled olives from once well-groomed trees. The gate opens with a rusty creak and I knock on the arched wooden front door. No answer. I chew a third Vicodin while I wait. The speakeasy, a smaller arched door with wrought iron bars, opens to reveal Kitty's face.

"What's the pass code?" she says.

Déjà-vu. Same charade with Barbara. "Music is magic," I say in a daze.

The door opens. "Let's make music together."

I look around the old familiar house where I came often for lessons, from the time I was five, until just before I left for college. Barbara always wanted me to be exposed to several different pianos as I learned how they all had sound qualities of their own. The black, parlor grand Baldwin piano remains in its usual place in the sunken living room beside the burgundy velvet sofas and the ornate dining table cluttered with dusty china.

"This place, it's . . ." The high from the pill I just crunched takes over, it's the euphoric high I only occasionally get. I think it's from being here and feeling the light Barbara always shone on my discipline for music.

Kitty jumps in. "I know, right? I thought this would be the perfect setting for us."

"I've been practicing your song," I tell her.

"Good, but we'll get to that later. I want to show you something."

Kitty takes my hand and leads me to the studio in the basement. A place Barbara never invited me to explore. I'm lightheaded. But my shoulders slump when I see it. Compared to Kitty's place, this studio is seriously outdated. It feels like a tomb where music would go to die. The mixing board is wide with over a hundred analog controls. I rub my chin and look for the best in it. There are two chairs with a monitor between them. Captain's chairs I think, with the view onto the studio floor beyond the glass, like the view captain Kirk had into the unknown universe, from the USS Enterprise.

"We could make a lot happen here. Musical magic I mean." Kitty's fingertip strokes my collarbone.

I clear my throat. "Instead of the corporate studios Dirk wants me to record at?"

She nods. "Of course, it needs upgrades."

And now I can practically feel the thrust of the spaceship as it launches. Kitty begins on a list of the upgrades. All technical terms that mean nothing to me, though I nod, and shake the pills in my pocket, wondering if it would be rude to take one while she talks. A fourth would put me into light speed, which is the same rate she rattles on at.

"Do you think you'd like to be partners?" she asks.

The coquettish tone of the question brings me back.

Wait, is she asking you to pay for the upgrades?

"I don't get it. Partners?"

Kitty presses me down into one of the captain's chairs and takes the other. She steeples her hands and takes a business tone. "We would form a production company. You would earn producer's credits and royalties. And we split the cost of the upgrades 50 50. You can name the new company."

"Tempting, but no." Yet, production names are already bouncing across my mind: DeAngelo Presents, Enterprise Adventures. *No dumb, besides you don't even have access to your money.* And I recall, with dread, Dad also pushing me into a chair at his dining room table not long after I bought my Camaro, and the airplane, followed by the piano.

"No more retail therapy!" Dad had said and made me sign over what remained of my settlement into a trust fund *he* holds the purse strings on.

"How much are we talking?" I ask.

"One hundred and fifty thousand dollars."

My stomach somersaults. I stand up.

"Sit down, for you it's only seventy-five."

I jeer. "Only seventy-five *thousand* you mean."

Sweat sheens on Kitty's forehead. "This is the big leagues, Santiago. You've already seen what Vicky is doing for you. With the royalties our deal would provide, this one song could set you up for life." She leans back in the chair. "I don't even know why I'm asking." She stares off into space. "Because of Barbara, I guess."

Heaven Sent Song Works, Musical Promise. I rub my

face.

How can we get Dad to give you the money?

My mouth is dry. I can't reason this out, but I can't decide without the money so what's the difference? I just know I want it. I can taste it. Mom's song, written by—produced by—performed by—Santiago DeAngelo. "I'll get the money. We call the company, Redemption Records."

"Get the money, DeAngelo. I'll drive you home."

In her car, a white Audi R8, I posture for the conversation with Dad. Do I go obsequious? Confident, analytical investor? Demanding? Dad likes me smart, so I'll lay out the numbers. Calculations crowd my psyche, where a shriek rings out. I screwed up the re-bar order.

"Take me to the church, I've got some work to finish," I say.

"You haven't quit that gig yet?"

BACK IN MY office, just as my mouse wavers over the submit button on my computer screen, Dad clears his throat as he closes the door behind him.

"Measure twice, cut once," he says. "You under ordered and we didn't get our quantity discount when I supplemented."

I'd just confirmed the error and was kicking myself for the mistake. But compared to the negotiations I've already managed this is nothing I can't handle. "It was a miscalculation, but we'll just make a call."

Dad crosses his arms the way he does when he wants to make a point on principal. "*Your* miscalculation to be exact. The difference is coming out of your trust fund."

"Speaking of . . . I suck air through my teeth.

"Yes?" Dad says.

I stall. "I can fix this with a two-minute call to the owner, a guy you play golf with."

"I don't take advantage of my relationships, and my partners pay for their mistakes."

"I'd never run the company the way you do."

"So, you want a shot at that?"

Is that hope I hear in his voice? "Let me make the call."

"I've already made the call, Santiago. It's handled."

I jump out of my seat. "Why do we gotta play games like this? You know what? Forget it, it's not going to matter."

His forehead wrinkles with confusion. I walk around the desk and approach him.

"I'm leaving the internship, and starting a production company, I need to make a withdrawal on my money."

He walks closer and points his finger right in my face. "You won't get a cent."

Blood rushes to my face. "It's mine, and I have a solid investment opportunity."

He grips me hard by both arms and shakes me. "Son, don't you get it? This is your future you're gambling with."

I press my elbows up to try to and escape his grip. I can't. I grab his upper arms. "Dad, music is my future."

His grip strengthens as I struggle in vain. The effort, along with the four Vicodin I've taken in the last hour, coupled with Dad's pretense at reason—even amidst our physical anger—infuriates me.

We move forward and back like a well-matched tug of war. "You would have listened to your mother. Why is it so hard for you to trust me?"

"It's not about trust. It's about making my own way." I break free by pressing his arms out as hard as I can with my elbows. His arms flail and I grab him by the wrists.

But he breaks my hold and grabs me at the neck and collar bones. My own grip is lost. "If I let you make your own way that money would already be gone." His voice is a growl as he works to keep it below a yell that church personnel won't be able to hear in their own offices down the hall. Then the pressure of his grip softens along with his tone. "Don't you see what I'm setting in motion for you? A career as an artist."

I catch my breath in the relaxed hold. He sounds so reasonable as he reinforces this idea. But mention of a *career as an artist* reminds me of the fear he forced on me as a teenager that my future as a musician was a pipe dream. When Barbara got sick, his fear became my own and I gave up my dreams to follow his. My resentment turns to rage, and I rush him and pin him against the door with my forearm against his windpipe.

"You've never believed in my dreams. But I'm not scrounging for your fucking approval any longer. I've found someone who does believe in me, and now I'm gonna take my shot. And, if I fail, I'm gonna try again until I get it right, because that's how much its always meant to me." I release the pressure of my forearm from his windpipe, and he clutches his throat and gasps for air. I pull him by one arm away from the door. He trips and falls. I look down on him as he struggles on the ground to breathe, let alone believe what's transpired.

I take a moment of my own to breathe and straighten my rumpled clothes. My opiate high becomes euphoric.

Dad says, "You won't get another dollar of that money."

"I know and that's okay. It was only a crutch anyways."

I open the door with a sense of victory and close it

softly behind me in the hall.

Fortunately, there is no crowd in the hall. I have no way of knowing if we were overheard, but I have to believe we were. I shrug this concern off and see Sophia enter the hallway at the opposite end. I stop. She seems shocked to see me. I advance towards her quickly. The high spirits building to punctuate my triumph with her presence.

"You aren't supposed to be here right now," she says. In her hand is a small ivory colored envelope with my name on it and a bird of paradise. She holds them up for me. "I was just going to leave this on your desk to say thank you for everything you've done. Everyone is really impressed and grateful."

My eyes dart to the flower, which reminds me so much of my mother that inspiration joins the elation as a song lyric. I need to try it with the Steinway, but I know it's been moved from the cathedral to tear the structure down.

"Where did they take the Steinway?"

"What? Why?" Sophia says.

"You've inspired me."

"It's in the rectory," she says.

"Come on." I clutch her hand and drag her with me.

The rectory is packed with boxes, everything that was in the church is stuffed in here. People even had the audacity to pile the boxes atop the piano. I growl and move them one by one to another corner stacked up to the ceiling. Sophia assists. Then I sit down and play the chorus while I sing the lyric, "Bird of paradise, I long to feel your touch."

The words don't boom back to me like they would in the cathedral, but they resonate in my heart. My angel in heaven. I feel so close to Mom through the music, like she's there watching me. The words continue to come, and I sing them as they do:

"When I gaze out my window, I know you're watching me."

"It's wonderful," Sophia says when I stop.

I stand and turn to her. "It feels like every time something good happens for the song, it's because you're there."

"Don't be ridiculous." She looks down.

"It's because you make me so happy, Sophia. I wish I could be with you all the time."

She looks up at me. "You do?"

"Come out with me tonight, to celebrate."

"Tonight? I want to but I can't. I have this presentation in class tomorrow and I still have so much to do to get ready for it."

"Saturday then? We could go flying."

"What do you mean, flying?"

"I have an airplane and my pilot's license."

Sophia shakes her head and grins. "You never cease to amaze me. Isn't that scary?"

"It's thrilling!" I take her hands, and the electricity that pulses between us is just as thrilling.

She rakes her lower lip with her teeth and titters. "Okay, let's do it. That sounds amazing."

I put the knuckles of her hand to my lips and kiss them. "Saturday, 9 a.m. Until then, good luck on your presentation."

Part 3
Who Do You Love?

CHAPTER 13

SANTIAGO DEANGELO

She Lets Herself be Found

IT'S 9:07 A.M. AND Sophia's not here. I pace the open hangar. The faint smell of oil and fuel sits at the back of my throat. I survey my space to be seen by Sophia. It's about thirty feet by forty feet, with my white Mooney M20 airplane parked in the center. God, I love this plane. Morning light pours in through the open hangar door that faces the direction Sophia would come from. I rub the prickling heat off the back of my neck and overhear the father-son duo in the neighboring hangar snicker that my date's a no show. I check the time and search the horizon again. My confidence flies on fumes. My withdrawals show up as further punishment, but I wouldn't risk piloting the plane high with Sophia along for the ride.

Kyle, the younger of the pair next door, walks by my space on his way to the trash bin with an arm load of junk. He stops. He's about my height and twice my width. A steroid eating, bald, behemoth who spends half his time in the gym and the other half wrenching on his Dad's eclectic collection of planes. "What's the matter Romeo? This Chica actually mean something to ya?"

My lack of a comeback proves his case.

Kyle prods on. "Oh shit, she does! Too bad she didn't show up."

His dad, a grey-haired, well-groomed man of fleshy pink face and small round glasses steps out of his hangar. "Leave him be, Kyle. I want him in a good mood when he gets back from this flight."

"You don't give up, do you, Bob?"

Bob's been trying to part me from my plane for the last six months now. And for a price that's twenty-grand less than the hundred thousand I originally paid. He's always had a thing for the unique body style of the Mooney. In my estimate, given the repairs and maintenance I've done, its worth about a hundred-and-ten thousand dollars.

"Looks like you shouldn't either," Bob says, and points toward the horizon out the open garage door.

In the distance, Sophia pumps a mountain bike towards the hangar. I skip into a run.

"You came." My breath is short a pant between words.

Sophia's breathy too. "It was a lot further than I thought. But it was such a beautiful morning, I didn't want to miss a chance to really be out in it. So, I rode my bike."

She gets off the bike and unwinds a long, yellow, silk scarf from around her neck, but keeps her puffy, grey down jacket on. The February morning is brisk with plenty of sunshine. The scarf flutters in the light breeze as we stride side by side back to the hanger. Her bike clicks as she pushes it, and when we arrive, she parks it in the corner and turns to the airplane in the center of the hangar.

I run my hand across the leading edge of the right wing. "What do you think of her? She's a Mooney M20."

"What year?"

"'91."

"She's beautiful." Sophia fidgets with the zipper on her jacket, sliding it up and down, up and down, and I see red blotches of nerves spread across her chest.

I tilt my head towards the plane. "Come here, I still get a little nervous before I fly. But preflight checks remind me our fate is determined here."

I begin my routine. Sophia pays attention, no fiddling with an emery board, or her cell phone, and though I've never been inclined to walk anyone through it—I describe what I'm doing step by step. Sophia's at my side listening like there might be a test later and touching the plane wherever I do. I test the flap and rudders, and she tracks their movement.

As we move through pre-flight, Sophia's hives recede. I tug on the nose to pull the plane forward and inspect the tires, but they catch in a divot in the concrete. I struggle, and Sophia gives the plane a nudge that rolls it forward. "Thanks."

She squats and looks over the tires. "Tread looks great. You take good care of her, Santiago."

I drag the plane from the hangar and fire the engine in the open air. In the cockpit, I continue my descriptions through the headphones, adjusting her microphone so I can hear her questions. No detail is too mundane for her eager mind. We check in with control and get the okay to taxi out to the main runway.

"You want to taxi out?" I ask her.

Her face is beat red in an instant. "Me?" But in another she's got control of the left and right foot pedals swerving at first but correcting thoughtfully.

"You're a natural," I tell her.

I accelerate down the runway and tell Sophia to pull back on the yoke. She doesn't hesitate, though she squeals as lift propels us into the blue. Then she scans the many analog gauges and switches with a touch of panic.

"Just relax, now and enjoy the view," I tell her.

She looks out the window to her right.

I tip us slightly to the left. "There's the University of Redlands there."

She peeks out my window and beams.

"I have two flight itineraries." My voice goes up a pitch. "One, we fly around for about half an hour. Two, we have brunch in Catalina. It's less than an hour's flight."

She exhales a static screech in the mic, the first itinerary a given. She stares down at the world below. About this time, I'd pull a stunt to get her attention: a zero G drop, or an engine stall. I've put some passengers through some pretty-sick maneuvers and if I were alone, who knows what I'd try. But peace settles over me and I fly on, smooth and level.

Sophia stares out her window with the childish amazement of the world from this view I love most in passengers. But then she turns from the window and touches my arm. The touch sends waves all the way to my chest.

"I've never been to Catalina before. Let's go."

I bank hard to the right and she giggles with the sensation the turn produces. She turns back to the view. The loud sound of the engine makes the silence between us easy.

Before we know it, we are flying over the ocean. I point out a school of dolphin diving in the surf.

"This is so amazing. How'd you get into flying?"

My face adopts the jocular smile that always

accompanies the story I tell when people ask this question. A story of searching for thrills and a skill to dedicate my time to. But the smile falls away because with Sophia I *think* I have a chance to be more honest about it.

"It was kind of an accident. I didn't plan to. I just ended up in a plane when I was searching for something to pull me out of the apathy I was falling into."

"Apathy?" she asks with concern. Her voice cuts through the static of the headphones.

I want my own voice to cut through the harsh static in my head that I've been struggling alone with since my blowup with Dad. I'd spent the first few days reveling in vindication but woke up this morning wondering where it all went wrong between us.

Sophia puts her hand on my thigh. I take her hand and squeeze it then forge ahead with the words I'm trying on to make sense of things.

"Painful loneliness, really. I mean, not only was I lonely for my mom, I was also aching for my dad. Because when she died, we couldn't figure out how to talk to each other. And then I had the song to keep me connected to her, and Dad couldn't figure out a way to stay connected."

Sophia catches my meaning and jumps in to complete the thought. "So, he was angry with you for maintaining a connection and you were angry with him for holding that against you."

"Exactly! And living with that anger made us both destructive." I think on how the pills exacerbated the situation, but I don't want to admit that yet. "I guess flying was a way to test how destructive I really was."

"You don't mean suicidal, do you?" Her voice in the headphones is hard to read. Is she expressing concern or judgment? I turn towards her. Her eyebrows are lifted high on her brow. She retrieves her hand to her own lap.

She's judging you. She knows.

I laugh it off. "God, no. I just needed a little danger to remind me how much I wanted to live, even without her."

Her hand goes to her heart. "It sounds like you two were very close."

I clear my throat; I can't cry right now. "Look!" I point out the windshield to a long strip of land emerging from the dark blue ocean. "Here comes the fun part."

As we get closer, the ocean brightens and what was a long grey rock becomes a golden hilled land mass specked with grey-green brush. There is a bluff and then a runway. Beside me I notice Sophia tense and grip the sides of her seat with shallow breath.

My own breath remains calm with a light grasp on the yoke to make the difficult landing I know so well look easy. In my peripheral, I feel her watching me, noting my confidence, and relaxing because of it.

The wheels touch ground and bounce over the asphalt. She titters into her hands.

I communicate with the flight tower and then look over at her. "Were you afraid?"

She presses her lips together and nods. "But you weren't, and that helped."

AFTER BRUNCH, WE walk the beach. We both carry our shoes in our hands with our jeans rolled up mid-calf. As we stroll the sand by the sea, we slip into forthright conversation about our parents. We speak more openly than I thought I ever might. But I've met Dara, so I get Sophia's concerns. And she's worked with my dad, so she has a reference for what I'm dealing with. She takes my hand when I choke up telling her the story about how he collapsed in the hospital after we took Mom off life support.

"We shouldn't have been alone," I tell her.

Clouds roll in and the sky greys.

Sophia says, "I feel alone with my mom too. I don't understand why she turns to drinking when I'm right there for her. Does she think her pain is too much for me? I just don't get why she keeps going back to it. Or why *I* think each time she gives it up something will be different—and this time I'll be enough of a reason for her to stay sober."

The conversation is freaking me out a little.

"Can I ask about your dad? Where is he?" I say, as I guide us closer to the sea.

"He's a fairy tale. My mother fell in love with him at an artist's retreat. But he was from Italy and went home long before she even knew she was pregnant. They had never planned to keep in touch after he left the country. And she says she has no idea how to find him—or doesn't want too. I've thought about trying to find him myself, but for now, I prefer him as a fantasy."

A wave rolls in and soaks us mid-thigh. Our shrieks dissolve into laughter as we break towards the sand dunes covered in sparse grass and toss our shoes in the sand.

Then she says, "I loved the lyric to your song. Is bird of paradise a metaphor for your mother in heaven?"

"Yes."

"Since you played it the other day, the music has been running through my mind non-stop. And when you were talking about her on the way here, I was thinking of some new lyrics you might try. I mean . . . since you asked."

"I would love to hear them," I tell her as I take both her hands in mine.

"Maybe you can play it after the next committee meeting."

I look down at our bare feet covered in sand. "I left the project, Sophia."

She lets go of my hands. "What? Why would you do that. You said yourself how happy you were to be this close to your dad again."

"I need my dad to love me no matter what I choose to do. And right now, I'm going to start a production company and pursue a future in music."

Her face reddens. "You just do whatever you want, don't you?"

"Yes," I say, as I take her face in my hands and kiss her lips.

The kiss is soft and seeking. She lets herself be found. We fall into the sand dune rising behind her and her yellow scarf flaps over us in the rising sea breeze. She pulls away, a little breathless. I can feel her heart drumming in her chest. I kiss her forehead, stand, and pull her to standing.

"Let's head back. It's cold out here."

"Could we come back here again?" she asks.

"We'll have to take the ferry."

"What? Why?

"I'm selling the plane to Bob for the money to start the production company."

CHAPTER 14

KITTY HOLLADAY

Yo Boy, You Got Chops

"NICE WORK PUSSY cat," Dirk says. There's feedback from his cell.

"Take your phone off speaker." It clicks clear. I eye the screenshot I sent Dirk in a text. A wire deposit in my personal bank account for seventy-five thousand dollars from Santiago. "You doubted me?"

I'm sitting in Barbara's basement studio in the dark. The only light comes from my cell phone. I slide the dimmer light up the control panel for the studio. The room brightens. I slide the dial down into darkness, and picture it and the control board updated. Finally, it's going to happen. The installers are arriving today. I needed the wire to pay them in full at the time of install as agreed. Dirk said if I got him to pay for it, he'd let us record here. Three sleepless nights wondering if the scheme would come off.

"I just don't know why he'd go for it. He's paying for

the full upgrade with no promised return," Dirk says.

I brighten the room. "Don't underestimate the lure of fame, Dirk."

"Send me the docs on this production company you've formed."

I dim the lights again. My finger is slick on the analog slide. Lying to my husband directly takes nerve. If he knew I'd made Santiago an equal production partner he'd flip. That will mean a lot more money for him if the song is as successful as I think it will be. Far more than the seventy-five he paid. But I owe it to myself to do things my own way for once. If Dirk does use his control of Santiago's song against him, I need to know I at least treated him fairly.

"I've got this, Dirk." An incoming call beeps. "Gotta go, D, I've got another one coming in."

I switch over to Santiago's call and brighten the room again.

His voice brims with excitement. "Did you get it? I sent the wire over an hour ago?"

"I got it. We're officially partners. You should come and watch the installation. Bring a bottle of champagne.

A few hours later, in Barbara's avocado green galley kitchen, I twist the cork from the bottle of Perrier Jouet he brought with him. I pour 2 glasses, and hand Santiago his.

"To Barbara, my personal hero," I toast.

His eyebrows knit and then he nods. "To Barbara. *Our* Hero."

There's a knock at the door. I down my drink and dash across the room. As I let the installers in, I glance back at Santiago swallowing something from his pocket with a gulp of his champagne.

I lead the crew down to the studio and head back to the

kitchen to find Santiago finishing his glass. "You drink alone?" I ask him.

"I thought we were celebrating."

I give him a hard stare. He shrinks back. I slip my hand down the front pocket of his jeans. He puts his hands up in surprise then flinches when my searching hand glances his groin.

"That's not what I'm looking for," I say.

He steps back. My wrist bends backwards, and I wince, retrieving my hand with one of the many pills I felt in his pocket. I read the inscription, VICODIN. "The name brand is expensive."

He reaches for the pill.

"What, you don't want to share?"

"I only brought a few," he says.

"Greedy and secretive. All the makings of an addict."

He licks his lips and crosses his arms. "I was in an accident. I've had a lot of surgeries."

"Justification. That was over a year ago. You have several in your pocket for a couple hours out of the house."

He looks up at the ceiling for a beat and grips his right wrist. "The bones in my right arm were crushed. It still hurts when I play the piano."

"But you don't let it stop you." I move forward and touch his cheek with an open palm.

We make tight eye contact.

He says, "I just need them for now. I don't have a problem. I swear."

"I get it." My thumb strokes the swell of his cheek. If only someone had reached out to me in sympathy about my addiction before it was too late. And he's still so young. I shake off tough memories and remember my place. "Just remember, Santiago, sometimes the things you think give you power, are really taking your power away."

"What takes your power away?" he says.

"Nothing!" My face feels hot.

His hands fly up. "Sorry, my bad. It's just for a second, I didn't feel so alone."

My own loneliness surges out of the cracks I force it into with every line of cocaine. I feel the blood drain from my face. I exhale and hang my head.

When I look up, he sees me. I want to be seen. My lower lip trembles.

He squeezes the ball of each shoulder. "Maybe we can give each other some power back, Kitty." He shakes me a little. "So, tell me—what is it?"

"Cocaine," I say, "will you have a line with me?"

"It's not my thing. But we can get high together." He takes a few pills from his pocket. "It will be fun. We're celebrating right?"

We settle into the well-worn blue leather sofa in the den. I lean over floral throw pillows that still smell like the Chanel no. 5 Barbara used to wear daily.

He notices it too, holds one up close to his nose and says, "God, it smells just like her."

"I bought her those pillows when I was about fifteen."

"You've known her that long? How did you meet?"

"I won a contest that Barbara put together for kids who were taking violin lessons in public school."

"What did you win?"

"A chance to perform at the local symphony. But it was terrible. I froze up on stage and didn't even finish the piece. I was in tears. I thought she'd be furious with me. But she just comforted me and asked me if I'd like to take private lessons with her. My parents agreed. The more seriously I took mastering the violin the more interested in me she became. She loves discipline most."

"That's for sure."

"When she found out that I was attracted to writing music she got even more involved. No one has ever paid that kind of attention to me."

"What about your parents?"

"My parents are good people, but they spent most of my childhood managing their careers. I think they assumed the private schools and music programs they paid for would be enough for me to turn out 'just fine'." I do the air quotes and he laughs in response. "I don't think they meant to have children. They never had any more."

"No brothers or sisters? That sucks. I would hate being an only child."

"I didn't know any better, and it gave me plenty of time to focus on music."

"What's it been like writing and producing music all these years?"

I stand and go to the window to pull down the fringed mint green roller shades. With them drawn the room becomes comfortably dim. We lean in and let the stories start. Old stories with someone new are so much fun. I tell the cool ones. The tales that make being a coke addict in the music business *seem* glamorous. And that leads to my success stories. The stars I've worked with. The awards I've won. His black eyes sparkle at details Dirk would shrug off. And then it's his turn. There really was an accident. His recollection is gripping. I wipe tears when he tells how his mother sent him the song.

"When I first heard those notes the pain meds were the only way I had to feel good. And I had to try to feel good—to feel the music again."

"Yes, I totally get it." I snort another line from the glass coffee table a few feet in front of us. "Do you know what we're about to do? About the crazy-wack-funky trip I'm about to take you on? My song is going to change your life forever."

The trip we take into the future of Redemption Records makes the writers of *The Secret* look like pessimists. By the fourth line of coke I think, *I'm not alone anymore* as I force the feeling further into the fissure.

We check in with the installation crew. A duo of dorks, one in his forties with his long blonde hair pulled back in a ponytail and a scraggly beard. He reminds me of Shaggy, but his younger counterpart is no Scooby. He's a twenty something bi-racial kid, light skinned with green eyes. He's clean cut with a tight fade and thick glasses. His name tag reads Darren. He pushes his glasses up his nose, and nods at me. The sight of all those state-of-the-art digital controls makes me giddy.

Darren says, "Ma'am—"

"Do I look like a Ma'am to you?"

He smiles. "Pardon me, Miss Kitty. We'd like to get a sound check on the mic if we can."

I touch Santiago on the arm. "Sing us something, Santi."

"Okay, like what?"

"Something from a musical."

He belts out the romantic opening to "Your Song" by Elton John in the style of *Moulin Rouge*.

Blood pricks my cheeks; I cover them with my hands.

Darren says, "Yo boy, you got chops."

"Isn't he fabulous?" I titter.

Shaggy claps. "I guess we got everything plugged in

right."

"Me and my engineer will dial it all in," I tell them.

When they've left, I say to Santiago, "Now we just pick a recording date. I'm thinking next Wednesday.

He pulls his phone out and checks his calendar. "Wednesday the fourteenth?" He hesitates. "Can we do it the fifteenth? Wednesday's Valentine's Day."

I cross my arms. "You have some kind of cliché Valentine's date planned?"

"I don't want it to be cliché. But there's this girl." He walks towards me with a silly grin.

My jaw muscles tighten. I wanted to record the song with him that day. I'd tried to make the date sound random, but it wasn't.

"I can't let this holiday go by if I'm going to have a chance with this girl. Will you help me?" He settles into one of the chairs.

I drum my fingers against my forearm and sigh out loud. "Fine, we'll do it Thursday, but you owe me."

He pumps both fists. "But give me some ideas. I want to make the day special."

I uncross my arms and attempt to soften my jaw. "The thing with Valentine's is honoring the traditions while doing something unique that shows you know what your Valentine loves most."

He rocks back in the chair, searching the ceiling with his tongue poking out the side of his mouth.

He rocks forward. "I think I've got it." He jumps up. "You're the best, Kitty. I'll see you next Thursday."

He scrambles out the door and I hear his light spree up the basement steps.

I turn the new dial that controls the lights until I'm in darkness again.

CHAPTER 15

SANTIAGO DEANGELO

Tough Love

THE LIBRARY? OUR Valentine's date is at the library?" Sophia says with the excitement I was hoping for.

I get out and open Sophia's door for her. "I arranged a private tour for us." I offer my hand for her to exit the car.

"I've always wanted to do that." She pecks me on the cheek. We head towards the A.K. Smiley Library, a prominent architectural treasure of the downtown area. The unique Moorish styled brick-red exterior is vibrant against the grey of the day.

In the lobby, Sophia takes my hand and we both gaze up at the high ceiling where several lavish oak beams arch together some twenty-five feet over the librarian's desk. "It's gorgeous, isn't it?" she says.

The tour is glorious. I don't know which of us appreciates it more: Sophia for the philanthropic commitment the Smiley family made in bringing literature to the community, or me, in soaking up the building's architectural past.

When the tour's complete Sophia says, "Shouldn't we check out a book while we're here?"

"I have three in mind."

Her eyes grow.

"Three great love stories. I was hoping you could pick one and we'd both read it at the same time."

She looks like a vibrating espresso machine that's about to boil over. "And what, pray tell, are these three books. You've already picked them?"

I lead her through the aisle of fiction to the first selection. My knees quiver when I take it out and hand it to her. Jane Austen's *Sense and Sensibility*. I want her to like that it's on the list, but I'm not pulling for it as *thee* one.

She holds it to her chest. "I adore this book, but it's not the right one for us. Too obvious I think." She winks and slides it back between Austen's others.

I lead her to the next aisle and search for my next choice. For a second, I think it's gone. A contingency I've worried over and let go. Then I find it and deliver it into Sophia's waiting hands with held breath.

"*Love in the Time of Cholera*?" Her brows squish together.

I tug it from her grasp. "Moving on then?"

"No, Gabriel Garcia Marquez is one of my favorite authors. I'm impressed. I've planned to read it, it's just—" her head bobs side to side "—kind of a tale of unrequited love."

"We're not the characters," I tell her.

"No, but tell me why you put it on the list."

I exhale into my fist. "My mom had this bookshelf in her room with all her favorite books. Important books she wanted us to read together. That was one of our things." I drop my head.

Sophia touches my chin with one finger to lift my face. "And this is one of those books?"

"I can't read it with my mom. But will you read it with me?"

"Then I'll check out this copy and you can read the one from your mom's shelf."

I pull out a single yellow rose I cut short and tucked into my jacket's inner pocket. I hand it to her. She rises on her toes to kiss me. I kiss her back with all the constrained passion pent up in this scheme.

Breathless, she says, "Why yellow?"

"Yellow is the color of hope and friendship."

"You didn't kiss me like you want to be friends," she says.

I tow her by the hand through the aisles of books back to the librarian's desk, where the other eleven roses both yellow and red are waiting in a glass vase with a giant golden bow and a note. She giggles when she sees them and reads: *I hope to be your friend and your lover.* She kisses me again. Behind the desk, Fatima, the elegant Syrian librarian who helped me pull off this escapade claps a palm silently and gives me two thumbs up.

"Let's go back to my place," she says.

I tense. "What about your mom?" I don't feel like running into Dara again after our last conversation.

"She's shooting a Valentine's wedding. She won't be home for hours. We can start reading." Her mouth drops open. "Wait your copy."

"I had Lucy get it for me. It's in the trunk in case you chose it."

A gentle mist of rain veils me and Sophia as we walk hand in hand from my car to her house. A stout red Doberman joins us at the separate entrance to a building to the left of the main house. Sophia rubs the dog's ears and scratches it beneath the throat.

"This is Ginger."

I let her sniff my hand, and she licks it.

"I always thought Dobermans were fiercer than this."

"Oh, she's plenty fierce if she senses the need to be," Sophia says as she opens the door.

The dog follows us in and lays in an oval bed against the far wall of the den. We cross the large open space of dark walnut flooring. I stare out the windows through the diamond bevels of leaded glass which emit tiny rainbows into the room.

Sophia stands beside an oversized brown suede sofa several feet from the fireplace. She says, "Let's push this closer to the hearth and I'll start us a fire."

The pegs of the couch screech against the floor as we move it into place. When it's close to the river-stone hearth I take off my shoes and flop down on the sofa. She tosses her pink leather coat over the back of the couch and slips off her heels then leans in to light the firewood that was already in place with crumpled paper beneath it.

When the fire is kindled, she turns to the sofa and says, "Any room for me?"

I scoot back and rest my head against the high arm of the couch and tuck my legs into my chest. She sits facing me against the opposite arm. Our feet touch as we advance them towards each other in an exploratory way. Mine are on the inside against the back of the couch. She leans hers against mine and I want to feel more of her against me.

I open my book and peer over the top of it. "Alright,

Sophia, no funny business. It's reading time, I mean it." I laugh and pretend to read in earnest, though I know we are both using the pretext of reading to pace the sexual tension that has been building since she read my card. I see that she's using it to keep her place in the book.

The fire crackles like my nerves. I spy over my book at her eager to make a suave move.

She feels my glance, looks up, smiles and pulls her legs into her chest. I creep my fingers like spider legs towards her naked foot. It tenses, I seize it and tickle her arch. She squeals and kicks. The top of her foot catches me under the chin hard. My head snaps back and I see stars for a second.

She pops up and crouches over me. Her hair falls over us like a curtain.

"I'm so sorry. It's just my feet are so ticklish."

I shake it off and sit up a little. "No joke," I say, rolling my head until my neck cracks.

"I'm sorry," she says again.

"Nothing a little kiss couldn't take care of," I tell her as I tap my chin where she kicked me. She chuckles and leans forward to peck me there. I pull her onto me smoothly and kiss her with the same flame ignited between the bookshelves.

She pulls away. "We won't get much reading done this way."

"We can read each other though."

Her body, soft and relaxed against mine, feels like a puzzle piece that fits perfectly. My arms across her back hold her to me. But she pulls further away, a playful grin on her face. "Oh really? What are you reading from me right now?"

"That you'd rather talk." I soften my hold on her and let her sit up.

She scoots back. "I want to know you."

The fire hisses, and we both turn towards it. Our hands find each other. Our books lie side-by-side on the floor.

"Do you?"

I want to be known by her but worry she won't like what she finds. How much can I tell her? With Kitty, confessing my addiction led to a connection. But can I expect the same here?

She says, "Tell me more about the song you're writing. Have you written other songs before?" We both turn our heads towards each other. The firelight dances in the center of her eyes.

"No, I'm not sure I'm a natural song writer. I was trained to interpret the music of others, not create my own. But something happened that made it easy at first. Then after a while, there was this block. But when I met you, Sophia, it was like you threw me a rope."

I have a feeling Sophia could help pull me out of my addiction too. But can I be honest with her about it? There's a tightness in my chest. Perhaps her experience with her mother will be enough to understand.

"How did the song first come to you?" she asks.

"I'm not sure if you'll believe me."

"Try me."

"My mother sent it to me."

"I know the song is about your mom, but what do you mean she sent it to you? She inspired it?"

I take a deep breath and blow the air out. "It was a very dark time after the accident. I was in a lot of physical pain, and my emotional pain felt physical to me too. Before I knew it, I couldn't distinguish between them and was taking too many pain pills as a result. Mom was gone and my dad wouldn't even speak to me. I got to this point where I was desperate. I wanted to die, and that was when she reached out to me with the notes the song is based on. I feel like she gave me the entire song and it's only my job to *remember* it. I sometimes get this crazy idea that she rewards me with pieces of it when I do things that help me—I don't know—heal, I guess. But when I'm doing things that work against that, I can't scale the wall."

"What are you doing that you shouldn't be?"

The fire pops. She squeezes my hand.

"Tell me," she says.

I turn towards her. The fire is too hot now. I release her hands and rub my face. "I don't know."

She takes my hand again and kisses the knuckles. "I think you do."

I withdraw my hands and suck air through my teeth. "I don't think you want to know."

"I told you, I want to know you." She crawls onto my lap and pushes the damp hair on my forehead back. I lean towards her to kiss her, but she leans back shaking her head. "You can tell me anything, Santi."

"I'm still taking the pain pills. I can't stop."

The playful look she's worn the entire time vanishes. She stands up, tripping over our books and sitting on the edge of the hearth.

"Why can't you stop?"

My excuses are lined up like soldiers ready to deploy. But they feel useless. "I . . . I don't know how. I've tried, but it never lasts, and I only end up taking more."

Why are you telling her this?

Her look of judgment increases with each word.

She lifts her dark mane of hair off her neck and walks around the sofa to get away from the fire. "I don't think I can be with an addict," she says.

I flip around and lean over the back of the couch. "What are you saying?"

Her face is pained. She hesitates. "My mom—well you saw her—I told you how I feel. I don't think I could handle having someone else in my life that's an addict."

"Are you kidding me right now?" My tone escalates.

From the corner her Doberman begins to snarl in response and rises from her bed with a deep bark that I shout over to be heard.

"Sophia, I want to get help. That's why I told you." I climb over the back of the couch.

She backs away and her dog comes to her side, barking at me. She puts a hand on the dog's head and the barking subsides. "You don't know what it's been like, being raised by a single mother with a drinking problem. I can't take on the responsibility of another chemically dependent person."

"You're overreacting. I don't need you to rescue me, just accept me."

Ginger barks again and I flinch.

"If I accept you there won't be any reason to quit."

"I will quit. I'm just not ready."

"Then I'm not ready either. I can't be your lover or your friend right now."

"Don't you get it! That's what makes it so hard, being alone."

She shrugs. "I just can't, Santi. I'm sorry. I think you should go."

"No. I'm not going."

"I need you to go."

I move towards her. Ginger snaps and I jump back, grab my book and shoes and retreat to the door. I look at her one last time before I open it. Her chin juts in defiance. I can only assume some well-intentioned book she'd read on helping loved ones with addiction gave her this line of *tough love* she thinks she has to follow. I shake my head and walk out the door.

Outside, the cold rain stings my hot face.

CHAPTER 16

KITTY HOLLADAY

Love is Bigger Than the Rules
We've Built Around It

I STAND IN Barbara's formal living room beside her Baldwin grand piano. I tuck my violin between my chin and shoulder and kiss the bow to its strings. I play "Cinema Paradiso" as I wait for Santiago to arrive to begin recording. It's a song I know Barbara taught him. My insides quiver. All week long I've laid down the basic tracks to my pop song with studio musicians and Otto, my engineer. Smooth and easy. But today is special. The vocal tracks Santiago will provide are the soul of the song. My fingers tremble over the violin strings. I sense him and look up as he enters the room.

"Is that 'Cinema Paradiso'?" Santiago asks.

"Play with me?" I slink towards him and lead him to the piano. The music book is propped open to the piece.

He takes a seat. "I haven't played this Baldwin in

years. I learned Paradiso on it." He spins his body around on the bench. "But I'm pumped up about *your* song right now. Why this?"

I let the violin speak for me. My emotions ride the wide movement of my bow arm as it provokes the strings. My bare feet grip the wooden floor as I sway at the torso to the nuance of the tune.

Eventually, Santiago faces the piano again, his hands poised over the keys. I stop, and he begins the duet with the piano intro. I hold the violin in wait while he plays. Expectation churns from my belly to join him in the music. When I do, it feels like falling into bed with a lover.

There's a pregnant pause when the music ends. I put my hand on his shoulder and bend to his ear. "Thank you, that was beautiful."

"It was amazing," he says.

I reach into the deep pocket of my loose maxi dress and clutch a small package. "I have something even more amazing if you're game?"

He stands up and eyes me intently. "You know I'm game."

My heartbeat rises. I proffer the package, a handkerchief tied with a ribbon. "This is something I thought would be *both* our thing. I've been saving them for a day like today." I untie the ribbon.

He rises from the bench and squints down at the two white capsules. "What are they?"

"MDMA," I say.

He's baffled.

"The magic ingredient in ecstasy without the fillers to fuck it up. This is pure bliss in a capsule, Santiago."

He runs his hands through his hair. "Holy shit. You

want me to record high?"

I grab an arm. "Not just high, happy."

He rolls his eyes. "What's that?"

I clap. "Exactly. I want to remind you. I want to heighten your emotions and capture them on digital file. When people hear the music we make together today, they'll feel that too." I hold them in an open palm.

He shakes his head and laughs. "I've never known anyone like you, Kitty."

"And you never will again." I hold one pill to his lips and the other on the tip of my tongue.

"Let's make music," we say in sync, before we swallow the pills.

Otto arrives, and I introduce him to the talent. "Santiago, this is my engineer. We go way back. He's a genius on the control board, so trust what he tells you."

They shake hands. Santiago looks him up and down and I see Otto through his eyes. The years of partying etched on his tan face. The nose ring in his septum like a bull. The kinky-black-curly hair that falls past his shoulders even though he's bald on top. He covers that with a Chicago Bull's cap. I tense at the thought Santiago won't respect him like I do.

Otto pats him on the back. "If you're half as good as Kitty says, you just do your thing and I'll dial it all in on my end."

"Sure-thing, man. I'm just gonna warm up." Santiago opens the small door between the studio floor and the engineering room and takes the few steps down to the lower level. The soundproof door closes behind him.

"So, he's the one huh?" Otto pops open a can of sugar-free Red Bull.

I slide it from his hand and suck some down as I stare absentmindedly through the glass at Santiago, still sober before the MDMA hits either of us. I look at my watch, probably another twenty minutes or so before we both come onto it.

Otto jerks the can back. "You think he'll come through today? Is he professional?"

"Huh?" I shake myself out of a daze. "You should know we'll both be rolling soon. I gave him that MDMA I've been saving."

"No shit? What happened to staying clean in the studio like Dirk the jerk wants?"

"There's just so much I want from him. I think this is the way it has to be."

"I want to trust you, Kitty. Just let me know if things get out of hand."

"I'm in control."

In the studio I mark where Santiago should stand with a piece of blue tape about a foot from the mic. I adjust the sibilance screen in front of the mic. He toes the line. I hand him the headphones. Before he fits them on, I ask, "How are you feeling?"

He shrugs.

"Me either, but don't worry, it just takes a while to kick in. We won't miss it when it does." I retreat to the sound board with Otto, fit my own headphones on and say, "Let the magic begin." He puts a thumb up to confirm he can hear my voice in the cans.

Otto says, "Sing something, let me get a reading."

Santiago sings the first lyric, "I've got a lust for trusting on a dark night."

Otto stops him there and we adjust accordingly. A

pleasant swirl radiates through me as the drug kicks in. I sink back in my chair and beam ear to ear. *Hello happy, I've missed you.*

I lean over the mic, my voice like honey. "Santi, I'm going to play you the basic instrumental tracks. I want you to sing the song straight through. The lyrics will appear on the digital screen above you. Ready to go to work?"

"I feel it now, Kitty, it's beautiful."

"Everyone here loves you," I say, watching Otto from the corner of my eye. He mocks me with a chuckle, and I smack his forearm with the back of my hand. "Five, four, three . . ." I hold my fingers up for the final count. Otto can't mock what comes next.

Santiago melts into the microphone. At one point he takes the crescendo of the chorus, high, high, high to a new octave. The song ends, and we cut. Otto looks at me and mouths the word *fuck* with total awe. I stand and feel like I'll hit the ceiling.

"Was that okay?" Santiago asks through the mic.

I run down to him and clutch him to me. His heat sends desire through me. "You amaze me. A few more takes like that and—"

"Stay with me while I sing." He holds me tight to him.

I push him out to arm's length. It isn't far enough away. His biceps tremble beneath my grip. I lock into his gaze. My stomach twirls. The sensation surges all through me. It's the high I asked for and didn't know what I'd get.

"You did this to me, Kitty, see it through, or I'll just lie down on the studio floor and let the pleasure ripple through me."

"Do your thing, Kitty Cat. I got it in here," Otto says over the speaker.

Santiago says, "I love you man."

"I love you too, bro. That's an amazing set of pipes you got." Otto rubs his hands together and whoops. "Let's do this."

I tell him, "Turn up the orchestration. Especially the violins." Then I step behind Santiago and run my hands along his spine for the next take.

Five to six takes later he's lost all inhibition. Dancing, crooning, and performing for my entertainment. I laugh so hard it reaches the place inside where laughter stands a chance to heal anything.

"I think we've got what we need," Otto says over the speaker. "I'm gonna take off for the day." The music he'd been playing back for us cuts out.

Santiago approaches in the sudden silence. "It's gonna happen for us with this song, isn't it?"

I nod with the assuredness I'd been faking before now.

"I always knew it would happen for me. I kept it right here." He taps his chest with a loose fist. "Barbara never wanted fame for me. She said my music would serve a bigger purpose. But what could be bigger than that? And you're giving it to me."

"We're giving it to each other. But Dirk oversees it all."

He snickers. "Yeah, I guess so." He looks away and back. "Will you help me finish my song too?" He sits at the Yamaha in the center of the studio and plays the emotional opening to his song. The bass rich chords seem to vibrate through me as I stand beside him. He looks up at me hopefully.

"You'd owe me," I tell him, and run my hands through his hair.

He takes my hand and kisses it. "Thank you for this

feeling. I didn't know I could feel happy like this ever again. Not since the accident. I tried, but it backfired bigtime. I don't know if it's the drug, or studio magic with you, or knowing how close I am to this lifelong dream. But I feel like I know something I didn't know before."

I draw his hand to my lips and kiss it softly. "What's that?" I put his finger in my mouth and suck it gently.

"That love is bigger than the rules we've built around it."

I bite his finger. "If that were true, I could love you and my husband, and it would be okay."

"But it is true," he says.

"Don't be naïve." I fling his hand down and walk across the studio. At the door I turn back to him. "Are you coming?"

I'm shaking as I descend the hall. My hand rattles the knob of Barbara's bedroom door. His breath is hot on my neck as I force the door from the swollen jamb.

This time the duet is between the sheets. My notes are high and vibrate over the melody he continues to play on cue. As he kisses me, while we make love, I think, *this is love, and what if he's right? What if love is bigger than I ever thought. He makes me feel like it is.*

I'm straddling him, joined at the sacral chakra. He's deep inside me. I run my thumb over his closed eyelids.

As he opens them, he says, "I love you, Kitty."

The unexpected intimacy of those words startles me. Despite waxing lyrical on love, I didn't think him bold enough to claim his for me. The vulnerability of that intimacy burgeons a hidden longing triggered when we began making music together. I believe him. What's more I know I love him too.

Tears fill my eyes as my long-held desire for a child breaks free from the deep recesses I'd resigned it to. I feel that to have our baby grow inside me would be the culmination of a love I've never known but longed for.

Is it life itself that manifests love beyond reason?

I sense that, like me, he's close to climax. I fall forward over him and say, "If you love me will you give me your baby?"

Beneath me he convulses, the length of him quivering with the delivery of his precious gift.

Alarm accompanies it.

I'm not free to feel this way.

CHAPTER 17

SANTIAGO DEANGELO

The Real Price of Addiction

MY EYES ROLL back in my head. *My baby?* My body and brain spasm several times. Is she insane? Maybe. But inspired imagination foretells of a child imbued with our talents. Who knew I could want a child?

Yet right now—in this moment. I want ours.

Is it just the drug?

Kitty kisses me one last time and rolls onto her back beside me. When her rapid breathing subsides, I roll to face her. "Did you mean that about a baby?"

"Why do men confuse the primary purpose of sex?" She runs her index finger along my hairline.

"Guess it's a woman's job to remind us." I draw circles on her shoulder. "Right now, everything feels possible. Even our baby. But is it? I mean, you're married."

"Don't go crazy. I don't think it's even possible for me to conceive a child. But you're right—it would be impossible—outside the bubble of your *infinite love*." She chuckles with gentle mockery and taps my lips. "A bubble which will likely burst in another few hours. So, let's just enjoy it while it lasts."

She kisses me then, with so much emotion that her words bewilder me.

"You could leave you know. With the money we make from the song. You could leave him."

Kitty rolls away from me. "It's not the money I would need," she says so quietly I can barely make out the words.

I wrap an arm around her. "What then?"

"I lost my mind for a moment. That's all. Don't ruin the little time we have left? I can't leave him, so please don't ask."

I cup her small breast in my hand and caress her nipple. "Then what do I do with the feeling I have for you?"

She makes a tiny sound of joyful laughter beneath her breath then encloses my hand with hers. "Remember it. Treasure it. Transfer it." And then she flips around, and her mouth is on mine to shut me up. She climbs on top of me and arouses me again. "Promise me you'll remember me just like this forever, Santiago."

Afterwards, we fall asleep. I wake to the sound of a buzzing phone on the nightstand near the bed. A couple texts on vibrate. It's dark out but the city lights give a faint glow through the sliding glass door with the curtains drawn back. It feels late. Pleasure still dances through my muscles—from the drug—though its fading. Kitty stirs. I kiss her cheek.

"What time is it?" She yawns.

I reach for my phone and wince at the brightness of the screen. It's 8:36 p.m., which surprises me. But not as much as the text preview from Sophia that reads, "Sorry about yesterday."

I bolt up and hang my legs over the side of the bed. Kitty makes her way to the bathroom from her side. I feel thirsty and guzzle the half-full liter of Aquafina between the lamp and Kleenex box on the bed side table.

I stare at Sophia's text. The undulating bliss that moves through me focuses its attention on Sophia. I pull on my lower lip as I click on the message and read what comes next:

"I did overreact. I haven't changed my mind. But I didn't mean to hurt you."

I rub the faint stubble on my chin.

Kitty switches on a dim lamp on her nightstand and crawls back in bed from her side of it. She kneels behind me. I put the phone face down and drop my head as she massages my neck.

"Santi, tomorrow you'll experience what I like to call a dopamine deficit. Don't be alarmed, it's to be expected when your body's just unloaded its serotonin stores into your system." She pecks my neck. "You'll be alright. Nothing an extra Vicodin can't take care of."

I crane my neck to watch her lie supine and pull the floral sheet over her bare breasts. Then I lie beside her and interlace our fingers.

"It's not even 9 yet? What should we do tonight?" I ask her while my thoughts wander about how I should respond to Sophia's text.

Kitty bounces our joined hands against the mattress. "I thought we'd just lie in the shadow of our accomplishments." She turns on her side towards me and props herself up with her bent arm. A sly grin on her face. "By the way, what happened on your Valentine's date yesterday? You were so excited." Her flashing eyes indicate a playfulness I fear prodding.

My legs twitch. "I can't tell you about it?"

"Why not, don't you remember how *big* love is?" She snorts in jest.

Angst gains a foothold. "It's wearing off, isn't it? I don't want to forget."

She becomes serious again. "Then don't"

"But it already sounds so stupid."

"No, it's not stupid. It's the best thing anyone's ever said to me. But it's safer as a secret. When you find someone to love you can share this feeling with her."

"So, loving you is not an option? Is that what you're saying?

She moves her head to indicate that it isn't. Her eyes are cast down.

"Is that why you asked about my Valentine's date?" I bite my thumb nail and rip it off with a wince.

Kitty pulls my thumb from my mouth and kisses its tip. "I'd be lying if I didn't admit to a little envy. But I can handle it. Tell me about her."

I exhale and stare up at the ceiling. "Something went wrong, and it re-activated all the cynicism I thought she'd free me from. For a minute there, I thought she could make me happy again."

She clutches my chin and makes me look at her. "No one else is in charge of that. You oversee your own happiness." She releases my chin. "How do you feel right now?"

"Confused. Like I'm under a spell I'm afraid to emerge from. Sophia really hurt me. And now you're doing the same. But I have no one to blame. You're married for God's sake. I didn't think I'd ever do something that stupid."

Kitty laughs again, and my face begins to burn. I flip

onto my side away from her. She reaches her hand around and fondles my chest, cooing an apology, I move her hand away.

"I'm sorry, Santi. I'm just more surprised by what happened between us than I can say. And to be honest, more jealous than I expected to hear about Sophia. What went wrong?" She kisses my back. "Please tell me, I want you to be free to love her. Because we can't love each other in the real world."

I roll flat on my back and sigh up to the ceiling. "She just rejected me. Everything was going so well until I told her about the pain pills. I just thought . . . I could tell her. I thought she could help me. I told you, and it felt so good. Not just the relief from the lie, but the connection. You understood me. You accepted me. She didn't."

Kitty lays her head on my chest. "She doesn't have the context to understand you like I do. And what you experienced with her is the real price of addiction."

"I can't live like this anymore."

"Then get sober and take your power back, Santiago."

"I just can't do it alone. And the crazy thing is Sophia just texted me that she's sorry, says she overreacted! Hasn't changed her mind though. Now, what do I do? Here I am lying with you, feeling the most intense pleasure of my entire life, followed by the most seriously mixed signals it's possible for you to send—only to get that text."

"What do you think you should do?"

"If I can't be with you, I should go after her."

Kitty sits up and looks down at me. "Then do that! But promise me something, Santi."

I look her in the eyes. "What?"

"Promise me you won't forget what happened between us today. Because it made me believe what you said, love *is* bigger than the rules we make for it."

"How could I forget?"

And to ensure I don't she kisses me again.

CHAPTER 18

SANTIAGO DEANGELO

Love Letters

I FEEL STRIPPED down. Thank God I'm not, since my sister is with me when I wake. She's propped on her side. Her cinnamon brown eyes fixed on my waking face. I blink at the morning light shining in a halo around her head.

"You're alive," she says.

"Close the blinds."

She hops up on my bed and twists the wand on the dark oak blinds. Her short un-brushed hair stands up on the back of her head.

My mouth is so dry that my tongue feels like Velcro against the roof of it. It's like all the water in my cells transferred over to my bladder. I gotta pee.

In the bathroom, Lucy's arranged the mess into order. Even the spots on the mirror are wiped clean. Nice. I brush my teeth and drink directly from the faucet. I open the cabinet and count out my Vicodin like Scrooge counting coins. Sixteen. A chill runs down my spine. I chew two.

"Coffee. Must have coffee." I mimic a cartoon mummy shuffling into the room with my eyes shut and my arms stretched out in front of me.

Lucy laughs. "It should be done brewing. I'll get it. But drink that water and take those vitamins first." She sounds just like Mom for a second. I swallow them all in one mouthful and chug the water. Then I look around. The clothes I've strewn about the room all week are gone. I hear the mechanic swishing of the washer humming through the walls. I should invite my sister over more often.

Lucy was all too happy to come. In my emotional state, after leaving Kitty—and still high as a kite—I began texting Lucy with a confession of my fraternal love. Followed by all the compliments I'd ever meant to share but never thought necessary.

She comes in and hands me my coffee. I sip. "Damn, sis, you make it better than me."

She raises an eyebrow. "I do most things better than you and you're still the one Dad puts his hope in."

"Do I detect some jealousy? I thought you'd surpassed that on a higher spiritual plane."

She flicks my nose. "Dad's falling apart since you left."

I flinch and rub my nose. *Oh God, here we go.* She'd been holding her tongue all night. Biding her time. Building my compliments into a pedestal.

"Dad's doing what he wants—" I sip the steaming coffee "—and I'm doing what I want."

Her nostrils flare. "So, this Kitty person giving you drugs to record, and tricking you while dicking you doesn't seem a bit suspicious? Jesus! Dad's right to be insane with worry."

"That's really not what I said happened."

"Consider it an astute observation on my part."

I sit at the edge of my bed and feel the caffeine mixing with the opiate in my blood, but my engine is idling low on the fuel. Dopamine deficit.

"It wasn't like that," I insist.

She inclines her head.

How to put it? I sip more of the coffee while Lucy taps her feet. My phone, on the dresser buzzes and I lurch for it.

It's a text from Kitty that reads: "What if I did leave my husband and we lived in a bubble of your infinite love, with a baby to make it real?"

I laugh out loud, and a sense memory of last night's pleasure returns to me full force.

Lucy eyes me suspiciously. "Hey, we're talking."

"Just a sec, Luce."

She sticks her tongue out at me and that makes the moment even better.

I text back. "Only if we can have more than one, siblings are the best☺!!"

I toss the phone back on the dresser, walk over to Lucy, and sit back down on the edge of the bed beside her.

"That was Kitty, wasn't it?" she says. "What is it with her? Why are you smiling like that?"

"It's like Kitty opened up a portal into a variation of my life where I could be happy."

The phone buzzes again. I look towards it and back to Lucy.

She narrows her eyes. "Don't you dare, Santiago."

But I can't help myself. I lurch for the phone. Kitty writes. "I'm serious. Would you love our baby? Could you really love me?"

I text back. "Yes, and Yes!"

Her reply is immediate. "WHY?"

I type. "Because no other woman has ever made me feel like you. And just think of the music we could make together."

Lucy throws a pillow at me.

I release the phone and sit back down on the bed, humming Kitty's song.

"What is she saying now?"

"What?" I shake off the daydream Kitty's texts prompted. "Nothing."

"Well, what you were saying a minute ago? About a version of your life where you could be happy? Instead of what?"

"Pissed off all the time."

"It's the pills you know."

"Yeah, I know."

She stands up. "Then why are you still taking them? Are you that much of an idiot?"

I shake my head. "I wish I could let you feel, for just a minute, what the withdrawals are like. Or what the itch for a pill feels like when any emotionally stressful situation comes up. Not to mention the illusive euphoria that each pill promises. And I'm so alone."

"God, that sounds horrible. But you're not alone! I've been here the whole time."

"Don't blame yourself, Luce. If it wasn't for you, I probably would have crashed my plane a long time ago."

"Why is it so hard for you?"

"I don't know. I wish I was more like you, but I'm not. I've always been so sensitive. Barbara said that's what made me such a good musician." The coffee is cooling, and I take larger pulls from the mug.

Lucy walks to the end of the bed and falls straight back onto it with outstretched arms. "I'm gonna pray for you. *And* talk to Mom about it."

I jump up just in time to keep the bouncing mattress from spilling my coffee. "Wait, *what*? You talk to Mom?" I stare down on her.

She lies on her back with her hands clasped behind her head. "Not exactly. I mean I talk, but I mostly just *feel* her answers. I get this strong intuition about what she would say."

"I don't hear shit," I sneer.

"That's because you have to be sober."

I roll my eyes. "Well, put in a good word for me."

"Only if you do something for me." Her voice pounces on the opportunity to insert the request I could feel queuing up all night.

But I can't refuse her. She knows it too.

"The old bell tower's coming down soon. It's the part of the project Dad's been super stressed about. I just want you to show up and help out."

"Me being there won't be a help. He doesn't want to see me. You get that, right?"

Lucy takes a deep breath, then blurts out, "Mom thinks it will be good."

"You just said—" I rub the back of my neck "—okay, so you have a feeling? Because I have a feeling—*your feeling*—is a recipe for disaster. Don't look at me like that, Luce."

Her lips twitch. "Please just try to be there. It's probably still a month away. I'll remind you about it." When I don't respond she adds, "And I wish you wouldn't pretend to be so nonchalant about things with you and Dad. I know it's killing you. You can talk to me."

I just stare at her, thinking *and say what*? In the dopamine-deficit, the despair in me whimpers, *I just want him to love me. It's not fair.* I can't say this. Not even to Lucy. I pace.

"Fine. Remind me and I'll be there."

She leaps off the bed and kisses me on the cheek. "You're the best."

WHEN LUCY LEAVES, my loneliness becomes an itch I'm trying not to scratch. I leave my fourteen pills alone and simmer in my loneliness instead.

I text Sophia: "I understand your reaction. Can we get together for a cup of coffee and talk?"

But when hours pass, and she doesn't text me back I feel helpless because basic rules-of-engagement require me to wait out Sophia's next text. But, if I were sending her quotes from the book we're supposed to be reading together, well I mean, that would be totally okay.

I scour the book for an irresistible quote. The thing is, while I'm reading to connect to Sophia, I'm also fully aware of Mom's voice in my head. And the reasons she wanted me to read this book. Is that what Lucy was talking about? I don't think so. I'm putting together my beliefs of what Mom would say in a situation we'd been in before, discussing literature. Lucy is asking Mom about things that haven't happened yet.

I close my eyes and imagine Mom's voice saying something she told me often as a child.

It's okay to be sad sometimes, Vita Mia. If we take care, our emotions will work for us, not against us.

I give in to the sadness and feel it fully. "I just miss you so much," I say aloud. Then I release the emotional strain in a few silent tears.

When I return to the book, I struggle with quotable options to lure Sophia into communicating with me.

My anxiety deepens in the following days. An edgy feeling of shaky restlessness from my gut to my trembling hands. I take as few pills as I can until my unanswered calls and texts to Kitty initiate a kind of obsession I've never fallen victim to before. Since our text conversation about having children together, I haven't heard from her at all. What the fuck? Even when I text about the song.

In addition, I'm narrating a tragedy of injustice with my dad that Lucy set the stage for. But I can't talk to her, because I know I've taken the tale down the opposite road she intended.

There's no one I can talk to. At night I crave a warm body to curl up next to after mind numbing sex.

But after what I experienced with Kitty and want to recreate with Sophia I won't go there.

Masturbation is the obvious choice. But my dick goes limp in my hands. My ego, who lives between my legs, calls addiction out. *This shit is not cool. It's happening half the time now.*

I surrender to the book again and the idea comes. The story is about love letters. I could write Sophia one. I sit up in bed with a spiral notebook and a pen. I need to plan it out. And do I send it on paper? No, I need the immediacy of a text. But I plan it out on paper before I start typing on my phone. I scratch out lines and circle ideas. I cross out whole pages and start again. I learn something.

Only the truth matters.

I text:

"Sophia, it was selfish of me to not think of how my confession would make you feel.

But when you said you wanted to KNOW ME, I couldn't bear to hide something like that from you, like I do from everyone else. I understand your need to put a safe a distance between yourself and fragile people like me and your mom. I just want you to consider that maybe meaningful connection is what we need to be strong enough to stop believing the lies the alcohol and pills tell us.

But your mom doesn't just need it from you. The same way I don't just need it from my dad or my sister.

Humans thrive by connecting with people in physically loving relationships that family cannot provide alone. I think your mom is as lonely as I am.

I don't expect you to save me. I won't lie and tell you that I'll never take another pill. But I will say that you're the first person who ever made me feel like I could quit. And I want to. I hope you'll hold a place for me in your heart when I have."

After I hit send, I set the phone down and realize I'm holding my breath. I don't know how long it will be before she replies. When twenty minutes have passed and I haven't moved from my place at the kitchen table, I accept the fact that she may not return the message at all.

I click over to my message strand with Kitty. The last two messages are from me.

The first sent two days ago. "Hey, how's it going? How's the song coming?"

The second sent today. "You there??"

I scroll up to our messages about the baby and question the joy I initially felt when we sent those messages back and forth. What happened? Do I really want to be a father? Am I anywhere near ready for that? Probably not. I mean, of course not. She just fucked with my head. So, why can't I stop thinking about it?

Thing is, I think I could love our child the way Mom loved me. That it would be a chance to let that kind of love back into my life. The thought of which makes Kitty's radio silence that much harder to bear.

I mean, did her husband read our messages? Is she okay? Would he hurt her? Would he stop the song from being released?

My erratic thoughts turn to mixed projections about my future following the song's release. I imagine flashing cameras and raving fans with outstretched arms and open limousine doors. But what would it really be like? And what if the song fails to impress the right people? Maybe that would be better. I could sink into the shadows and check into a rehab facility. An option I don't think I have with all the intense publicity Victoria Thompson has stirred up for me. I check in with social media to see what's brewing.

After a few minutes browsing, my major thought is, thank God Sophia isn't on social media! As she puts it, her time's too valuable for voyeurism. So, she won't see the golden calf Victoria Thompson has made of me. If she does, she'll never text me back.

The Holladay site hosts a ticking clock, counting down the moment of the single's release. Forty-two hours, sixteen minutes and twelve, eleven, ten . . .

The excitement is manufactured. The social media groups that follow the hype circle the clock like sharks.

They're not my fans but fans of the Holladay Records pop production machine. They'll either devour the success of the song—or they'll devour me—as they see fit to satisfy their hunger for new music trends.

The clock has me queasy.

It's past 9 p.m. when Sophia's message chime pulls me out of the social media rabbit hole.

She texts:

"I appreciate your words. I can feel their truth.

I was disappointed to have my thoughts of you turn so suddenly. I guess I was holding my own fantasies about who you are and what you could be in my life. That was selfish too.

You are right, my mother is terribly lonely for romantic companionship and that is NOT my fault. Thank you for helping me see that.

The truth is I've over analyzed every relationship I've ever been in to protect myself from being as lonely as she is. I get that now. And it helps.

But, right now, we are both lonely because you were honest. It's not fair of me to need you to be OR NOT BE a certain way when I'm already holding a place for you in my heart.

Please don't hurt me for being vulnerable enough to say that."

I write back. "Sophia, I'm honored by your vulnerability. I've swallowed a lot of pills to avoid being vulnerable, only to learn by your example, that vulnerability is letting love and faith take over to protect us from life's pain. I like that better. Don't you?"

She texts. "I don't know yet . . . my hands are still shaking."

I write. "I wish I could hold them."

She replies. "I'm afraid of getting even closer to you when there's so much that's about to happen to you. I don't follow social media, but my mom says that the publicity Holladay is churning up right now will either make you a huge star or a huge failure. Either way, being a fragile artist in a sudden spotlight can be dangerous. I don't think either of us have any concept of what your immediate future holds or how it will affect your need for the drugs, you're already dependent on. Will I even factor into your thoughts when that lifestyle grabs a hold of you?"

I start to type. "I couldn't stop thinking of you if I tried." But I backspace because she's right. I have no idea what to expect and I don't want to make promises I can't keep. Suddenly my future fame feels frightening.

I put those thoughts into words and send them. We spend the next few hours corresponding that way and when my eyes begin to blur with sleep I text:

"Will you be there for me like this in the unknown weeks ahead?"

She writes:

"I want to be, but it would hurt me to think of you with other women when we're becoming this close. Is it fair to ask you to be exclusive? Because after everything we've said to each other tonight it would be dishonest to act like it was okay to hold your hand through this if you were sleeping with someone else at the same time."

There is a rush of emotion when I read her words. I want to be in an exclusive relationship with her! But on the heels of that thought is my sense memory of Kitty and the imaginary *bubble of infinite love* I've held intact in my mind. But, as Kitty said, we aren't free to love each other in this world.

I text. "I want to be exclusive with you!"

My eyes grow heavy while I wait out her prolonged response. I drift off and startle awake when the phone chimes next.

She writes:

"I want that too! But I have to admit that I'm not comfortable being involved with you sexually before you've gotten help for the drugs.

I can't tell you how awkward it was to type that. Especially because I'm so attracted to you. But it's important to me. Not as a punishment or an enticement, but just because I wouldn't feel comfortable otherwise.

Hitting send with an anxious heart."

I can feel her nerves and I want to calm them. I write back. "I want you to be comfortable. Sweet dreams my beloved, Sophia."

Then I surrender to a deep and heavy sleep like I haven't known in forever.

CHAPTER 19

SANTIAGO DEANGELO

Creative Process

D O YOU WANT to hear it?" Kitty purrs when I answer her call the next night.

"Where the hell are you?" The hand that holds the phone shakes a little. A combination of early withdrawals and the funky blend of relief and excitement hearing her voice again kick started.

"It's a private hell called creative process, and its invitation only. You coming?"

I drive immediately to Barbara's house where Kitty has been staying during postproduction. When I see her; I re-interpret her words. Since I've last seen her, Kitty's lost several pounds she didn't have to lose. The skin under her eyes appears bruised. The whites of her eyes are yellow, and there's dried blood in the rim of her nose.

But still, her eyes dance, and she forgets herself for

what it is she wants to show me. She drags me by the hand into our musical den, and presses play to hear *our song*. She calls it that for the first time.

I dance to it. The song asks you to dance to it, and the lyrics further lure you. But when I pull her out of the chair, she surprises me with her strength of refusal. She turns down the volume and we study sections. She describes her postproduction handiwork while I exhaust my mental thesaurus on the word 'awesome'.

"You hear that?" she asks. "I added the synthesized snaps because you started to snap when you started to roll." She chatters on. I zone out, smiling in time to the cadence of her babbling.

"It sounds amazing," I say.

"You have no fucking idea, do you? It's not amazing, its alive! You feel that? Half of the music—no—ninety percent of the music that gets recorded, never sounds good enough to release. A product like this is the miracle of pop music. Something so alive, people come alive, when they hear it. This song is going to be a monster.

"I'm like Doctor Frankenstein, trading my life, for the life of the song, and tomorrow you trade the life you used to know for the life I'm offering with it."

I make the mistake of laughing.

Kitty drops her head, the top of her scalp greasy, her fine hair a mess. I see what she means. Spun out as she is, Kitty really is trading her life for the music's.

Her nose starts to bleed and blue veins pulse in her temples. I lift her head. Her eyes roll back. When I remove my hand, she falls forward onto the sound board.

I lift her. She's limp in my arms. And difficult to carry given her height.

"No, Kitty, no." Her head bobs while I trot her into the house and down the hallway to the bedroom. I flop Kitty down onto the floral sheets and rumpled comforter and attempt to revive her. Shaking, slapping, threatening, all fails me.

Think man think!

I grab tufts of hair and pull while pacing. Kitty's phone seems to be the answer. My chest pounds as I search the bed clothes, the dresser, and the kitchen, which reveal nothing. So back to the studio where I find her cell phone along with the uncomfortable number of eleven missed calls from 'Husband'. I can hear the blood rushing in my ears. She has several unread texts and I read only the last from Dirk:

"Got the sound file. AWESOME. Vicky has major push lined up tomorrow. Call me! Need 2 know U OK."

Searching the contacts, I find Otto, and dial.

"It's a girl!" Otto says.

I'm confused into silence.

"How's you and the boy's love child? You know, the song. Any cries from the delivery room yet? I have cigars ready."

"It's me, the boy."

"Oh shit, where's Kitty?"

"Unresponsive."

"I'll be there in twenty."

Otto charges the door with a duffel bag, and like the matador in this drama, I pull it back in time for a graceful entrance. Within minutes he erects an IV stand and inserts a needle in her arm. I look away and then back at his forehead which irrigates its furrowed channels of fear with sweat. He answers my assumed question without looking up. "I used to be a medic in the army, Gulf War. Had a job as an EMT all lined up before I surrendered to music's underbelly."

"Underbelly?"

"Any time you mix drugs with your passion you transform it to Hades. That's where Kitty's at right now. We need to get her stabilized and then let her rest."

"What the fuck happened?" I squat down beside him.

He keeps his eyes on Kitty. "She's been on a binge for post-production. That's her thing man. She doesn't need it, but try telling her that. We gotta get Dirk off her back or he'll find her like this and commit her again. I was worried, but she said she had it under control."

I pummel my forehead. "And you believed her?"

He looks at me. "We all do, that's the way it works, man. Besides, I'm guessing the song is worth it. It's her best work. And you're the one who benefits the most."

"Why does everyone keep saying that? How do we pacify Dirk?" I jiggle Kitty's arm and she inhales deeply, and her eyes roll beneath their lids.

"Leave her man. We'll just send Dirk a text from her." He grabs her phone from the bed and reads the messages. "Shit," he says under his breath, a few burst of laughter, a couple sighs of distress, then both thumbs twitch. "Let's see what he says to that. I'm late, man, you gotta stay with her all night. Alright?"

"That would not be okay with my girlfriend."

He gives me a hard stare.

"What? Okay, okay, alright."

He puts a Ziploc bag next to the phone. "She'll need this in the morning, and if she's restless in the night inject that needle in the IV."

"I can't do that, dude."

"You have to."

When he's gone, I check the text he sent to Dirk from Kitty: "I love you, Dirk. OK I promise. Resting now. Fingers crossed for tomorrow."

While I'm holding the phone, it buzzes: "You need to come home tomorrow."

I peel off my jeans and climb under the covers, pulling them over our heads. I put my arms around Kitty and rock her like a baby. Our song plays in my head. Our love child truly.

Kitty moans in discomfort and twitches in my arms.

"It's okay, Kitty, I'm here."

In the morning, light peeks through the cracks in the lined draperies. My head pounds with deepening withdrawals. I'm still holding Kitty and my morning salute is nestled against her like a hotdog in the proverbial bun, albeit through the cotton of our clothing. A boner is something to be thankful for. Even if I do need withdrawals to get one.

Kitty's warm and damp against me and smells like celery. I take a deep breath of her armpit, capturing the earthy un-showered essence. It's wonderful. She's wonderful. She makes the smallest sound of laughter in her sleep.

"Stay sleeping," I whisper.

She interlaces her fingers in my hand and draws my arm tighter around her. "You stayed." Her voice like a bull frog's.

"I stayed. Now stay sleeping, or I'll have no choice but to tranquilize you." I laugh.

"Otto?"

"Yes. Are you okay now?"

"You two may be my only friends," she says.

I start to pull away.

"Please stay," she says.

"I have to go."

She presses her butt back against my incensed groin.

My desire for Kitty feels like a sin given my promise to Sophia.

"Kitty this is not okay, your husband texted you like a thousand times."

"I love you for staying," she says grinding now.

"Kitty, I don't want this."

She lies still but presses herself against me tighter. There's a pulse in my groin.

"The song comes out today," she says. "I wish I could protect you from the fame that's coming."

I chuckle nervously. "Why? I thought you didn't care what happened to me. Besides it's not like anyone ever gets famous overnight."

"Not organically. This is something else. And I don't want it for you anymore because I love you too much."

I squeeze her tighter. My throat is too thick to talk. I want her so badly, not just because I'm hard as hell, but because I love her whether I should or not. Thing is, I'm falling in love with Sophia too, and one love is not cancelling out the other like I expected.

Kitty grinds against me again and I'm burning for her.

"Make love to me one last time," she says.

"I can't. I'm with Sophia now. I told her . . ."

"Don't tell her you love her like you told me so soon."

My face reddens with embarrassment. "It was your damn drug—"

"I know," she says to soothe my shame. But we both know it was also the music we'd made together that had primed that confession. "Just don't tell her so soon. That might ruin it."

"Okay, I won't. But, but . . ."

But as I try and protest, she's slipping down her sweats and wrestling me from my underwear. Guiding me like a missile to my defeat. Then I'm inside her and she begins to move against me in a way that forces me to concentrate.

God damn woman.

She glues my forearm and hand against her chest. "Your fame won't be like you ever thought, Santiago."

"What will it be like?"

"That depends on you," she says.

CHAPTER 20

SANTIAGO DEANGELO

The Beating Heart of Music

BEHOLD THE FATTED Calf.

A headline delivered via the pop pundits who insist: "Holladay's latest sacrifice won't divert attention from the rising number of pending lawsuits against it."

To which I check the response to my own tweet: "This idol aint gold plated." With a screenshot of the song's rise from its debut two weeks ago on the charts at number 17 to its current place on the pop music chart at number 5.

When I chuckle at my own audacity Victoria Thompson puts her hand on my forearm to get my attention. We are in the back of the company Maybach with vanity plate HOLID8.

"We have people for that. Stay off Twitter. I didn't design things to have you destroy them in the car before interviews. Just keep to the notes I messaged you."

And before I can respond, Victoria is answering her phone with her earpiece. It took me a while to get used to her wearing hers 24/7. She speaks to it more than me, though the calls never last longer than a minute.

I stare at her. She's always dressed in a shade of pink power suit. She reminds me of the Energizer bunny that keeps going and going. I can't help but guess her endless drive is to prove her value as a woman in a man's world. She certainly works harder than any man I've ever met. But I wish I could tell her that a little feminine charm would make her a lot more approachable. As it is, I don't feel any connection to her, and that sucks. Beneath the hard exterior of her ambition is likely a fun-loving woman that I could be friends with.

My phone dings, it's a text from Sophia, and a ball of warm energy expands in my core.

"You don't have time to answer that. We're getting out now."

The brakes on the car click as we pull up alongside the iHeartRadio studios where I'll conduct the first of sixteen radio interviews on my promo day. Victoria looks at the time on her rose gold Apple watch, it's 6:28 a.m.

She looks me over. "Why are your eyes so red? Put these drops in."

I glare at her. "It's a radio interview, the listeners can't see my eyes."

"Wrongo, kid, the whole thing is also being filmed for YouTube. So, play up to the cameras while you're at it."

She answers another phone call with her headset. "Yes, we absolutely want the MTV news interview. Make it happen! We can squeeze it in this week."

I squeeze the drops into my eyes. They burn. And my right wrist aches. My injuries are my weak points, and they're always my red flag to when too many pills and cups of coffee are being used to replace sleep and down time.

But filming the music video for the hit single has been listed a priority above sleep. Three days of feeling like a dancing marionette on a plush Hollywood set before the music video director said he had a new vision of the video that would include filming on a mountain top at sunset. It was several days before the light was just right. But I gotta admit, the footage I saw overdubbed with the vocals made the lyrics more poignant than ever. As the sun sets into darkness, I sing, "I've got a lust for trusting on a dark night." And with the lyric, "but relief keeps shifting", the special effects show the edge of the cliff I'm standing on give way. Meanwhile the chorus is dramatized by the camera angles which make the mountain top appear much higher than it was. It was a surreal experience until my exhaustion made it all too real.

While Victoria Thompson instructs the driver to pull up another ten feet I glance at the message from Sophia. It reads: "Just be yourself today. They'll love you."

But who am I? I feel like I know when she and I are texting. Our honesty with each other feels like a saferoom inside this storm. But everything else that's happening is happening so fast I'm not sure who I can trust.

It's cold inside the studio. I'm glad I wore the black cashmere sport coat over the white dress shirt, untucked, with the top two buttons undone. Growing up in classical music, performance always meant a suit and tie if not a tux. As I greet the morning talk show hosts, Toni Tone and her counterpart Rockin' Ron Kay, they seem impressed with my attire. They are both dressed very casually. A bonus to radio work, I guess. An intern goes to work setting up my headphones and mic.

Toni, the female headliner is an attractive woman in

her early forties with her dark brown hair in a sleek ponytail and barely-there makeup. Her warm smile breaks the ice.

She says, "We're gonna keep this real laid back. And I'd like to lead into the live performance like it was a spontaneous suggestion on your part."

"Sounds good," I say.

"You nervous?"

"Nah." I titter. "Yeah, I guess I am."

She laughs with me. "Don't worry, I'll make it easy. *Love* the song by the way. We're coming on after this traffic report ends."

I meet a guy in his early twenties with reddish brown hair that he brushes out of his eyes before he introduces himself as Andy. He gives me a brief rundown of how things work and hands me a pair of headphones. I slip them on and hear the jingle, "It's Toni Tone and Rockin' Ron Kay in the morning on KSXY an iheartRadio Station" before Toni's voice announces me.

"As promised, we have Santiago DeAngelo, the new artist behind 'New Kind of High' in the studio with us. I'm glad *he's* a morning person. Well, I guess anyone can be with enough caffeine, right?"

"You better believe it," I say with a snicker thinking not only of the tasty double shot cappuccino I ordered up to my hotel room this morning but also the pill I crushed and snorted to overcome the fear my looming schedule held over me. Now though, between her casual, conversational opening and the high that catapulted me out of that anxiety, I feel at ease and glance around the room at posters of hip new artists and the radio show's rising ratings to the number 2 morning drive time.

"What's your drink of choice?" She asks me.

"Definitely cappuccino."

"I think the cappuccino machines at Starbucks are going to be working overtime this morning now that the listeners know that."

I beam, aware of the YouTube cameras shooting from my peripheral. "You think so? That's nuts."

"Your fans love you! And they're very active. When we announced your coming on the show, we got *so* many tweets. It's amazing the way you've been able to interact with them on social media and form a following off just the success of this single. Tell us about that."

I replay Victoria's notes like a pro. "It's been so cool to connect with the fans in such a personal way. It's like I've suddenly got a few thousand new friends."

Rockin' Ron Kay chimes in, his voice smooth as velvet. "What I'd like to know is what the *new kind of high* is for you?"

"Ah, man, for me, it's about being back in the beating heart of music."

Toni says, "Back?"

I take a deep breath and feel my muscles twitch. Victoria Thompson didn't have specific notes on my musical past. But I remember Sophia's advice to *just be yourself* and relax into the question.

"Well, the thing is, I spent most of my childhood totally immersed in music. I mean, my mom even homeschooled me up until high school so I could spend six to eight hours a day between the piano and voice lessons."

"Nice, so your voice is real then?" Toni says with a grin. I get the impression she's already cleared this line of questioning with Victoria. Playing up my voice is part of the marketing scheme.

"My voice?" I pause. "My voice coach always said"—
I chuckle—"this is gonna sound over the top—but she always
said my voice was a gift from God that we had a duty to
develop. She committed a ton of time to teaching me to sing
through my break and warmup properly. And she was always
on me about core strength and abdominal strength to support
my diaphragm and enhance my range. She thought of me as a
vocal athlete and trained me that way."

"Oh, so you've got great abs then?" Toni says like a
flirt.

"I mean . . ."

She winks at me playfully, and I stand and lift my shirt
to reveal them.

"Wow, I wish you guys could see this. He's got a total
six pack."

Ron says, "Oh, that's nothing, I've got a keg right
here." He lifts his sweatshirt to reveal a hairy beer belly."

"Ron, put that thing away before someone gets hurt.
Thank God this is radio," she says.

But in this era, we're all quietly playing up for the
YouTube cameras all the time.

Then Toni turns to me. "Santiago, my crush on you is
now complete. But seriously, a lot of people are impressed
with the vocal range this song showcases, and the first thought
is that it's all created in the studio. What do you say to that?"

"The studio is magic, no doubt! But why don't I give
you a live performance and let you decide for yourself?"

Ron chimes in "You ready to go Acapulco on this baby
to prove yourself?"

I laugh out loud along with Toni, "Acapulco? You
mean, a cappella, man?"

"Yeah, man, like I said, Acapulco."

Andy hits a laugh track.

"Alright, let's do this." My heart takes off like a dragster.

An applause track plays. Rockin' Ron hoots with excitement.

Toni says, "Okay, calm down a second, you two. Apparently, your Acapulco abs have lit up the phone lines. You wanna take a call from a fan?"

"Abs-o-luteley," I say.

They click on caller 1. Toni says, "This is Monica from Sherman Oaks."

"Good morning, Monica," I say.

A young caller's voice comes through the headphones. "Oh my God, it's really you." She sounds like she's about thirteen.

"It's really me. You sound excited, I'm glad you called, what's your question?"

"Oh my God, okay, do you have a girlfriend?"

"I do."

"Does she sing?"

"No, but she does write, and I'm hoping she'll help me out with the lyrics I've been working on for a very special song."

"That's so cool."

Toni closes out the call and says, "Are you also a song writer?"

I blow out my held breath. "I mean, I'd like to be. I was always told my greatest strength was my ability to interpret music, vocally and on the piano. But there is a song that's on my heart I want to share with the world so that they'll know who I really am as a man."

"Wow, I can't wait to hear it!" Toni says. "You also

mentioned you play the piano. Are we going to get a taste of that in the upcoming album?"

"Oh man, I hope so! Musically I feel most authentic behind a piano. In fact, the song I'm working on is a piano ballad, so fingers crossed it makes the cut. Other than that, we've been pumped about the songs we've been offered. I just can't wait to get in the studio and record them."

"What was it like recording 'New Kind of High'?"

"It was easily the most thrilling experience of my life. Working with Kitty Holladay who wrote and produced the song was like a dream."

"If you're just tuning in that's Santiago DeAngelo everyone. We'll be right back with a live performance of his new hit single, 'New Kind of High'."

We cut to break.

Toni slips off her headphones. "Time to get warmed up."

I eye the exits.

This is the high you asked for.

I go through my vocal warm up, totally aware that the YouTube camera is still running with this behind-the-scenes footage. But given my mention of the importance of the vocal warm up I give it the full treatment for the camera even though I spent half an hour warming up before I left my hotel room this morning.

When the last commercial plays Ron points to the performance mic. I rub my hands down my pant legs as I make my way towards it. Then I close my eyes and revisit the feeling in the recording booth when I sang it for Kitty and Otto the first time. I remember her reaction and live inside that feeling when I get the cue to start singing.

It's true, this *is* a new kind of high.

Performing the song with only my voice forces me to focus and I feel on fire as I deliver what I know is a clean a cappella cut. I love this. I love being back in the beating heart of music. When I'm done, I hear the live applause of everyone in the studio.

"You're the real deal, man!" Ron says with genuine respect and possibly relief. After his big joke, singing it a cappella was a risk that paid off for both of us. People will be talking about what happened on his show today.

Toni moves towards me with open arms. "Can I hug you? That was unbelievable!" She squeezes me tight; I only hope she doesn't feel me quaking. "We've got a couple extra tickets to the iheartRadio Music Awards this weekend. Would you be interested?"

"Abs-o-lutely." I tell her, and we both laugh.

CHAPTER 21

SANTIAGO DEANGELO

Superstar

LATER THAT NIGHT, alone on the white, curved leather couch in the living room of my hotel suite, with my feet up on the brushed chrome coffee table, I feel the exhaustion creeping up beneath the wave of adrenaline I've been riding. I think over the big moments the day's interviews created. I can't discern how well *the real me* I tried to give them will be judged. I remember detailing my foundation of classical music and my connection to Holladay records through Barbara Holladay. Was that okay? One of the interviewers teased me about my looks, asking if I'd be able to get by on my musical chops without them. I answered her playfully. I *think* it went over well.

Throughout the day there was this natural emergence of a fun loving, humble, new artist eager for more. Right now, I'm eager for sleep, but too keyed up to expect any. I could use some more Valium and Ambien to get the rest I need and do it all again tomorrow. My body aches with fatigue. I pull my legs onto the couch and rub my thighs while I do a mental tally of my Vicodin count for the day.

Nine pills. Up one from yesterday. The first one that I'd snorted had been an exciting new experience. Instant euphoria followed immediately by the need to puke in the bathroom sink. But it was supported by elation that lasted through the interview before the bottom dropped out as I departed iHeartRadio studios.

I spent the day chasing that high by chewing my pills. It seemed too risky to crush and snort another in a public place.

I text Zenon to tell him I'll pay double plus a delivery fee if he'll drive out to LA with my usual order. Seconds later my phone chimes and I'm stoked he's responding so fast. But it's a text from Sophia. Even better.

"How was it? I only caught the early morning interview. I was SO PROUD to know you."

"Just be myself was my mantra. Was it okay that I told everyone about you? I wasn't expecting that question about having a girlfriend."

"You kept me anonymous, which I appreciate." She texts, followed quickly by, "Truth is, I was super jazzed that you were talking about ME. I could just feel the envy of all those teenage girls."

As I'm typing a reply, I get a message from Z: "Sure thing, Bro. Be there tomorrow. Text me your addy."

I send it, then toss the phone down and raise both fists in victory.

A minute later it rings, and for a second, I catch myself hoping it will be Kitty. An entire day discussing our song made it impossible not to fixate on her MIA status. She's the only one who can really appreciate what my life is like right now or celebrate the song's success. Which we haven't gotten to do yet.

My heart drops a little when I see the call is from my sister.

"Hey, Baby Bear, did you catch them?"

"I caught a few, *Superstar*." She giggles. "I couldn't help it; I showed my friends that a cappella performance on YouTube, like, a thousand times."

"It's crazy, right?"

"So crazy!" Then her tone takes a turn. "But how are you? I know you get kind of moody when you get tired and lonely? I could drive out this weekend and stay with you."

"You're just hoping to get invited to the awards show that Toni and Ron gave me tickets for."

I'd texted her about the tickets soon after I left the station. I stand, stretch, and walk into the bathroom.

"Can you blame me? Who are you taking?"

"Don't know yet. It's not like I'm up for an award. It's just a work thing I've gotta do."

"Whatev. As if you're not just as excited as I am to see all those stars. Anyways, how's the pill count?"

I switch the phone on speaker, set it on the white marble counter and squeeze more toothpaste onto my toothbrush. "I wanted to go down one from yesterday, but I went up one instead." I start brushing my teeth.

"That's not good."

My words are garbled by the toothbrush in my mouth. "No, but I need them to get through this." I spit and rinse. "I'm just a zombie when I try and cut back." I start brushing more vigorously. Growing up together with a shared bathroom, Lucy and I are used to having heart-to-hearts over a bedtime routine, so she isn't fazed.

"You're going to turn yourself into a real zombie if you don't figure out how to cut back soon."

I keep brushing, knowing she's right, but not knowing how to clean up my act. I rinse my mouth and stare at myself in the bathroom mirror toothbrush held midair. "Do you know if Dad heard any of the interviews? Has he heard the song at all?"

"I bet he's secretly watching a replay of them all on YouTube right now. But, no, he hasn't mentioned it. He's working major over-time to distract himself from it all."

"What about Mariano? He hasn't returned my text."

"Well, it would help if you didn't lead with, 'Did you hear me on the radio today?'"

"I didn't! I asked how he and the family were first." I put the toothbrush back in the cup and start flossing.

"I haven't talked to him in a few days. By the way, I seriously hope you weren't talking about Kitty when you said you had a girlfriend to help with the lyrics."

"I was talking about Sophia."

"You mean the girl you took to the library? I thought that whole thing blew up in your face."

"We reconnected. But it's kinda weird because we haven't seen each other in the weeks since the song came out, and yet, these long texts we're sending each other are getting intense."

"Shouldn't *she* be your date to the awards show?"

"I'm going to ask her, but somehow I don't see her agreeing to a thing like that."

"If she says no, you better take me."

"It's a deal."

"You gonna be able to sleep tonight, Santi?"

"I'll be good. Love you."

"Love you too. Take care of yourself."

I dial Sophia as soon as I hang up. After several rings it goes to voice mail. I don't leave a message, but I do scroll through our recent texts and reread them. There's one a few days ago that had really hit me hard.

She wrote:

"I feel like your struggle with the song runs parallel to you figuring out who you are as a man."

To which I'd written:

"It means a lot to me that you understand that."

I stare into the mirror at nothing, the phone in my hand pressed against my heart as I try and recall each detail of her face. When I can't do it, I scroll back through our messages to a selfie she sent me of her lying in bed, her hair artistically arranged, her eyes reaching through space to find mine.

I climb into bed and lose time gazing at her photo as an ache spreads across my chest while I acknowledge how awkward our words are without a physical foundation of affectionate touch. I just want to lie my head on her chest and feel her heartbeat echoing in my ear.

Well, that's not *all* I want. I close my eyes to envision her with me and become aroused.

The ringing phone disrupts my fantasy. She's calling me back!

"Sorry, I fell asleep reading." Sophia yawns. I picture her with her hair spread across the pillow and nothing on beneath the sheets, though I can't envision her naked body as its secrets have yet to be revealed to me.

"I didn't mean to wake you," I say.

"No, I'm glad you did. It's good to hear your voice. I sometimes think it's silly that we don't talk more," she says.

"Or see each other more," I tell her, forgetting—in the

moment— the logistic difficulty given my schedule. Electricity crackles through my aching body. "I want to feel the weight of you pressed against me."

"I want that too," she says.

I throw back the blankets. "I'll just drive out." My mind races as I look for my shoes with the phone pressed to my ear. It will probably take about an hour and twenty minutes this time of night with no traffic to reach her. Then I realize, she hasn't answered. I hear her exhale heavily.

She says, "I mean, you know I want that, but . . ."

I don't want her to have to say it out loud, remembering how anxious she was to be honest and insist in text on the commitment I'd agreed to—in writing—not to be sexual before I get sober.

I drop the one shoe I'd found and sit down wearily on the edge of the bed.

"I know, but couldn't I hold you and feel your arms around me an entire night?" I crawl back under the bedding and pile pillows around me to feel less alone.

"It would make our words mean more, wouldn't it?" she says.

"Yes." I bite my nail and say, "Would you come somewhere with me this weekend. I've been invited to the iHeartRadio Music awards this Sunday. I'm not up for an award or anything crazy like that, and it's, really, just a publicity thing . . . but . . . I'd like you to be there with me. Will you come?"

She's quiet, again.

"I would have asked sooner, but they only just invited me. The tickets came last minute from Toni and Ron."

"I want to be with you, I just don't think I'm ready for something like that. All those cameras and pictures that last forever on the internet."

"No, I get it. I'll just take Lucy," I say more sharply than I mean too.

"Don't be mad."

"I'm not mad. I just really want to see you."

"Soon," she says, and we say good night.

THE NEXT MORNING, I get to sleep in since the big act of the day is a spot Victoria Thompson landed us later this afternoon on the Zach Sang show. It's a sign we're on the right track because Zach is the biggest name on the radio for listeners age twelve to twenty, which as Victoria Thompson puts it, "is the sweet spot of our target audience."

Around 10 a.m. I hear a heavy-handed knock on the door. Looking through the peep hole I see Zenon in the hall. The distorted image makes his tall muscular body appear to bulge beneath the black Under Armor work out wear he's got on. He raises his fist to knock again and I let him in.

"What's up, Z?

He strolls into the entry way of my hotel suite and whistles at the ultra-modern room decorated in grey, white and cobalt blue.

"Your what's up, bro? I guess all that singing and piano playing finally paid off. But I mean, what the fuck? I heard your song on the radio three times on the way over here. It's on all the XM stations."

"Three? That's cool. You want something to drink?" I move us towards the bar/kitchen area where there's a fridge full of choices.

He sits on a stool on the opposite side of the counter from me. "For you it's cool, but not for me. I can't come out here again. I had *no* idea."

"What's the problem?" I ask. "You want an orange juice? I've also got Red Bull."

"Give me a water."

He takes a bank bag out of the red-and-black backpack he had slung over one shoulder and tosses it down on the counter. The pills tinkle inside. He unscrews the lid on the Fiji water bottle.

"It was *one thing* getting you a few pills now and then when you were just a kid I grew up with down the street. Now, you're some kind of fuckin' superstar and I can't risk that kind of heat. You get me?" He gulps the water and sets the bottle down.

I shrug.

He runs his hands through his hair, long on top, short around the ears and neck, bright with natural bronze highlights from all the time he spends in the sun, on the road, with his professional road bike team.

"Dude, you're livin' the dream. Whaddya need this shit for anyway?" Zenon points at the bag.

I shrug again. There is no good answer. "You wanna hang out a while? I've got a few hours."

"No, bro, I'm gonna take off."

I toss a wad of bills on the counter and he pockets the cash. "Thanks for making the trip."

"I'm not coming out here again, so, make those last."

I figure that will force me to cut back, especially since Sophia is holding her ground, but as the week stretches on, I need the jolt to face the daily grind.

Sunday morning, an elegant white box with a red satin ribbon shows up from Versace. That afternoon, there's another from Tom Ford. Both on lend for tonight's red-carpet appearance.

The Versace, a silk dress shirt in vivid colors and patterns, is a bit too bold. I go with the Tom Ford number, a white silk tuxedo jacket with a blue velvet lapel, black patent-leather shoes and black denim jeans that fit like a glove. The ensemble is complete with sunglasses with light grey aviator shaped lenses.

As I tie the definitive black bow tie, I swear to myself, I'm not gonna snort another pill to face tonight. But if I did, I might try crushing the valium up with it.

That would be perfect.

Just as I get the tie done right, I hear the *bump, baba bump bump* of Lucy's signature knock. I run to the door and throw it open. We both scream in childish delight at each other's grown up prom attire.

As a fashion lover pursuing a future in clothing design, Lucy does not disappoint in the black, square neck dress that shows off her pretty collar bones and Mom's solitaire diamond necklace. The dress sits just above the knee with a peplum flare at the hip. It's timeless.

"Mom would love this on you, Luce."

"We both went classic. Mom always said, you can't go wrong that way."

I love these casual remarks Lucy and I can toss around about Mom.

I grab us both a soda at the kitchen bar. We're still waiting on Victoria Thompson to arrive so that we can all take the limo, that brought Lucy here, to the awards show. Lucy sips her soda as she reveals her excitement about all the stars we're going to see. She's even memorized a list of who's up for which award, tells me she's most excited to see Taylor Swift and shows me how she's practiced her "chill-non-star-struck face" in case we get to see her up close.

We both practice the face together, and I crack up when Lucy slowly passes her hand over her face to reveal the uncomposed version she was working to hide. Then Lucy creates a spontaneous game where she shouts the name of any-given-star we'll see tonight, and we try and outdo each other with our over-the-top expressions of total star-struck awe, followed by the attempted poise we're hoping to pull off. I laugh so hard I forget to be nervous.

When Victoria Thompson enters the hotel suite, the mood changes. Lucy takes a minute to praise how well her apricot-colored chiffon dress compliments her dark skin. Victoria gives a curt thanks. You can read the stress on her face. She hasn't spent the day resting like I have.

I squeeze Victoria's shoulder. "Let's just have fun tonight," I tell her.

"Fun, what's that?" Victoria says.

"I'll pour you a drink."

"No. Tonight's work. None for you either."

Then she goes into detail about the spur of the moment interviews I may, or may not, be asked to give on the red-carpet (my desirability given the bigger names is hard to predict). But if I am asked, here she points at me and says, "You've gotta be cool, DeAngelo. Practice these phrases." She runs through a few canned clichés that are all a variation of, "It's an honor to be here."

'It's not like I'm up for an award." I tell her.

Lucy gawks. Our playful mood is a thing of the past.

"Just practice the phrases."

I excuse myself and go into the bathroom off the bedroom. I take out two 5mg Valium and an extra strength Vicodin and smash them with the brand new heal of my Tom

Ford shoe on the counter, sweep the powder into a line and inhale it through my nose. I shake with relief, spit a little bile in the sink and revel in the glory until I see Victoria's shape in the doorway beside me. In my haste, I hadn't turned the door lock all the way.

She shakes her head in disgust. "I knew it! This is not gonna work, DeAngelo. This is not the image I'm going for with this experiment."

"Will you stop referring to me as your fucking experiment! This is my life." I'm still holding the dress shoe and thinking about licking the extra powder I see on the heel.

"It's my job to think about you as a commodity! And my reputation is riding on marketing you as an asset. So have some fucking respect for the opportunity you've been handed. Most of the artists you'll rub elbows with tonight never had a hit single gift wrapped for them." Her tone escalates. Her words cut deep into the anxiety at my core.

They won't respect you. You haven't earned this.

Lucy runs into the bedroom and ducks beneath one of Victoria's arms to enter the bathroom. She stands between us her arms outstretched. "Hey, let's all take a breath and cool down." She turns to Victoria Thompson. "You have no idea how hard he's worked for this. My entire life I've watched him trade everything a normal kid does to develop his talent. And as for the drugs, he's still recovering from a bad accident our mom died in. So, you, have some respect!"

I beam at her ferocious defense of me.

"I knew something wasn't right with you," Victoria says to me.

"Why don't you help him then?" Lucy says. "His honed talent is still the product you're trying to sell. Don't you see he needs all our help? Everyone just expects him to shake this on his own." She catches her breath. And we make eye contact in the bathroom mirror. "Even me." She mouths, *I'm sorry.*

Victoria inhales deeply and blows the air out slowly. "We do not have time for a stint at rehab before the major recording work begins tomorrow. This album has got to be released this quarter. Besides, it would damage your image and sales with the preteen market share. We could possibly sell the story about your mama. But that's private and I think you're too sensitive for that." Her voice is calm and professional again. She's thinking it through. "We start with the Vogls' songs tomorrow. They don't put up with schedule changes and their songs are our biggest chance for another hit."

"I can do this. You just freaked me out about tonight, and the pills take the edge off. I was cool until you came in here and ruined the night."

"I have to stay in the zone."

"Do you have to be such a bitch to stay in the zone?"

Lucy says to me, "Hey, that's not nice."

Victoria says, "I meant what I said. I'll try not to be such a bitch. But if your drug habit gets out to the public, I *will* shift gears and use the bad publicity to keep our momentum going."

IN THE CAR, Lucy gives her all to keep the mood light. And Victoria Thompson really does transform as Lucy shares her non-star-struck face to big laughs from my publicist. Victoria has a big, bold, beautiful laugh, and when it subsides, she shares her own stories of attempts to stay cool while working with some of the biggest names in the recording business.

As we near the red-carpet, Victoria is on her phone, messaging non-stop. When Lucy inquires, Victoria says she's tweeting—*as me*—about our imminent arrival, trying to stir up the fans who line the streets for star sightings. She tells me that she's worried that, amongst the well-established artists up for awards tonight, my arrival may not drum up any response without some serious effort on her part.

Before we arrive, I tell Victoria, "I really am glad to have you on my team. I get that I wouldn't be here if it wasn't for you."

She's about to brush it off, but the sincerity of my words reaches her. She looks me in the eye and says, "Thank you." Followed by, "By the way, DeAngelo, you can call me Vicky."

CHAPTER 22

SANTIAGO DEANGELO

Stay True to Who You Are

WE ARRIVE. A security guard in a black suit and tie opens the door for me to climb out. There are no flashing cameras and no fanfare as I step out of the black stretch Chrysler 300 limousine. I stay cool and make my way down the red carpet, which is congested by the huge gathering around the photo-shoot-zone where arriving stars are photographed in front of the iHeartRadio 2018 Music awards back drop. There are a multitude of screams and stage direction from hundreds of paparazzi for Iggy Azalea, who's currently posing in a black and silver dress, her right arm has a long sheer silver sleeve and the slit on the left exposes her left leg to her waist. The camera flashes are like strobe lights under which she maintains complete composure until she's certain they've had enough and walks away casually. Thank God I practiced my chill face.

When I finally get up closer, with Lucy hemmed in

tight to me against the pressing crowd, Halsey—a singer, who is up for female artist of the year—is posing before a storm of lightning strikes from hundreds of camera flashes. I can't help but stare at her skimpy tiger outfit that looks more like a two-piece bikini than a dress. Between sultry poses she notices me and gives me a look that could kill along with a tiger's hiss.

The cameras turn to record the object of her scorn.

They don't respect you. They don't even like you!

"Whoa, what's that about? She does *not* like you," Lucy says.

The stint of photos dies out quickly as Halsey's boyfriend, rapper G-Eazy grabs his girl and starts kissing her for the cameras.

"Kitty told me that, before she offered the song to me, she'd tried to sell the song to Halsey, but she turned it down. Maybe she's pissed about that."

"I wouldn't worry about it, man," a voice behind me says. I turn to find it's Charlie Puth. Lucy and I both assume our practiced faces with an effort.

He says, "You've got a great voice and she knows you're up-and-coming. She thrives on drama like that. Just focus on the music, and let the drama go."

"Is that what you do?" Lucy asks, her eyes glimmering, her mask slipping big time.

"Yeah, the music keeps me grounded," he says, before he's pulled away for an interview.

After several minutes I'm asked to pose for the cameras, and I pull Lucy in for a few shots. Later when Bebe Rexha pulls me in for a quick interview, I boast about sharing the spotlight with my sister, which earns me a kiss on the cheek.

The show itself is a rush of exciting musical

performances, big star moments, and a variety of acceptance speech styles. I personally prefer the winner to speak more about the value of not giving up on your dreams then list a dozen names. Lucy leans over and asks me who I'd thank.

"I'd thank Mom," I tell her. She pats my hand.

I clasp it, grateful for a hand to hold and wishing my other hand was holding Sophia's.

We're seated up in the mezzanine, below us on the ground floor, the artists nominated for awards are seated around tables. Towards the end of the night, I'm uncomfortable in my little seat, and ready to go.

But it's worth the discomfort to see Bon Jovi accepting the Icon Award.

He says, "To all the new artists tonight, just stay true to who you are and they're going to make an icon of you someday."

I feel like he's talking directly to me.

LATER, ALONE IN bed, I recall his words as I reread Sophia's text about figuring out who I am as a man. How can I stay true to who I am if I haven't even figured it out yet?

I call Sophia and she answers on the first ring.

"I'm so glad you called. I thought you'd be out all night at the after parties."

"They wouldn't be any good without you there, besides Lucy had to get home for school and I've got my first day of recording at 9 a.m."

"I should have just come tonight. I watched the show, and every time the cameras panned into the audience; I was looking for you with my heart in my throat. I should have been there. I'm sorry. I could have been in the car that picked your sister up and be driving home with her right now. It's just that I might not have made myself leave."

"I wonder if I would have been as afraid if you had been there."

"You were afraid?"

"Yeah, and the thing is, maybe that's why Barbara kept me from this life. I think she knew I was too sensitive. Someone told me recently the pressures of show business either make diamonds or dust. What if I'm not up for this? I mean, it would be different if it had come at a different time in my life, or if I had more support."

"Is that what you're afraid of? Because I've heard you play and sing for years in the church and I think you were born to do this. As for the timing, use it to turn your life around."

"But isn't everyone thinking that I didn't earn this shot? I mean it just fell into my lap. It's not supposed to happen like that."

"Santiago, listen to me. You've spent your whole life preparing for a chance like this. Of course, it landed in your lap, that's how fate works."

I think of how Kitty had called it fate and I'd shut her down. I won't do the same with Sophia. Hell, maybe she's right? It's preferable to think of it that way. I undress and feel a chill that makes my teeth chatter. I grab an extra blanket from the closet and wrap it around myself before getting into bed with Sophia's voice still in my ear.

I'm about to say good night when I bring up Bon Jovi's words and express my concern about not knowing who I am before I record this album and expose that fact.

"Don't let it mean so much. Your growth will be marked by subsequent albums as a record of your discovery."

"You think so?"

"Let it be so."

I snicker to myself at the suggestion it could be that easy. I say the words I've text her so many nights. "Good night my beloved, Sophia." And the words mean so much more spoken with my voice.

CHAPTER 23

SANTIAGO DEANGELO

A Mother's Love

IN THE MORNING, I'm up early pacing before my first big day of recording. There's an uncomfortable tickle in my throat, and a chilling ache in my legs. I begin my vocal warm up. But I feel like I can't pull a breath all the way down to my diaphragm. If only Barbara or Kitty were here to coach me. If only they'd sent the music and lyrics in advance of today.

I'd had plenty of time to prepare to record "New Kind of High" and knew that I could count on Kitty to coach me like Barbara would have. She had, and since then, performing our song again has felt easy. Something I can do without understanding why. But as I prepare alone, for three songs that I haven't even heard yet, my fear has me locked out of Barbara's method. I don't want to overdo it with the drugs. I swallow a valium to temper the panic attack I feel coming on and two Vicodin to prevent major withdrawals.

In the car I share my concerns with Victoria Thompson on the way to the studio.

She puts her hand on mine on the arm rest between our seats in the back of the plush company car. "Don't let the Vogls intimidate you. Your talent is real. You deserve to be working with them."

"Why would they try and intimidate me?" My anxiety deepens. My head throbs. It turns out that two Vicodin are no longer enough to avoid a withdrawal headache.

"I'm just getting some strange vibes from the Vogls that may be stemming from Dirk Holladay. He's known them since he was a kid. They helped his parent's build the company. Even while they continued to work with artists from other labels. I don't think he expected us to get this far. And I've been hearing some rumors around the office that he's none too pleased about your mention—in interviews—of the chemistry between you and Kitty in the recording studio. I've even heard he's pissed about how close you talk about being with his mother."

"So, what are you saying? Is he trying to sabotage me? I thought your big experiment was supposed to save the company. Isn't that more important?"

"You'd think so."

"This is *not* helping me relax." I take a pill out and move it towards my mouth. She stops me by grabbing my wrist.

"Pursuing your dreams takes guts, Santiago. Use the fear!"

"I think the fear is using me," I tell her, while the idea strikes that I've become a host to the parasite of fear.

She squeezes my wrist so tight I drop the pill.

"You don't need these," she says.

"I've got a monstrous headache."

She closes her eyes to think, like a mother handling a difficult teen. "Give me everything you brought with you."

I set my jaw in defiance.

She raises one eyebrow.

I reach into my pocket and hand her the contents.

"Other pocket," she says.

I roll my eyes and comply. She hands me back one extra-strength Vicodin and I gobble it up greedily.

It is just enough to diminish the headache.

Inside, a couple in their sixties sit rigid at a high-tech sound board. Their space is dark; the counters and walls are black granite flecked with gold.

The woman shifts her cat-eyeglasses down her nose to look me over. Her short hair is like orange sherbet, her skin an expensive sprayed on tan I imagine is named apricot. Her sea-foam-green eyes narrow in on me. My Adam's apple rises to meet her.

Her husband, who looks a smidge like Christopher Plummer circa *Sound of Music* (thanks, no doubt, to the help of a Beverly Hills surgeon) offers his hand.

"I am Friedrich Vogl." His accent and his air suggest I'll recognize the name.

We shake hands. His grip is firm, his gaze penetrates my fears.

Vogl exhibits a dozen or more framed albums in gold and platinum with the number of album sales engraved in the frames.

He's worked with a wide range of talent over a long span of time. Some of them legends: Mariah Carey, Heart, Lionel Richie, Pink. I scan them with a deepening sense of dread that should be excitement.

You're an amateur by compare.

"This is my wife, Eliza Vogl."

She nods at me and doesn't extend her hand, which is for the best considering how clammy mine has become.

Vicky clasps her hands in prayer position and says, "They are the vogue of songwriting, Santiago."

Behind us the door from the hallway opens, and the crew of YouTube videographers that seem to follow me everywhere slip in and set up their cameras.

"Turn that off," Friedrich says. "Get out of here." The camera guys look at each other, then at Vicky who moves her eyes towards the door. The guys turn and go.

"I don't like this whole publicity stunt your people are trying to pull," Friedrich says.

Vicky forges an ear-to-ear smile. "Let's just hear the first song, shall we?"

Friedrich sweeps his hand. "Put him in the booth," he says to his wife.

Eliza points the way with a curt nod of her head. I open the door and walk down the few steps to the studio floor. She points to the flexible microphone stand weighed down by a pair of headphones. A long, covered piano is only a few feet away from my station.

How did I end up in the singer's spot when I've always thought of myself as a pianist?

It's your voice.

Once Barbara taught me to use it properly, she marveled at it and said the world would too.

But she's not here to walk you through this.

Eliza lifts the headphones and the stand bobs up. Maybe I will too when the music plays. I fit the headphones on.

Eliza says, "We wouldn't be working with someone as unproven as you if your song hadn't made the top ten billboard charts."

I pull the ear cover away. "It's number three now."

She arcs her painted brows at me, her forehead doesn't even crease. I wonder if she has as much Botox, as blood running through her veins.

"I know. You're, here aren't you? Warm up while we do a sound check." Eliza returns to the command center.

Once again, I struggle to pull a breath all the way into my diaphragm, and I feel a desperate thirst.

Friedrich's voice cracks into the headphones. Once we establish clear communications, he lays out the rules of engagement. He will play the song once through, the lyrics will scroll on the monitor at eye level. The second time through I will sing with the basic tracks. If he is dissatisfied with my interpretation, he will stop and instruct further.

The song rolls.

Why am I only hearing this for the first time?

I concentrate. I like the song. It's more of a ballad than I expected. The key changes.

Do they expect you to sing that high?

This is not an easy song to sing.

Friedrich says, "Rolling in three, two . . ."

I'm not ready. My bladder is going to burst, my throat is dry, my whole body is dehydrated beyond recognition. I miss the cue.

He halts the music. "Something the matter?"

"No."

"Then let's go."

The music rolls again. *He knows you're a fraud, he's going to expose us.* I miss the cue again. The microphone is still on when he tells Vicky, "I can't work with him. He's too unprofessional."

"Let's give him five," Vicky says.

"He hasn't been in there for five. I told you I wanted Sam Smith for this song."

My throat feels scorched. Burned by their desire to cast me off. I want to sit down.

"Let me sing it," I say. They don't seem surprised that the microphone was on. I don't think it was a mistake. "The song is brilliant. Let me sing it."

The flattery works. I don't miss the next cue.

Friedrich interrupts. "Not so angry, the song is not supposed to be angry."

You're not using your breath right; this doesn't feel right.

Friedrich tells Eliza on the open mic, "He's out of shape."

We go again. Take after take—until I hear a rasp in my voice that shouldn't be there. I feel weak, my forehead is damp.

"His voice is shot," Eliza says.

"He's all wrong for this," Friedrich adds.

Vicky says, "Look people the ink is dry."

The mic switches off. My knees buckle. I take off the headphones, schlep over to the piano and fold my upper half over it.

Why am I even here? All I ever wanted was to write Mom's song.

Behind the glass the animated argument continues without me. The covered piano stirs my curiosity. I tug a corner up to reveal a bright white finish. Nice! I rip the fitted cover away. In the control room, no one notices. I uncover the keys with reverence. They are real ivory, almost yellow against the bright white of the piano's lacquered finish. The golden letters read BÖSENDORFER. I wheeze. The action seems too wide and I recall Bösendorfer is unique in that it makes a ninety-two key model. And this is one of them. I sit and count. Then run my fingers across the action until I can no longer contain myself and play scales and arpeggios. The cloud of inferiority lifts and I begin to play the Vogls' ballad on the piano from memory.

Friedrich says, "What do you think you're doing?" on the intercom speaker.

Eliza slaps him on the shoulder. "Listen, Friedrich."

Vicky says, "I told you he had talent. If you can't work with that, then you aren't professional."

The trio trip down to the studio floor. I don't look up. Eliza rests a gentle hand on my shoulder. "Who taught you to play?"

"Barbara Holladay."

Her eyes light up with her suspicion confirmed and she pats my shoulder. "Barbara was one of my friends. I think I remember her mentioning you now. She taught you to sing as well?"

I nod, trying to swallow, but failing.

"Your voice is shot for today. That's not good."

"I don't feel well."

She does a double take then puts her hand on my forehead, first with her palm, then with the back of her hand like my own mother would. I feel like Mom is reaching through this woman to comfort me. Maybe she'd reached through Vicky in the back of the car too.

That's crazy.

Is it?

"You've got fever. They've run you ragged." Eliza says with a mother's love.

Friedrich throws his hands up.

Vicky crosses her arms. "Boy, you can't get sick."

Eliza shushes them both. Holding them off with extended arms. "Santiago, I want you to go home and get well. Rest your body and your voice. Be silent for three days."

"Silent?" I say, clutching my aching throat.

"To heal your voice and hear yourself think. Ya?"

I nod.

BACK IN THE Maybach Vicky is busy with phone call after phone call to recreate our schedule. I stare out the window, finding Los Angeles grungy in the grey day's light.

I text Sophia to share the news of everything that's happened including my theory:

"I think I've gotten to a point where the pills are causing the fear instead of combatting it."

Sophia texts: "Knowing that is a big step towards your freedom. I'm proud of you. I think a three-day vow of silence would be so healing, and if you'll let me, I'll be with you."

"I would like that more than anything."

AFTER A JAUNT in urgent care, a diagnosis of laryngitis, a prescription for antibiotics and—holy of holies—liquid Tylenol 3, I spend an entire day sleeping with the shades drawn.

When Sophia knocks, I can't get to the door fast enough, though the sprint fatigues me. I open it. Sophia smiles and holds up a paper bag that smells like minestrone.

"You're an angel—"

She puts her finger on my lips. "Shhh."

I kiss the finger and take the bag giving her a wolf-whistle and an affected once-over. She's wearing yoga pants and a snug hoodie in baby blue. Her hair is in a ponytail. She kisses me once on each cheek, holds my face in her hands and penetrates my eyes with hers.

I grasp her to me, her head rests over my heart.

"Your heart is racing," she says.

I nod and place a finger over her lips. "Shh."

I set us up at the kitchen nook. We giggle, slurp, and smile silently through dinner. Afterwards I hold up my DVD copy of Westside Story and she nods with glee. We sit-side-by-side on the sofa and she traces her finger up and down my right arm. When the scene arrives where Tony sings, "Maria," Sophia can't contain her mirth. I lean in to kiss her, but she covers my mouth.

"You're ill."

I withdraw. She settles back into the sofa while a headache settles into my right temple. I press my thumbs against the throb. She notices and sits up on her knees beside me and takes over the job, massaging both temples with a circular motion of perfect pressure. She kisses my damp forehead. My eyes shudder shut.

I wake to a ringing phone. Sophia hands it over. I touch my throat and take the phone—private number. I let it go to voicemail.

I nod back off. A minute later the phone alerts me to a voicemail. Curiosity steeps. Who would leave such a long message?

Maybe it's Kitty. We need her help.

I wait a little while then excuse myself to the bathroom and dial my voice mail. Kitty's voice is eager and bright:

"Santiago, it's me. I'm sorry for disappearing, this is my first phone call. I called you. Dirk found me and checked me in to a, uh, a facility. But I'm glad to be here. I've made it past the first stage. It was easy, really, because of what we made together. I'm staying for the second phase of treatment. I feel as though each day's the first day of the rest of my life. I'm so happy. I wish you could give up the pills and feel what I feel right now. But I won't lecture you. Timing is everything. I just want to thank you and ask you, if you need me . . . I thought without Barbara, you might need me. God, I hate missing the aftermath of the song's release. How's it been for you? Did we make the charts? If you need me, I want to be here for you. I owe you that. I'll call you again when I can."

CHAPTER 24

KITTY HOLLADAY

Overcoming Fear

ALONE, IN MY cell, dark thoughts close in on me. This facility is different from the last few drug treatment centers I've been to over the years. It's heavy on finding your truth and light on luxury. The room is spare. A twin sized bed pushed up against a four by five window, a small wooden writing desk and a dresser near the bathroom door. Bright colored posters on the white walls show beautiful ocean scenes with motivational phrases. My thoughts are miles from the ocean.

What will I tell Santiago about the baby? I almost told him in the voice mail I left.

What will I tell Dirk?

Nothing, nothing, nothing, nothing.

You're not even sure yet.

But the soreness of my breasts and the days since my period have me certain.

My addiction insists, *I've always been here for you. You can't live without me.*

I don't need you. I have the baby now.

I claw at my scalp so hard that blood trickles from the tracks I forge.

TWO DAYS LATER, I push my plate of runny eggs away, nauseated by the sight and smell of them. I'm exhausted by the constant cacophony of group meals where voices echo off tile floors and wooden tables.

In group, our folding chairs in a circle, I clutch my knees to my chest and glance at the grey-green chalkboard, where our stick-thin, middle-aged male counselor, in a sloppy grey suit, has scrawled the subject of today's session:

OVERCOMING FEAR.

Stick asks us to consider our fear at its source. While, I've surrendered to the profound questions this facility has posed, often writing paragraphs on the back of pages when I ran out of room on the front, *this* topic is not open for discussion. I leave my clip board with its sheaf of stapled yellow papers beneath my chair and reopen the infected wound in my scalp. A little blood and puss ooze from them.

Stick says, "Katherine why don't you share your fears with the group."

My fingertips are warm and gooey. I drag them down my face, leaving a trail of slimy blood down my cheek.

"Stop that," he screeches, his face full of his own fear. The other girls lurch from their chairs and gape at mine. I claw at my face.

He grabs me by the wrists. "I said, stop that. Security!" he calls.

I'm strapped down, and a nurse needles me.

"No! No drugs. The baby," I say. The sedative blooms, and I'm folded inside it's petals like a fly in a Venus fly trap.

When I regain consciousness it's to a bed in the facility's infirmary. I hate the hospital.

A pretty Latina with ombre hair, gold and black, enters the sterile white room in burgundy scrubs. "You're awake Mrs. Holladay. Your husband's here to see you."

I bolt to sitting. "My husband?"

"Yes, we called him after we sedated you. I'll bring him in?"

My heart thuds.

Dirk's face is hidden behind a vase exploding with pink roses and orchid lilies. My stomach turns at the cloying scent. He plants the vase at my bed table, near a pink-plastic-pitcher of water.

"Pussy Cat," he coos, with an equally cloying tone.

I cringe and pour myself a cup of water from the pitcher.

"Have you heard the news?" He rubs his hands together.

"Tell me."

"Number one with a bullet, baby!"

I clasp my hand over my mouth. It's been part of my work here to release the outcome of my song. But I hadn't given up hope that it would go all the way.

"That's right, Pussy Cat. You did it. And the video just came out and it is getting a ton of hits on YouTube. Things will really heat up with that."

He runs his thumb tenderly along the scratch on my cheek. I soften beneath his touch. He lowers the bed rail and sits. "That damn kid doesn't look like he can take the heat though. I had the Vogls go hard on him. Then we had to reschedule everything for a case of strep throat, or some such atrocity. And when that happened, it hit me—we can't let him fail, no matter how much I hate the kid. So, I had this idea." Dirk pulls out his cell phone. "I've been following Santiago on Twitter. Turns out he's a pilot. Check this out." He punches up a video. "Since we made him famous, people are posting a shit-load of random videos they've got of our guy."

I shake my head as Dirk puts the phone in my face, I push it away, hearing the buzz of an engine, and a shriek of frightened laughter.

Dirk snorts. "Santiago put the plane into a zero G drop. Guy filming loses it."

I think Dirk has become as infatuated with Santiago as I have. Then my worry deepens. Is he only carrying on about him to test my reactions? I grimace.

He notices and lays a light hand on my leg. "Point is, Pussy Cat, what do you think if I have him fly the G-36 from Burbank to a concert in Vegas? It would be his first live performance, opening for Rihanna! Vicky's doing the leg work to set it all up now. How's that for a publicity stunt? Kitty? Kitty?"

I pout. "Is this what you came out here for, to talk business?"

He takes my hand in his. "No, babe, no. I'm so proud of you. But now this?" Once again, he lightly touches one of the deeper scratches in my face. "I'll order some scar cream for those."

I hold his hand to my cheek and relish the comfort that has always come from this pose.

What have I done?

A woman invades our space clad in white, stethoscope for a necklace, Dr. Arden embroidered on her breast.

"Mr. and Mrs. Holladay let me be the first to congratulate you."

Dirk shifts towards her. My stomach clenches, I twitch my head no, and mouth no, but the bitch doesn't even look up from the clipboard at me.

"Remarkable under the circumstances really"—she flips through pages—"but our tests confirms your suspicions, you are pregnant Mrs. Holladay."

Dirk stands.

I ball my sheets in my fist.

Dr. Arden finally looks at me. "Do you remember the date of your last period?"

I press my lips into a white line and shake my head at her.

Her eyes dart between us, as she registers the error, backs out of the room closing the door and mutters about giving us a minute.

Dirk cracks his knuckles. "You wanna tell me what the fuck she's talking about, Katherine?"

Adrenaline shoots through me. My breath is shallow: in, out, in, out. My thoughts won't line up. I inhale deeply. "A miracle."

He stares hard.

My voice comes out like a child's. "I just needed to know I *could* be pregnant."

His chest heaves. "You betrayed me? Who with?" His eyes close. "It's Santiago, isn't it?"

His eyes open and he expects an answer. I stare into his eyes, expecting to see the veins of gold, bright with anger, instead they become dull, and his shoulders drop.

"How could you do this to us?" he says.

Both surprised and touched by his sadness, I lay my hand over my heart. "Dirk, I . . ."

He glares at me and the gold finally appears. My weak response to his submissive posture initiates his fury.

"You get nothing, Katherine. I leave you like I found you."

I find my rage as easily. "It won't be *nothing*. I finally have what you denied me."

My words are a slap in his face. He expected me to cave beneath his bluff. More than that, he knows I have a point. His cheeks flush and his pupils narrow in on me as he changes tactics employing the control he's always had over me.

"You're not keeping it, Katherine."

Since I've been in treatment, reclaiming my power and considering this very question, I've been rehearsing a life without my husband. The thought of it both frightens and thrills me. Emboldened by my right as a woman to choose what happens inside my body, I lift my chin. "Yes, I am keeping it."

In one leap, he's on me, clutching my shoulders with both hands and shaking me. "I won't let you do this to us," he says.

I reach for the pitcher on the side table and bash the side of his body with it.

Water gushes. The vase of flowers teeters, and crashes. He steps back and brushes water from his clothes, glass crunching beneath his feet. "You can't have *his* baby."

"You owe me this, Dirk. No one has to know it's not yours." This is one variation of my projected life that surprises me to voice aloud to him. I really can't imagine life without him. I don't want to hurt him. After all we've been through together in the last twenty-five years maybe we can get through this too.

He squeezes the sides of his head, breathes like his therapist taught him, and says, "I never thought you'd go this far."

IN THE AFTERMATH, I'm assigned four sessions back-to-back with psychiatrist Dr. Octavia Sole to address the pregnancy and my husband's reaction specifically.

She seats me in a large high-backed oxblood-leather chair across from a sumptuous mahogany desk. I study her trustworthy face as she describes the way our sessions will unfold. She is in her mid-fifties. She has skin the rich color of dark chocolate, dark black eyes set in bright whites, short hair above her ears that suits her handsome face, prominent cheek bones that she plays up with bronzer, and full lips painted with a clear gloss. She neither smiles nor frowns as she listens to my unfettered rant.

Session one: I unfurl fermented rage at Dirk. Name the betrayal of his vasectomy the root of my addiction and blame him for every one of my character flaws. Time's up.

Session two: I further lament on Dirk's failures as a husband. His sly nature, our difference in philosophy, his insistence on making everything up to him with sex. Time's up.

Session three: I fantasize about my future with baby and anonymous daddy while holding my belly with two hands.

When asked how I think the divorce will unfold I launch into my means of getting the upper hand in that process.

Dr. Sole leans forward and says, "So, you want to go on punishing him then?"

"Me? He's the one . . ." My eyes find the floor.

"It sounds like the two of you have been punishing each other for a long time now."

I draw my legs into my chest in my deep, high-backed leather chair and rock as I consider her words.

Every time my husband disappointed me, I turned to cocaine. Not just to cope, but because *it hurt him*. Even in his pain, he was determined to keep helping me. But in his frustration, he also found ways to punish me. That went on for years before I'd ever fixated on becoming a mother. Had his clandestine vasectomy merely been a counterattack to the abuse I'd hurled at us both with my addiction? Or was it also a means of protecting an unborn child from a mother whose addiction could harm it as well?

After a long time, I look up at her and say, "I don't want us to keep punishing each other anymore."

"How do you think you stop?" the doctor asks.

To avoid the question, I stare past her. Behind the desk, matching bookshelves line the walls. So many books, so much knowledge, has she read all their lines? She's certainly read between mine. Session ends early.

Session four: Over the last twenty years I've controlled these types of sessions by hearing and saying only what I wanted. But now, for the baby, I am ready to bare my raw heart and heal the wounds of my life. I've never been so ready.

I take ownership of the character flaws I'd mentioned in session one. I admit that it had always been my idea to try and make everything up to Dirk with sex. I detail our best years and question Dr. Sole on the possibility of Dirk's accepting the child as his own.

"Can't I just explain how important the baby is to my health. What the baby means for my sobriety?" I blow bangs (that I personally chopped) from my eyes and await Sole's intelligent response.

She rubs her chin. "You could show Dirk that your pregnancy impacts your health and sobriety with your cooperation in the program. You were doing so well before his visit. Do you think he'd be willing to join us for a session?"

I hang my head. I'm not ready to face him. Even though I feel a hollow place in my chest every time I reach out for him in bed at night and find I'm alone. I want to fill that ache with the love I still believe in for us. Anxiety shoots through my arms at this thought. He'll never take me back with the baby. And I can't take *me* back without it.

"Could I contact him?" Dr. Sole asks.

I curl up.

"Kitty, I'd need your permission to speak to him. Let him know how much this rift between you is affecting your results here."

My forehead on my knees, I peek up at her. She cranes her head, her cheek nearly touching her desk to make eye contact with me.

"Please call him," I say.

"Have you thought about how you can stop hurting each other?"

I've spent all my time thinking about this. I nod. "But will *he* forgive *me*?"

The session ends with me earning a phone call.

With my marriage in good hands, I address the other concern that keeps me up at night.

Santiago answers. "Kitty, thank God. I'm under siege. I was supposed to go back to the Vogls' studio last week. They don't believe I'm still too sick. Truth is, I'm too afraid. Vicky says if I don't go back to the studio, she's worried the label will drop my contract and I'll be liable for the breach. I don't know what to do, I can't make my voice work under this pressure. It feels like everyone's against me. I'm fucking freaked out. I need to see you. Can you help me?"

I clasp my hands over my tiny tummy and breathe. "We can do this, Santiago. They need to make the album fly under the flame of the single. It could blow out at any instant. You're out of shape, you need to get your lung capacity and your diaphragm strong again to rely on the method Barbara taught you."

He exhales audibly. It crackles in my ear.

"Remember the reason you can bridge your falsetto and sing through your break is because Barbara taught you to sing while holding your breath. They heard that in our song. The Vogls wrote their song because of the range you showed in ours. But the second you add breath to those notes . . ."

"I haven't done it that way in years, Kitty."

"That's not true, you did it with me in the studio. Subconsciously."

"So, what? Get high before I go into the sound room?"

"No, you've got to get in shape. You need to ditch the pills."

"I'm trying, but I need to see you, so you can remind me how to do it properly. I'm like an athlete without a coach."

"It's like a bicycle. You had mastered it. That's why Barbara loved you so much. You were the proof that her method worked." I sigh. "How did Barbara train your diaphragm, Santiago?"

He scoffs. "Power-breathing, martial arts shit, and she'd take me to the YMCA and make me swim laps underwater the length of the pool. When I came outta the water she'd make me sing the impossible note *before* I took a breath. Total fucking torture."

"You still have a membership at the Y?"

"No way, I'm not doing that shit again. I'd drown."

"Really? You won't do it?"

"I just need to see you, Kitty, please."

"Okay, this Sunday I can see visitors."

CHAPTER 25

KITTY HOLLADAY

Connection to Her

IT'S SUNDAY, AND I wait in the dayroom for both Santiago and my husband to appear. I cross and uncross my legs as I flip through an old Star Magazine. Dr. Sole thinks Dirk will come today for a visit. They've spoken on the phone several times. I lick my lips with cautious hope.

The tint on the wall of windows to my far left lends a sepia toned glow to the room. The Day Room is a vast space, with polished hard wood floors and over a dozen groupings of brand-new furniture. It reminds me of an upscale furniture store. There are about four other patients who have visitors today. They all speak in low voices in assembled living rooms a fair distance apart. I've chosen an overstuffed grey suede couch that faces the door, with simple modern tables and rugs of a grey and white color scheme to accompany the set. I'm dressed in jeans and a snug t-shirt with freshly washed hair that smells clean and makes me feel beautiful for the first time since I've arrived. The door buzzes and my moist fingers rip the corner of the magazine page.

Santiago walks through it. My womb flutters and my lips part. He looks haggard but still beautiful. I cover the tiny bump of my belly with the magazine and effect a careless pose that works to hide the anxiety of my secret.

I wish I could tell him about the baby. I think he'd be so happy.

But I can't make that mistake before I've learned what it would mean to Dirk for the pregnancy to remain a secret. It may be the deciding factor for him to take me back.

In the days I've had to reflect on my past and future with my husband, I know I want to give our marriage a proper shot. We both deserve a chance to understand our dynamic without cocaine's interference. And if I'm honest with myself, I'm too afraid to face the world as a suddenly sober, single mother.

Santiago spots me and rushes over. I fight the urge to stand and greet him with a hug. He sits on the plain white wooden coffee table in front of me.

"You look good, Kitty." He cups my shoulder and feels the back of my arm with a kind caress that makes me want to cry. "I can't see your bones anymore." His right eye twitches.

"I was so hungry when I first got here." I remember how I'd eaten to fill the void in ways my addiction hadn't allowed in years. My pregnant body was truly starving. I needed that food. But with the rift with between me and Dirk, I've stopped eating again. My stomach growls.

"It suits you." He leans back and rests a foot on one knee. "And you're even more beautiful without makeup."

"You can't talk to me like that, we're not lovers."

I can read the hurt in his face, but I can't apologize.

He looks around, like a spy just learning his craft. "What's it like here?"

I squint at him. "Why, are you worried someone will see that eye twitching and smuggle you into the program? You haven't ditched the pills, have you?"

He rocks back and forth. "I need them while I figure this thing out with my voice."

I raise my arm and crane my neck for a staff member. "We could talk technique for hours if you were locked up."

He wrestles my arm down. "It's bad enough I had to sit through that stupid-ass course on addiction before I could see you today. I don't need a lecture."

"Really, you came here for help. Maybe that's exactly what you need."

He leans into my personal space. "Are *you* going to stay clean?"

I palm his forehead and push him back. "Yes." And because of the baby I know that's true. "Now tell me what you made the drive for, I really don't know what you expect."

"Tell me why the method works. Barbara never explained it. I was just a kid then so whatever, but now I gotta get it, to believe in it."

I flick my tongue against the roof of my mouth while I think how to put it to him. "You know how a baby can cry for hours without going hoarse?"

He shrugs.

"Babies do that using this method, it's the most natural thing in the world. Without the air, the vocal cords remain a vacuum of pure sound, and they can reach that high note that pierces every mother's heart. You can too." My belly flutters talking about babies with him.

Santiago rubs his face. "I can't do the Vogls' songs first. They're too hard!"

"Move them to the back of the lineup. The other songs will be easier."

"Vicky's trying, but no one is cooperating."

My bladder loosens, and I cross my legs. "They're trying to sabotage you."

He wrings his hands. "I knew I wasn't imagining it."

The door buzzes. I look past Santiago at the door with my heart in my throat. Dirk appears in the doorway about thirty feet away. The blood drains from my face. Santiago is talking, but I don't hear him speak. I keep my eyes fixed on my husband, stand, and walk around the groups of visitors in their makeshift living rooms and towards him with a hopeful heart.

Dirk surveys the room, takes my hand, and leads me to a door that exits into a well-manicured rose garden with a small tinkling fountain in the center. There is a setting of comfortable patio furniture in beige with white stripes with a round table in the furthest corner. But neither of us are comfortable enough to sit down. We stand beside the fountain in the shade of the tall building that flanks the garden.

Dirk's nostrils flare as I look into his eyes. "Why is Santiago here?"

The battle begins on steep terrain. I try to disarm him by nuzzling into his chest. "*You're* here, that's all that matters."

Dirks arms rise over his head. He doesn't want to hug me back. The familiar beat of his heart is in my ear. I wrap my arms around him and hold him tight. His strong body in my arms is a refuge from the change I fear.

"What is he doing here?" Dirk asks, heart rate rising.

"I want to come home, I can't sleep alone anymore, Dirk. I need you beside me."

"You should have thought of that shouldn't you, Katherine?"

I nod against his chest. The cotton of his dress shirt smooth and warm against my face.

"Tell me what he's doing here, Kitty. Have you told him you're pregnant?"

"No, I don't want him to know, not if there's a chance for us."

His arms fall cautiously onto my back. They rest there lightly.

I hug him tighter. "I'm so glad you're here, D."

"Are you?"

I burrow into him. His heart rate steadies. "I know I went too far. Can you forgive me?"

His arms lift millimeters away from my body. "Why would you do that to us, Kitty?"

There are so many ways I can answer this question. I want to keep him close with the honest gratitude I have for him, but also address the pain that needs to be faced to see if we stand a chance. I'm frightened, but in my sobriety, the gentle lapping of the water at the base of the fountain calms me. I pull away from his chest and look into his eyes. "Dirk, I love you. Thank you for the life you were trying to give me. Because of you I got to follow a dream. I'm just so sorry I sabotaged our chance at happiness with drugs."

His arms relax into me and he rests his head on top of mine.

Steadied by his affection, I forge ahead with the harder truth. "But there was something missing that I wanted so much more than music."

I feel him tense against this truth. I step back and we face each other. "You knew how much I wanted to be a mother."

"Kitty, you weren't fit—" He steps back.

I take a step back as well. "But you lied to me about your vasectomy." My voice rises with my feeling. I pause and realize we're moving away from each other and I don't want that. I brace myself to say the words that I'm finally able to say. "Listen, D, all I really want to say is that, I get it now, and I forgive you."

His head jerks back, and he stares at me incredulously.

"I'm sorry that I punished you for that for so long. I was just so angry and high all the time."

He takes both my hands and pulls me towards him, laying our hands over his heart. "I really am sorry."

"D, there's been so much wrong between us that I was willing to throw our marriage away to at least save myself."

"I know you're right. I've been trying to save you for a long time, Kitty, but in all the wrong ways." We lock eyes. "Does Santiago know about the baby?"

I shake my head, then rest my forehead in the middle of his chest, that wonderful valley where my husband protects me from the world.

"No, Santiago doesn't know. He's just here for vocal coaching." My words are muffled into his shirt, but he hears them.

Dirk clutches a handful of hair at the nape of my neck to turn my face up to his. "You can't know how much you hurt me." He strokes my thrumming throat.

"I'll do anything for another chance."

He presses my face back into his chest and strokes my hair. "Anything, Kitty?"

I nod against him.

"Would you give up the baby for me?"

I place a hand over my belly. "I . . ." Cold creeps over me. I take a deep breath that catches as I begin to cry silently. "I don't know, Dirk, I may not get another chance to be a mother, and I need that kind of love in my life."

He cups my head with one hand, my back with the other, pressing me tightly—too tightly—into him. I whine. He grasps the back of my arms and moves me away from him. I cast my eyes to the basin of the fountain. He strokes me under the chin, and our eyes meet, mine glassy with tears, his sparkling.

"I just needed to hear you say that," Dirk says.

"What do you mean?"

"Kitty, we can have this baby if *no one* ever knows it isn't mine. Especially him."

I suck back the mucous in my nose. "Are you saying?"

He nods.

"Oh, D. Oh, D. Do you forgive me?" I spring to my toes and kiss him a dozen times all over his face. My hands tingle as I fidget with his collar. "Dirk, you make me so happy, what can I do to make it up to you?"

"You can spend the rest of your life making it up to me, Kitty." He snickers, and I kiss him again.

Then he becomes more serious. "But right now, I need your help with something else."

I giggle, still too happy to guess what he might want. "Anything."

He hesitates. "Believe it or not. I need your help with Santiago."

There's a heavy feeling in my stomach. "You're kidding me?" I worry that my feelings for Santiago will disrupt the difficult decision I made to heal my marriage if I'm made to work closely with him again.

He reads my reluctance and sighs with what I believe is relief. "I know. It's just that I worked so hard to undermine him when I thought you might leave me for him . . ." His voice cracks.

"D, I was never going to leave you for him."

"You weren't?"

"No." I realize that I will probably spend the rest of my life trying to convince him of this lie.

He's eager to believe it though. I watch his face shift as he decides to. In a moment he's all business again. "We've staked too much on one artist with this experiment. While I'm getting everyone lined up to support him again, can you coach him vocally?"

I falter. "No one else understands your mother's method like I do."

"Right, and the company *needs* this album to chart."

"Okay." I explain the plan I've already formulated. "We need to move the Vogls' songs to the end. Hook him up with the Reagan Myers team next, those songs will be easiest for him. And give me a couple hours with him today." Dirk nods at every note but this one. He narrows his gaze.

"I love you, D. You don't have to worry."

Dirk kisses the vein that pulses over my temple. Then we leave the serenity of that peaceful garden.

Santiago is seated on the grey suede sofa reading the Star magazine I'd left behind. He jumps to standing as we approach hand in hand.

"Sir, good to see you," Santiago says with marked decorum.

They shake hands, Santiago winces, rubbing his hand

when it's released.

"We're going to move your schedule around, Santiago. Kitty will tell you about it. The whole Holladay team's behind you now."

"We start with technique," I say. "We'll sit at that little table in the garden and I'll coach you through a proper warm up."

Dirk says, "Mind if I sit in on this little lesson?"

Santiago tenses. I want to reassure them both it will be okay. This is business and a little more decorum is all we need. And besides, I don't like the idea of being alone with Santiago. Who knows what I'm still capable of? It may take forever to stop loving him.

Meanwhile, I'm hoping the tranquility of that setting will be as useful for the three of us as it was for Dirk and me.

"Good idea, Dirk. You can help us pinpoint what he's doing wrong. You know how your mother taught us all. I think it's just a matter of getting his vocal fitness back."

"Barbara loved the pool for that. But why does it matter? With the equipment we have in the studio, we can dial anyone in," Dirk says.

"No. His voice, with the right coaching is so much bigger than that. Half the battle is getting him confident enough to do this. Barbara babied him. Without his connection to her he's struggling. Let me get his voice solid again. He's going to be on the stage soon, Dirk, where it's just his voice and the people who love it. When they hear him in person, they'll buy *everything* he records."

"I'm sold," Dirk says.

Santiago lifts his head. "I'll right, I'll swim the goddamn laps after this."

CHAPTER 26

SANTIAGO DEANGELO

When Did Your Song Become Less Important?

SUNLIGHT PIERCES THE pool as I slice through its depths. I swim towards the surface as I approach the wall and gasp for air. I've been at it for hours.

Beneath the surface on my next lap, I ask myself, *How many pills have you taken today?* No clue. Three quarters of the Olympic length pool my legs cramp painfully. I kick to the top, suck a deep breath of air and sink. Eleven, I think as I plummet. Eleven pills and still all this pain. What's the point?

The question stays with me before I fall asleep in bed that night. In the morning, well before dawn, I'm aware of having slept heavier than usual. Turns out the physical exertion is better than drugs for real rest.

As dawn breaks, I daydream over the last few days with Sophia. Those three days, before the anxiety of returning to the studio set in, were heaven. Not just because she fed me soup, and honeyed tea, and kept a cool washcloth on my forehead, but because her loving touch penetrated my pain. The first two nights I was unable to convince her to stay with me. Little does she know; the pills make it all but impossible to get a lasting erection, and the last thing I would do is embarrass myself like that. So, in a way they're all the protection she needs from our desire for each other. But even without that, I would never ask more of her than she was comfortable with, and I think her reluctance to stay had more to do with her *own* resolve.

On the third night, just before 11p.m. I panicked and called Vicky to explain I was still too ill to return to the studio. With reluctance Vicky agreed to buy me some more time.

Sophia kissed me as I set the phone down then pulled me towards the bedroom. "Let's go to sleep."

"Let's?"

"I want to stay with you tonight, Santi."

We lay in each other's arms all night.

I hug a pillow to my chest to keep the memory alive. But just as it had then, my joy fades. The next day, she'd lost patience with me when I'd shared my paranoia that everyone at the label was against me and admitted that my declining drug use was on the rise again.

She'd said, "You need to postpone everything until you've gotten some real help for the drugs. Why won't you do that?"

"I don't even think my usage is enough to get into rehab. People there, are taking like twenty or thirty pills a day, or they've switched to heroin."

"You know that's not true. I've heard you say over and over that you can't live like this. That means however much you're taking is too much. I think the drugs and this stupid album are keeping you from your own music. When did your song become less important?"

I'd known then the answer was fame. The dream which has been drawing me towards it since I first knew my talent was real and that I had the discipline to do something big with it. I want that fame, even though it keeps me from writing my own song.

I may have surrendered to Sophia's insistence if Kitty hadn't called again.

I RETURN TO the pool at sunrise. Barbara always said my biggest strength was faith in my coach's training. I give myself over to the exercise.

Days later, my body has responded, and my confidence has grown in kind. As I glide beneath the water, I envision the Vogls' studio. My voice in my mind glides over their notes and beyond them. I touch the edge of the pool with enough air to sing the impossible note before I draw my first breath.

I STRIDE INTO Holladay headquarters for my next studio appointment. A smile blazes my path. I'm directed to Studio 50, a bright and airy loft, where Cindy Myers slips off her headphones and does a double take at my persona. "You're not at all like they said."

I grin. "You're not what I was expecting either."

She is thirty-something, ivory skinned with pale grey eyes, and a pastel rainbow of dread locks that fall past her wide hips. She wears lavender-framed, rectangular glasses on the tip of her long nose.

"Thank God. You have no idea how hard I work to shatter stereotypes." Cindy beams as her partner joins us. "This is Jamal."

He too wears dreadlocks, his as black as his eyes and skin.

Our palms slap together, and Jamal pulls me in for a man-hug.

"We're stoked to be working with you, bro. Show us how you warm up." They take notes on my process, Cindy tries it herself.

I take eight and a half pills that day and we knock out three of three songs. Dirk is in the studio as we wrap up. "I knew you had it in you, kid. Just make sure there's no more interruptions in the schedule."

Throughout the week I record three more songs with two different song-writing production teams in their studios off site of Holladay Records. I relax into the process and accept its challenges and highs. The greatest challenge is the understanding that my own song is unlikely to make the submission deadline. Between the hours of recording, the relentless schedule of promotion continues. Kitty's words at the beginning come back to me with new meaning.

Your song's not finished. Do you think you can complete it while recording nine others, because no one, but you, cares if it makes the album or not?

My only hope is that I can complete it in the two-day break that comes before I return to record the Vogls' songs. But I need that time to recuperate, especially if I intend to continue decreasing my pill count by half a pill each day.

I pass on first class hotel accommodations in Beverly Hills for the two-day break. Though I tweet that's where I'll be staying to keep any fans from gathering near my house. I don't know if they would, but someone leaked my home address on Twitter. With the growth of my social media following, due to Vicky and her team's efforts, crowds have begun to gather in the places I arrive for promo work. I sign a few autographs with the message, "Follow your heart."

Between autographs Lucy texts me about showing up at the bell tower construction site tomorrow. I silence the phone, but the texts keep coming. I try and think of a good excuse, draw a blank, then forget about it all together.

Sitting at a stop light, while driving my own car home that night, another car pulls up alongside on my left with their windows down and my voice singing through their speakers. The guy driving looks over at me at the same time I look over at him. He does a double take and I give a casual wave as the light turns green. He's too stunned to notice the light for a second then speeds up and comes back alongside honking and waving. The recognition feels good.

On the way home, I text Sophia to meet me at the house and explain my hopes of writing the lyrics together.

SOPHIA'S THERE WHEN I arrive. On the porch I hold her against me and breathe in long drafts of her hair and skin which smell of rose and ylang-ylang. Her arms constrict my ribs. I kiss the top of her head. "I'm so glad you're here," I tell her.

Inside, I plop down on the couch and close my tired eyes. My body is exhausted, but the pills have my head hyped and jittery. She strokes my face and my hair; her touch is so soothing I begin to drift off.

"Where are you going?" she asks. "I thought we needed to work on your song."

"I'm just so tired," I say with closed eyes.

There's a knock on the door. I flinch but pretend not to hear it.

"Are you going to get that?" Sophia asks.

"I don't want to." I worry that it may be fans. I'd like to ignore the entire world for just an hour or two. I stretch out long ways on the couch.

My phone rings. Exasperated, I dig it out of my pocket. It's Lucy. When I answer she says, "Are you going to open the door, or what?"

I lurch out of the comfort I'd finally found to let her in.

"Sorry, sis, I was falling asleep."

"Is that why you haven't answered my texts about tomorrow morning?"

I instantly recall the texts that I ignored from her about showing up at the bell-tower construction site like I promised her I would weeks ago. I close the door, but we don't leave the entry way.

"Look, Luce, I can't. Tomorrow's my only chance to get Mom's song written out."

"You haven't done that yet? I thought that's what all this was about with Holladay. But Kitty didn't help you with your song like you thought she would, did she?"

"No," I say as I give her a hard stare to caution further mention of Kitty in front of Sophia. "I can't spend my time there, and my time here, writing the song." I pound my fist in my palm.

Sophia joins us near the door. Her arrival doesn't halt Lucy's mission.

"Mom says you need to be there."

Sophia says, "Do you really talk to her?"

"Don't put on like you have some nightly séance with Mom."

"It's no *séance*. He's right. Just a feeling that's stronger than a normal feeling." She looks at me with piercing eyes. "Just like the *feeling* Mom gives me that your making peace with Dad is as important as the song." She narrows her gaze at me. "Maybe even dependent on it."

I rub my face with both hands in frustration.

Sophia says, "You did tell me once you thought the song was revealed to you when you were doing things you knew you were supposed to be doing."

Do I still believe that?

I read their earnest expressions. They believe it.

I try it on for size. What would it mean to never make peace with Dad? If I've decided I don't need his validation, do I still want his love? Is that the same thing?

They both squeeze a shoulder.

"I don't know." I groan and look up at the ceiling. "How do you see me helping, Luce?"

She smiles in triumph. "The principal arranged something with the engineering department to observe the process. You could interface with the class and keep them at a fair distance. That way, Dad can see you're there to help without you guys getting in each other's way."

"Dad can handle that on his own."

"I'm telling you he's a mess. The trial's done a number on him. He needed it to go his way, and it didn't."

"He should have just settled."

"It was never about the money; the lawsuit was Dad's only way of staying close to her. Mom didn't send him a song, just you!"

Sophia clutches my arm in support.

"Yeah, well, I think he's jealous about that."

"Jealous?" Lucy feigns shock.

"I think he's always been envious of our relationship, and to him, the song is evidence that I was closer to her—even after she died."

Lucy throws her hands up, ready to admit the truth. "How would you have felt if you were him? First, she calls you *Vita Mia* while she's alive and then she uses your connection through music to reach you from the other side?"

My head jerks back. "Wait, does he actually believe she sent it? He's always acted like that was just bullshit. I just meant that he's pissed I have such a powerful way to stay close to her."

"I think he does believe it."

"Do you guys talk about this stuff or are you just making assumptions?"

"He doesn't have anyone else to talk to. We talk about you all the time. That's how I know how much he's suffering since your fight."

Unlike Dad and me, Mom's death made Dad and Lucy much closer.

Are you jealous of that?

I ball my fists and pace the room. "I don't know what you expect from me. I can't apologize for Mom loving me more. In fact, I don't have anything to apologize to him about. I'm achieving something he said I couldn't and now he won't recognize that I'm well on my way, so fuck him."

"I get that! But it can't go on like this. You're both suffering. And I really believe it's part of your creative block."

"You're not going to give up, are you?"

"Just show up for a couple hours then go home and write the song. It will do a lot to soften him up. Please?"

Jesus, now she's begging. I don't want to let my sister down. Still, to me this feels like the kind of bad idea you want to go through with to let the worst happen and say I told you so. "What time do you want me there?"

"7:30 a.m., and I'll leave you this file to get you caught

up." She pulls a file folder from her purse and puts it in my hand.

CHAPTER 27

SANTIAGO DEANGELO

You Have to be Sober to Hear Her

THE FOG AT THE CONSTRUCTION SITE is a low cloud that mists. As I approach it, I can see orange hard hats swarming the site like worker ants. Water droplets cling to the chain link construction fence that surrounds the bell tower. Within the fence four manlifts flank the tower from each side with extended arms that reach out and up towards the top. Inside the elevated cages I can see the fluorescent-colored vests and hard hats of the construction workers at the top. They chip away at the bricks and slide them down a chute.

I find the group of students I'm supposed to meet. They're high school seniors all dressed in Catholic school plaid. My senior year engineering teacher Mr. Henderson, who we called Mr. H., is at their helm. He describes de-construction as a tedious method to disassemble and preserve a historic structure. His bald head sheens in the mist. He wears his usual grey polo shirt with the school logo. His pink complexion brightens when he sees me.

"Basically guys, the workers at the top are chiseling each brick and sliding it down those chutes. Why? Well, because it was built in the late 1800s and the cities' Historical Preservation Act requires sixty percent of the structure's material be re-used in its resurrection to code."

A dozen or so uniformed students, huddle into groups ranked by interest. At the back of the pack are three teenage girls that giggle about my presence behind a hidden cell phone.

Mr. H. introduces me. "Class this is Santiago DeAngelo, a former student, and son of this program's founder."

One of the girls in the back shoots her arm up, phone still in hand. She has long medium brown hair, hazel eyes, a small mouth which is too small given the wide tip of her nose and a tall athletic build.

"Yes, Hannah?" Mr. H. says.

She eyes me. "You're him, aren't you?"

I hesitate, unsure how to answer.

Mr. H. says, "Hannah, bring me that phone." She rolls her eyes and trudges up to Mr. Henderson, slapping the phone into his palm.

He turns to me. "Santiago, can you explain the unique challenges this structure poses for your firm."

I launch into the details from the file Lucy left with me last night. Reading that file (which I've brought with me) I'd gotten a better sense of Dad's stress. He had lobbied with the city to overrule the Historical Preservation Act. There were multiple emails sent to the city along with the scans Dad had taken of the building. The scans were included in the file. Even I could see that the bell tower showed too much instability to approach it with de-construction. But the bureaucrats at the city wouldn't relent.

I'm surprised my dad gave in. Maybe he is in as bad of shape as Lucy lets on.

A short, freckled boy in the front asks, "Isn't what they're doing today dangerous?"

"Yes, which is why we are using manlifts instead of scaffolding to protect the workers at the top."

"Is that enough?"

I scratch my head, becoming more alarmed by the moment. Lucy appears through the lifting fog. "Excuse me," I say, and walk towards Lucy.

"Thank you for being here, Santiago."

"I read the file." I slap the folder against my palm. I can see why Dad's stressed. This is too dangerous based on the scans I saw. The original builders didn't use enough rebar, and the mortar is eroded." I scan the crowd and see Dad amidst a group of workers. The skin beneath his eyes is lined and dark. His hair is greyer than I remember.

I see a group of men in suits approaching from the parking lot at a leisurely pace. The bureaucrats. "I'm going to talk to those guys about these scans."

"Thank you. I'm going to talk to Dad." She makes for the gate.

"You need to stay on this side of the fence, Lucy."

She turns and grasps the fence with one hand. "I came up with some breathing exercises for Dad's anxiety."

Hannah approaches me from the opposite side and touches my elbow. I turn to her. She has her two girlfriends with her. The first, is a short, curvy, dark-haired girl with big doll eyes. She bats her lashes at me. I look away, into the eyes of the other girl, a copper-haired, blue-eyed waif that blushes violently when our eyes meet.

"Will you friend us on Facebook and post a picture of us together?" Hannah says.

"I'm busy," I tell her with gritted teeth. Then I look back and Lucy is gone. I move down the fence toward the gate.

"You don't have to be an asshole!" Hannah shouts.

The fog lifts further as the morning sun strengthens. The gate comes into view as it creaks open. Then a brick falls from the top of the tower and bursts.

Dad screeches up to the workers, "What's going on up there?" There's panic in his voice.

Behind me I sense that Hannah and her friends are following me. I look back, the dark haired one slips a phone from the waist band of her pleated, plaid skirt and holds it up like she's videoing me. I dig my nails into my palm. Another brick falls and bursts.

Dad yells to Lucy as she enters the site, "You're not supposed to be here."

Lucy says, "Dad, it's okay. I'm here to help."

"This is a hard hat zone."

"Someone get me one then."

A worker trots one out to her. Several bricks fall one after the other. Lucy dodges them with a skip.

I shake the fence with both hands. "Lucy, get out of there."

Several more bricks crash and explode, the dust mingles with the remaining fog and I can no longer see my sister.

Behind me, the girls ask each other what's going on with a rising alarm that matches my own. The fence rattles and waves as I shake it.

"Keep filming," Hannah says.

One of the workers in the man-lifts shouts, "The mortar is eroded. The tower's not stable!"

And then the bell tolls as it tips in the unstable base that our work all morning has further degraded. I feel sharp pieces of rock pummel my face and body through the chain link. Dust mixes with the remaining fog turning it to an opaque grey brown. My ears ring. I cough until my stomach cramps.

"Lucy," I scream, then cough again.

In the melee I forget the gate and clamber over the fence. It sways beneath my weight. I jump to the other side, run toward the place where Lucy had been standing, and trip over strewn scaffolding. I hit the ground hard and land in a pile of debris. My forehead hits a jagged piece of rebar. I wipe my hand against the burning sensation and see blood, rust and dust on my hand. The blood runs into my eyes. Head wounds bleed a lot, though I don't worry it's severe. I wipe the blood away and continue picking my way through to the wreckage in search of Lucy. I fear she's buried beneath it. I look up and see the orange shirts and hats of the workers at the top still safe inside their man lifts. Adrenaline spikes and I dig through the heap while time slows down.

I reach a massive chunk of concrete held together with crumbling, rusted rebar. I can't move it. I grunt and pull, but it feels impossible. The drum beat in my head quiets and I sense Mom—all around me—part of the fog. It feels like she's urging me to keep searching for my sister. I slow down, wipe away more blood, then twist the hunk and it comes loose. I hurl it behind me. My chest heaves with the effort. I look up, as I catch my breath, expecting to see others swarm to assist with the search. Away from the dust cloud, the fog is now light enough to make out a group gathering around a prone body where my dad had been standing. I hold my hand over my brow and squint that direction. My brother kneels beside my father shouting at someone to call 911.

I take a step that direction, but I haven't found Lucy yet. I turn back to the rubble and hurl several small pieces away with an anguished cry. My hands are raw and bloody, but I don't know if they're are bleeding or it's just the blood from the cut on my head. My vision blurs and I taste copper in the back of my throat.

"I fucking told you so, Lucy," I yell at the pile.

"Told me what?"

I turn to the voice of Lucy behind me.

"We think Dad's had a stroke. Oh my God, you're hurt! He's hurt!" Lucy calls out for help.

"What? I fall to my knees and place my hand over my heart. It leaves a bloody print on my light-grey polo shirt. I'm not sure which shocks me more; Dad falling victim to a stroke or Lucy's not being buried alive.

Lucy examines the bleeding cut on my forehead. "This doesn't look good, Santi. Your whole face is covered in blood."

The siren of an ambulance whirs from a distance. I try to stand but my knees buckle. "I can't go to the hospital," I tell her, thinking on how I need to finish the song in the little time I have left.

"That's for Dad, but you are definitely going to the hospital."

When the ambulance arrives, the EMTs put Dad on a stretcher. I watch from a distance not certain he would want me there. As Lucy climbs into the back of the ambulance with Dad, she says to me, "They say there's another one coming for you."

I close my eyes and nod wearily then sit down amidst

the rubble. In my peripheral I see Hannah and her two girlfriends, their faces animated with excited horror. The dark-haired girl still holds the phone aloft to video the disaster and record the ordeal for countless viewers.

CHAPTER 28

SANTIAGO DEANGELO

Kick Up My Chi Force

MY AMBULANCE TAKES me to Loma Linda University hospital where I'm treated for my minor wounds. But, as I voice the overwhelming exhaustion I feel, I'm admitted for further tests.

Well fuck!

How to cut the testing short and tell them what's really wrong? How would I put it? Something like, "Look, I've been barrowing energy from my nervous system at an interest rate I couldn't afford and now I'm just about bankrupt."

As I developed my addiction to opiates my energy to function has become dependent on them. As I've cut back, my ability to get through the day has diminished at a similar rate. I know that if I could get them out of my system I could start to function normally again. But that's proven practically impossible. Since I'm this close to the finish line with the recording of the album I just need to assure them I'm good, get my hands on some more medicine, and get back to work. Though, I know that's not true. When I'm finished recording the real work begins. Live performances and more promotional work. The stress of it makes me want to go to sleep to escape.

I'm only allowed to rest a few hours. Then, my assigned doctor, a beautiful Indian woman with a hypnotizing red bhindi on her forehead, introduces me to the team of residents behind her. This is a teaching hospital. The residents trickle in with their sleep depriving questions.

Doctor Lampson, a sandy haired resident fresh out of med school who looks younger than me asks, "Are you taking any prescription drugs?"

"Tylenol 3 for throat pain."

"Any recreational usage?"

Don't tell them anything.

Maybe they can help us.

"I was in an accident, had four surgeries in one year, and several prescriptions for Norco."

He jots it all down. "That was over a year ago. Anything else you want to tell me?"

I press my lips together.

From ongoing interviews—in which I hide my addiction, but not my exhaustion—Lampson tells me he thinks my lethargy points to adrenal insufficiency.

"Ha! More like adrenal exhaustion!"

But that is a non-medical diagnosis. Lab tests are ordered. They need to rule pituitary issues out. They drain enough blood to make me queasy with sleep and I nod off mid-question. I rouse to hear one resident whisper to the other, "With this much opiate in his system *Homm* might want to have a look at him."

I wake to hospital beeps and yet another young doctor. This one with an Asian face wearing royal-blue scrubs. He smiles to find me awake. Tired of being probed for the benefit of their education, I say, "I want a real doctor."

"I am a real doctor, a fellow to be precise, so I can proceed as your attending physician if you are interested in my proposal." He has no accent.

"I just want my real doctors to sign me out of here. I have to be at work tomorrow."

He drags a chair over and gets close. My sleepy vision narrows in on his embroidered coat, which reads, DR. HAM.

He says, "Maybe it's those *real doctors* who got you into this mess." His eyes glimmer with conspiracy.

I activate the bed to prop me up. "What mess?"

He taps his papers. "Dependency on opiate pain-killers. Your drug panel came back very high."

"I just need some rest. I'm over stressed, but I've been cutting back."

"My research only shows one active prescription in the system, but your blood tests reflect a much higher dosage. Are you getting the additional meds from a street dealer or an online vendor?"

My eye twitches. "I don't have to tell you that. I don't have a problem Ham."

"It's pronounced *Homm*. And I think we can help each other."

I cross my arms. "I don't need your help."

Ham stands.

Goose bumps prickle my forearms. "Wait, what kind of help?"

"My fellowship is concerned with reducing chemical dependency on prescription pain killers, specifically opiates."

"How?"

"You could be a part of a clinical drug trial."

I wait a beat. "Nah, I don't think so."

"Are you sure about that? Because the way I have it figured, you're going to be wanting one of these in very short order." He holds up a pill between blue gloved fingers. "And I don't think your attending physician will release you until they can rule out adrenal insufficiency. It could be days."

I reach for the pill, and he pulls it back. "Unbelievable," I say.

"I just want to help you."

There's a light in his eyes that I want to trust. "Why?" I ask him.

"That's why I became a doctor."

I want to believe him. But he sees my skepticism.

"You're also an ideal candidate for my study and an article I hope to publish. Your inclusion in the study could help a lot of patients like yourself."

"Why should I care about that?"

"The opiate epidemic is going to merit some intense reaction. A lot of opiate dependent patients are going to lose access to their meds at a dangerous rate. The drug I'm offering could reduce a lot of suffering while the medical community takes the time to understand how to manage their pain more safely and effectively. But more than that I want to make non-opiate pain killers the first choice for surgical patients."

"You're crazy to think you could manage that. Why even try?"

"Would you be addicted to these drugs if you hadn't been prescribed such a high quantity with each surgery you had last year?"

"No, but I'm not sure that's the problem."

Ham inclines his head with genuine interest.

"If I hadn't been so disconnected . . ." I start to say, but I can see that loneliness is not Dr. Ham's field and we need to keep this practical.

"Do you want to recover from your addiction?" Ham says.

He's trying to trick you; he wants us to suffer.

I ball the sheets and breathe heavily. Ham stands at ease, waiting.

"Yes," I say. "But what if the pharmaceutical machine that steamrolled me crushes you and your trial too."

"That may happen. But my findings will exist, they'll support future studies, and that gives my life greater meaning."

"Do you really think so?"

"Yes. When we follow our intentions, we are equal to our greatest self."

That gets me like a knife in the heart because Mom's song feels like that to me too, and I was willing to let it go. I test Ham by saying, "That's just a stupid Chinese proverb."

"I'm Korean, and no, it is just my personal philosophy."

I snicker. "Why can't I piss you off? Does nothing insult you?"

He grins at me. "My intentions to restore your chi force prevent me from being offended in your weakened state." He winks.

I laugh out loud. "You didn't learn that in med school Ham."

"No."

"Street vendor," I say.

He's briefly puzzled.

"I get the pills from a street vendor. I won't tell you his name."

"Can I have a sample?"

"That depends on two things. One, what they did with my pants, and two, how you intend to kick my chi force up a couple notches."

He rattles off some acronyms and medical terms that make me go cross eyed. "Give me the idiots guide version, Ham."

"Basically, the substance under clinical trial will override the withdrawal sensation in your brain. That will help with the most difficult part of the physical withdrawals. The medicine will also help eliminate the drugs from your system much more quickly."

"So, I won't get a suicidal headache?"

"You won't, but that's just the beginning of beating your addiction. It's a three-day trial. We can start today."

I pull my hair. "Shit, I can't do it, Doc. I've got work."

"I'll write you an off-work notice."

"Fuck, I don't have three days. I was already sick once. No one will believe me. If I'm not in the studio tomorrow, it all falls apart."

"Like that bell tower?" Ham says.

My head flinches back. "You heard about that?"

Ham launches his YouTube app on his phone and plays a video from the construction site. I hadn't seen myself. My face was smeared with blood and dirt. I look pathetic searching for someone who wasn't even injured. I squirm in the hospital bed with embarrassment.

"They'll believe you," he says as he pockets his phone.

I pound my forehead with both fists. "What do I say I'm being hospitalized for? I can't tell them the truth."

"Why not? Bring awareness to the cause."

"I don't want to be part of your goddamned cause. This is private." I calm down, my voice drops. "Can you really eliminate the drugs from my body?"

"We've achieved that in ninety-eight percent of our patients."

"Give me your phone back. I'm gonna call my publicist. If she can spin it, I'm yours." The phone slides out of the doc's hands. I dial Vicky, she picks up on the first ring and I let her know it's me.

"DeAngelo. Where are you?"

My gut clenches. "Why?"

"So, I can drive there and kiss you, I'm so happy. I couldn't have got this kind of exposure if I sold my soul to the devil. Everyone's watching that video."

"I need three days, Vicky. I'm getting some help for the drugs."

"Good! Well . . . shit!"

"What?"

"Sleezy reporters will be on the prowl. If you give them something newsworthy after the construction site video it could put you in a dangerous category of stardom."

My hands shake. "What category?"

"Tabloid category. Which we want to avoid. Things can get out of hand. If people find out that you're there for drug related issues they may blow it way out of proportion and paste it across every check stand in America."

I hang my head. But I'm not turning back now. "We'll just deal with that if it happens."

"Right." She hangs up.

Ham tip toes over. "Are we set?"

"Sign me up."

He smacks his lips. "Okay, but after this I want you to consider the psychological aspects of the addiction, which are beyond the scope of the trial."

"I have something kind of like your article. A song I'm writing."

Ham lowers his voice. "Did you think the drugs would help you write it?"

I can feel my ears turning red. I look away. "But you're going to heal me right, Doc?

He makes a humming noise in his throat. "I'll do my part, it's what happens after that, that matters."

THE DRUG HAM personally administers during day light hours is a paradox that he asks me to expand on as he burns up his page with notes. I like fucking with him to break up my incarceration. He gleans pertinence from my mania.

His favorite question—*how are you feeling right now?*—has generated a multitude of creative responses. Empty as a raped cadaver, cloudy as an old chalkboard, like an Olympic bronze medalist in their thirties. And when my creativity wavers, like an asshole.

The paradox is this:

I feel okay physically, so much so, that it's harder to bear the specters of my soul that my sobriety raises. If my body were racked with the pain of withdrawal than my emotional pain wouldn't be so poignant. And there's no escaping it. My cell phone died long ago, and there's no land line installed in my room. Visitors are a security risk, if someone slipped me a pill, the whole trial would be lost. Even the TV has been denied me, not by Ham but by fate. Mine quit working the day I checked in, a fact that stumps even the TV techs.

The only consolation is Ham allows me coffee. Though he limits even that, citing studies of addicts relying on other socially accepted drugs like caffeine and nicotine in dangerous quantities. I curse the Seventh Day Adventists that run Loma Linda, where caffeine is treated like crack, and tremble for the hideous brew my nurses pour into my plastic mug. I burn the roof of my mouth and stroke it with my tongue while the caffeine reboots the cycle of my suffering.

At night, I dream of the accident, and horror that it is, I clutch at the nightmare because my mother is alive in it. I start a sort of game we all like to play, the time travel game. I pick recent instants in time I could go back and undo.

I don't make love to Kitty.

I don't swallow her goddamn pill.

Hell, I don't even sign the recording contract in the first place.

I don't slam Dad against the door to make my point about self actualization.

What the fuck am I doing? I have a time machine. I don't put Mom in that car.

But I did do all those things.

I chew the inside of my cheeks to a bloody pulp. The coppery taste of blood takes me back to the point in time I was digging for Lucy. A mysterious moment. I felt Mom urging me to heroism, but Lucy wasn't even trapped. My embarrassment magnetizes my pain, and I curl up with it, moaning.

Ham bursts into the room. "Are you experiencing physical pain?" He scratches his short-cropped head and takes a pen from his pocket.

"Yes, I'm in fucking pain, Doc."

"Your head, your stomach?"

"No, you asshole, my heart."

He scratches something on his pad and hums to himself. "Wait, are you speaking literally, your heart has physical pain? Or ..."

I throw my pillow at him. He blocks it with his forearm, and it bounces back and knocks the lukewarm coffee to the floor. I chuck the plastic mug at the TV; it clatters to the ground. He departs and I resume the fetal position to wallow like a pig in the mess I've made of my life.

A real pity-party.

The other pig at my imaginary party is Dad. His mud coat is thicker than mine. Without word on his condition, I take to imagining the worst; he's dead. That brings me comfort, until it doesn't. I downgrade his results to paralysis on the left side, since he drafts with his left hand, and a downward spiral for the firm. This too, pleases, then stings, like sour candy in reverse.

"Dad," I take to muttering into my fist. Which links me back to Mom and why she wanted me there with Dad in the first place. If it wasn't to save Lucy, it was to land me here.

Here is where I'm supposed to be.

Ham peers in the door. I'm sitting up writing possible lyrics for Mom's song. Most of the words are lined through.

"Can I come in?"

I put the pencil down and smile.

He smiles back and enters, closing the door behind him. "The drugs have been eliminated from your body," Ham tells me as he looks at his chart. "Perhaps that is why you're taking a more positive note with me."

"Or I've worked some shit out."

"Which you couldn't work out until the drugs influence was eliminated."

I shrug. He reaches into his pocket and holds up a pill. It looks an awful lot like one from my jeans. Saliva pools in my raw cheek. My abdominals tighten as I lean towards it, hand outstretched.

"Aha. We still have some work to do. Have you thought any more on who's care I can release you too?"

"My self, Doc. Why are you so hung up on this? Look my mom's dead . . . my dad's in the hospital, and my sister is too young."

"Huh? I see that your uncle is a chaplain at this hospital, so I am confused why you haven't mentioned him as a candidate."

"We have issues."

"You have issues with a Padre?"

"I'm not ready for what he wants from me. Never mind, I couldn't explain it."

Ham sends him in anyway. I'm ready when he arrives.

Uncle Carl peeks in the crack in the door. I nod him into the room. He wraps his fingers around my bed rail. I put my hand over his.

"How are you holding up, my boy?"

"Better. You know why I'm in here?"

I'd told Ham it was okay to let him know the trial I'd come through.

He nods.

"I haven't been okay since she died."

He leans in and hugs me. "I know. But it's okay to forgive yourself for her death." His gentle voice is right at my ear. He looks at me with so much love I'm taken aback as I recognize the same light in his eyes that he's had for me since I was a child.

I've worked hard to avoid him because I couldn't face

him high, or in the shadow of my guilt for his sister's death. But I see now that was a waste. He was always there for me and I squandered the chance to be bolstered by his love.

My arms constrict around his shoulders. My voice shakes. "I don't think I'll ever be able to forgive myself for her death." We release each other and I adjust the hospital bed to sit up straighter. "How's my dad?"

"He's going to be okay. I think it was more of a traumatic panic attack then a stroke."

"So, he can walk and talk?"

Uncle Carl laughs. "Yes, he can still walk and talk, but everyone's treating him like he can't. I think he's needed the break. He never took the time he needed to mourn your mother's death. He just dove back into work."

I close my eyes and nod my head. "Good, that's good. I'm glad he's okay." The relief starts in my head and rushes down to my toes like water downhill.

"Is there anything I can do for you?"

"Please let Sophia know I'm here. I want to see her before we leave."

CHAPTER 29

SANTIAGO DEANGELO

Make Peace

MOBBED AT THE gates. It's what the headlines should read. Vicky was right, sleezy reporters are on the prowl. The gossip columnists dart from hiding when we step foot from the hospital. I'm accompanied by Lucy, Sophia, and Uncle Carl.

I make out logos for TMZ, Gawker, Star, and OK magazine. Seedier varieties are hidden in the brush, waiting to feast on the bones the more powerful pillagers leave behind. Sophia, who arrived as soon as Uncle Carl told her I was in the hospital, freezes and drops my hand. Lucy rolls her eyes, and heads back into the hospital.

"Go with Lucy," I tell Sophia. She dashes back towards my sister.

Uncle Carl greets the marauders with subtle sarcasm that bumps his status in my book. "I didn't realize we'd receive such a warm welcome. I'd have shaved first." He runs his hand down his face while they throw rapid questions like darts.

I make out: *is it true you're being treated for a rare pituitary disease, leukemia, cancer, drug addiction, stress, your injuries at the construction accident? Will you be able to complete the album, are you cancelling your live appearances? Was that your girlfriend?*

Uncle Carl doesn't break a sweat. "Your concern is touching. A formal statement will be posted by the end of the day to satisfy your impressive imaginations."

He takes me by the elbow and leads me to his car, a beige Ford Fusion. We hop in and he looks over at me, "Think I can lose them?"

"Go for it."

We strap in and head out.

"You have a charger for my phone in here?"

He points one out. When I have enough juice, I get Vicky on the line.

"Don't say anything to them. If you keep a low profile for a few days, they'll move on to juicer prey. Listen, the Vogls want you in studio day after tomorrow, that gives them just enough time to record and produce the tracks by the album deadline."

"Is there any way to get a little more time?"

"Afraid not. Physical CDs and records still need to be produced and shipped to stores in time with the release to digital music platforms on the day of the concert. It's a big promotion."

"What about my song?"

"It has to be submitted by tomorrow evening. That's firm too."

I pound my forehead. Vicky clicks off. My insides

vibrate. "I need to get home."

My uncle glances over. "There's bound to be more reporters camped outside your door."

I clutch my tightening chest. I'm sure there're some pills at home that I've hid. I need them now.

"So?"

"So, I promised your doctor I wouldn't take you back there today."

"What? Why?"

He rolls down my window. "You look like you need some air."

"I know what I need," I tell him. But I do lean into the wind to fight my nausea.

Uncle Carl's knuckles go white on the wheel. "I'm taking you to your dad's place."

"Jesus Christ!"

"Our Lord's peace is always available to you, Santi." He smiles at me.

"Yeah, that's exactly how I meant it." I stomp the foot well. "I don't have time for peace! I need to get my song submitted."

He pulls to the side of a residential street and cups my shoulder. "You ever wonder why you haven't been able to write it?"

I cross my arms and stare straight ahead.

He sighs. "Either way, you've been avoiding the inevitable for over a year now, but not on my watch."

I turn my body towards him. "What do ya think's gonna happen, me and my dad are gonna join hands and sing 'Kumbaya'?"

We resume the drive, the reporters on our tail appear to be lost as he drives in circles through the neighborhood he knows so well.

On the detour we pass Zenon's house and I get the idea to meet up with him, score a few pills that will get me through the dad ordeal, and give me just enough inspiration for the song. Then I'll be done forever.

I shoot my hand out the window and let it ride the breeze. I can do this. If I can't get out of facing Dad, I'll either stand by his bedside and force a smile for the given amount of time or tell him all of the things that have been running through my mind like a polluted river. I text Zenon to see if he can meet up on Smiley Heights Drive.

He shoots back. "You're in luck, but I'm out in twenty for a ride. You know where."

I stroke my sweaty palms and begin to explain to my uncle why we should avoid the whole situation for now.

"Look, the last time I spoke to Dad . . ."

We turn onto Smiley Heights Drive and the words turn to dust in my throat. Like me, the car strains up the steep street of my childhood. I haven't been back here since I bought my house and moved into it. My uncle puts the car into a lower gear to make the climb to our family's single-story estate. It's styled after an Italian villa. Dad built it just before I was born, and Mom gave birth to me there in her bedroom. We approach the driveway. The hillsides that surround the place are ablaze with purple and fuchsia ice plant, and bright orange poppies.

Uncle Carl parks in the driveway.

"I can't go in there," I say. "I really can't."

My uncle puts his hand on my knee. "I'll be with you."

I pinch the bridge of my nose. "But Mom won't be."

He taps my temple with two fingers. "She's in here."

I wipe my eyes with the heel of my hand. "I'm pathetic," I say, "crying is bullshit."

"No. I wish your father would give into the tears he holds back."

"Now what? We're supposed to cry together, is that it?"

He shrugs. "Why not?"

Just a pill or two and we could do this. "Can I go for a quick walk first?"

"I'll come along," he says.

"I really want to go alone, Uncle Carl."

He studies my face. "No."

The shades are drawn, and the house is dark. My brother Mariano paces the living room on his cell, a conference call from the sound of things. He's handling the aftermath of the bell tower incident with a kind of thrill that tells me he's been patient for this kind of control all these years.

My eyes sweep the room. Mom's everywhere and nowhere. I stare at the double glass doors in the entry way, and picture bolting before anyone can stop me. Instead, I sink into the sofa. My uncle holds me in place with a hand on my shoulder.

Mariano ends his call. "Things aren't good with Dad. Your being here won't help."

"I think you're right." I make to stand.

Uncle Carl presses me down. "Things can't go on as they are, Mariano."

My brother crosses his arms. "The timing is bad, old man."

My uncle squeezes my tense shoulder. "Or . . . it's never been better," he says.

My phone vibrates, it's Z: "7 minutes man."

I type back: "Give me 9." I crack my knuckles and tell

my family, "I'm gonna get some fresh air while you two work this out."

Again, my uncle stops me from rising. "No, you're not."

"Just let him go," my brother says.

"You mean like the rest of you have? Why have you done that?" our uncle asks him.

I warp through childhood scenes with my brother. He used to be my hero; I was his side kick. It's really not supposed to be like this.

My brother runs both hands through his hair. "I can't add family intervention to my plate right now."

"Why not?" Uncle Carl demands.

"I have my own family now, and the firm to manage."

My stomach cramps. If they'd just shut up, Dad's room is at the end of the hallway, there are three bedrooms I could access windows from to catch Zenon before he leaves for his bike ride.

There's a weighted silence. Uncle Carl breaks it with a low baritone. "We're going to see him now."

"He's not ready to see anyone."

"Ready or not," Uncle Carl says. The line triggers the prominent song in my Mariano memories.

"I'd like to see him," I say. They both turn their heads. "Fine."

I enter the hall, Mariano follows closely. *So much for escape.*

Halfway down the hall Mariano clutches my triceps. "You've been a real troublemaker since the accident." He stares me down, and the truth is, I'm just glad to be in his presence. I want to remind him who we are together, and I only know one way to do it. I sing our song.

"Ready or not, here I come."

My brothers head jerks back and he looks at me funny, but I keep singing.

"You high?"

"Nope, clean as a whistle." And I whistle a beat, while Mariano rubs the back of his neck.

"Come on Mar, you know this one, The Fugees, Lauryn Hill." I start singing again,

He joins in.

I punch Mariano lightly on the shoulder. He punches me back playfully and our old vibe takes over.

"Santiago, just be cool, okay? It took me a long time to get Dad settled." His eyes dart over my face. "Oh and . . ." our eyes meet. "I'm sorry about not texting you back. I just felt like Dad had drawn a line in the sand and I had to be on his side. You know how he can be. That's why I'm worried about you going in there right now."

"Trust me, I don't want to."

"Maybe Uncle Carl is right though. He may be more approachable in this state."

I nod and change the subject. "Have you heard the song on the radio?"

He rumples my hair. "I've got it on all my favorite play lists. And I tell everyone that's my little brother."

He puts his hand out. I grasp it, and he pulls me into a hug. Then we head back down the hall to Dad's bedroom door.

I put my hand on the knob and hesitate. Mariano walks away down the hall and looks over his shoulder to question my hesitation.

I have to go in.

With my plan a bust, I'm on damage control. With any luck, Dad will be sleeping, and I can climb out *his* window.

Or set some things straight.

I scan the room. It is painted golden beige with a four-poster mahogany bed surrounded by matching furniture. The navy blue and gold striped bedspread is thrown back. The bed is empty. Dad's not here. Something's not right.

But I can still make it to Zenon's place if I run. Behind the bed is an eight-foot-wide window with cherry wood shutters tipped open to reveal the unruly rose bushes that block it as an exit like a briar patch. When Mom was alive those bushes were quaffed to perfection.

I tap the master bath door. "Dad, you in there?"

No sound. I inch it open, to be sure he hasn't fallen.

"Dad?" I open it all the way. Not here, not in the shower, I eye the shower window and imagine crawling through it. Stupid, way too small, but the closet window is huge.

I turn the knob of the door that leads into the walk-in closet and push. It barely budges. I press all my weight against it to widen a gap I can slip through. The door has been blocked by a barricade of Mom's sweaters and jeans. As I enter the large space, I see that Mom's side of the closet has been yanked down. Another pile is made up of evening wear into a nest that my father has burrowed into. I sneak past it towards the window.

Wait, don't you smell her?

I breathe Mom in. The scent of her fills my head with memories and I sink to my knees, overpowered by them.

Dad was too. He lies in the fetal position amongst her most special dresses.

I look up to the window and back to Dad, drawn by his vulnerability. He looks so weak and helpless curled up on the floor, beaten by the same loneliness I've been taken down by at times.

I summon my anger to fight the rising sympathy. Sober, it doesn't rush in.

I reach out and touch his back. "Dad?"

He doesn't stir. He's clutching an emerald-green gown the way a child holds a beloved blanket. It's the same gown my mother wore to my piano competition in D.C. I finger a silky corner, then put my nose in it, inhale, and tear up with the memory of Mom joining Barbara and I on stage to accept the gold medal. She'd had to hold the fabric in her hands to climb the stairs that led onto the stage. I'd watched her make her way towards me. Her smile overtook her face, morphed into laughter, then turned to tears. Did she, like me, think that was the moment Dad would understand that my talent was real?

I sink back onto my heels as I recall the force of her hug on that stage. "I'm so proud to have a son like you, *Vita Mia*," she'd whispered in my ear. Then, she took one of my hands and Barbara took the other and they both held them aloft. I thought they'd pull them out of their sockets with their pride. When I found Dad's face in the audience he was clapping politely in his seat while others were already on their feet.

I look to Dad in the closet. "Why couldn't you stand up for me?"

Dad rouses, sees me beside him, and looks around him in a daze. His face reddens. I can only assume he's embarrassed to be found in this state. He props himself up on his elbow atop the pile of gowns.

I eye the window, my escape route from dealing with the relationship everyone wants me to magically solve so they can feel better. If I don't try now, how will that look to Lucy or Uncle Carl?

I fight back my desire to flee and extend the only olive branch I see.

"I remember that dress, it still smells like her."

He looks down at the emerald-green satin twisted around his fist and brings it to his nose. His face momentarily reveals the ache of loneliness he's been living with.

My heart goes out to him.

He shakes himself from his reverie and looks to me with a grimace. "What are you doing in here?"

"In the closet? Same as you, I guess. It's funny the way the nose remembers."

"I mean, why did you come here today?"

"Come on Dad, it doesn't have to be like this. We're both just out of the hospital."

"You think that's an excuse for me to forgive you for trying to kill me?"

I snicker at his embellishment.

His eyebrows lift. He wants an answer.

"Come on, don't you think you're being a little dramatic, Dad?"

"Me? Dramatic? I've seen your interviews and heard your music. Do you think it's cool to boast about a drug addiction in song?"

I flinch with surprise. I didn't know that Dad knew about my drug problem. We'd certainly never talked about it before.

Was I that obvious?

I can feel my ears turning red with embarrassment. My legs are numb from sitting on them. "The lyric is a metaphor."

"Oh, I see, you're going to deny it." He maneuvers into a sitting position then stands with the gown at his feet.

I rise to meet him.

"No, I'm sober now. It was hard for me with all of those surgeries and losing Mom at the same time."

"Excuses, son. That's another reason I was trying to steer you away from a music career. What do you think a life like that is going to mean for an addict?"

"I told you, I'm sober now."

"We'll see."

I crack my knuckles to disperse my flaring temper.

Am I just angry because he's right? I did text Zenon for more pills.

"Besides that, fame comes with responsibilities I don't think you're up for."

My fear he's right makes me strike out. "Are you afraid for me, or do you really just hate me because Mom loved me more?"

"Don't flatter yourself." A little spittle comes out with the force of his words.

"I'm serious! What is your animosity towards me about?"

"You're a disrespectful little brat and the world you seek will chew you up and spit you out. But then you'll think because you've tasted that life, you're too good for this one and you'll be worthless after that."

"Wow, you really are afraid. You know what I'm afraid of?"

He glares at me.

"I'm afraid of never finding out how far I could have gone making music with people that believe in me."

He snickers.

"And you know what's funny about that? It's exactly what you set in motion for me when your passion built this very house where your children could dream dreams even bigger than yours if you let them."

From beyond the closet door, I hear the master bedroom door creep open, and Uncle Carl say, "How's it going in here?"

I leap towards the window above my mother's rifled dresser. I scramble up pulled out empty drawers and throw open the shuttered window.

"Where do you think you're going?"

"We're done, Dad, and I'm done answering to anyone else about it." I toss the wooden dowel that locks the window at him. Then I kick the screen onto the lawn. With the escape route clear, I leap off the dresser and feel it tip back towards Dad as I jump out the window. I hit the ground running and bust ass down the street. Half a mile in a side ache slows me to a walk. I lean into it and hobble towards tablet sized relief. As my pace slows so do my thoughts.

I pick up a trot towards Zenon's house, but the side ache cinches tight.

What are you doing? You can't prove Dad right and blow your sobriety.

But there's still so much to do and I don't know how to face my life sober yet.

I sit down on the curb beneath a mulberry tree and hang my head beneath the weight of my addiction.

Ham was right, the trial was only the beginning. But I can't squander the boost he's given me.

I breathe slowly as I watch the water in the gutter at my feet stream around my shoes and down the hill as my anger slips away with it. I'm too tired to move let alone hang on to it.

I replay the fight and recognize it was merely a

continuation of our first blow up. But instead of justifying my words and actions, like I had the first time, I find myself reflecting much sooner and chuckle that Dr. Ham would appreciate that detail for his study. I can hear his voice in my head.

Now that the drugs have been eliminated from your system.

What else might be different?

As I sit there open to the subtle shifts of my sobriety, the flow of clear water in the gutter increases. Up the street someone is probably draining their pool. The water rushes over my feet and soaks my shoes, but I don't jump up because its flow is almost melodic. I let everything else fall away and connect to its musical quality until I can hear my own song in its current.

Lucy was almost right.

While I never needed to make peace with Dad, I did need to make peace with not having him in my life.

Fifty feet away Zenon huffs up the hill on his road bike, he's wearing blue and yellow spandex riding gear. The bicycle sways side to side as he negotiates the grade. His bronze skin shines with sweat. I stand up and take a superman pose. He straddles the bike a few feet from me.

"Got your fix, yo." He tosses a baggie of pills.

I catch them, lick my lips, and toss them back. "I changed my mind. I don't need the pills anymore."

I hear the faint sound of a camera clicking. A hedge rustles several feet away.

"Fuck, dude, I left my teammates to stay behind for you. We were going on a fifty-mile ride. Who knows if I'll catch up?"

"Right. What do I owe you for showin' up?" I walk

towards him as I take my wallet from my pocket.

Zenon scoffs. "Hundred bucks, but I won't take your calls again." He rips the proffered hundy from my hand.

The hedge rustles again.

"Hasta la vista, *Superstar*," Zenon says as he pedals away.

I HOBBLE BACK to the house. Mariano is in a rage about the state they found Dad in. His face is red, and he points his finger at me.

"I'm sorry, bro. I tried to talk to Dad, but he's still in too much pain from losing Mom to think clearly."

Uncle Carl grips my shoulder with remonstration.

I turn to him. "It's like you said, Dad never took the time to mourn her and it's messed him up. He's afraid of any future he can't control."

Uncle Carl looks down and shakes his head. "Perhaps what he's most afraid of, is losing you too?"

"That's the thing about fear. When you give into it, it manifests itself."

Part 4
Sober

CHAPTER 30

SANTIAGO DEANGELO

I Don't Have to Live Without You

THERE'S A SWARM of reporters out front when I get home. I consider sneaking around the back, but I want to face my life head on.

When I near their outpost, I see there are at least a dozen people including camera men. As I wade through their ranks a low rumble rises to a fever pitch. I treat them with the same nonchalance that my uncle assumed at the hospital. As if their being camped outside my door couldn't concern me in the least. "Really honored you'd all make the drive and stand out here in the hot sun," I tell them.

At noon it's already in the low nineties as the first heat wave of April makes an appearance. A fit, dark-haired woman of average height in her late twenties wears a striped, grey polyester skirt suit that has her sweating more than just my arrival. Her makeup runs along her cheek as she thrusts the microphone in my face and says, "Is all of this worth it?"

I momentarily meet her eyes, green and sparkling with

ambition that reminds me of my own. That shared aspiration connects us, however fleetingly. I grin at her. "You better believe it," I say with a wink. She blushes and lowers the mic. Meanwhile, a ruddy faced man with thick silver hair, whose white-shirted belly overhangs his fine wool trousers, nearly pushes her over to get his mic in front of hers. But I don't hear what he says, intermixed as it is with the rush of the group to fire off questions about rehab and my health and my relationship with Holladay Records. I stand at the top step of my porch, the narrow entry of which holds them back and look over the motley crew. Half of them are women, half men, some young, some seasoned. All of them racking their brains to pose the one question I'll be too intrigued with to hold my tongue.

The moment becomes surreal as I pair it with memories of falling asleep to visualizations like this when I dreamed of fame as a kid. Their desire to figure me out and reveal me to the world feels almost as satisfying as it is annoying. They want to understand what's in my head. I don't even understand it. So, for now I've got to hold my tongue.

When I turn my back to them at the door and fit my key in the lock, I chuckle in triumph. It had been more frightening when I sat in my uncle's car down the street contemplating the walk to the door then the actual walk had been. Uncle Carl offered to come along, but I assured him he'd already done his part.

Inside the house, with the door closed softly behind me, I'm surprised to hear the movement and voices of Lucy and Sophia in the bathroom.

When they don't come out to greet me, I realize they don't know I've arrived. I creep towards the bathroom and eavesdrop on their purpose. I press my back against the wall to the left of the bathroom door.

I hear a plastic trash bag whizzed from the box. Lucy laments on how things may be going between me and Dad right now. "I just worry my dad will ruin everything. You'd think his nervous breakdown would soften him up, but he seems angrier than ever the last few days."

"That's terrible," Sophia says.

One of them shakes the bag open with a pop that makes me jump and Lucy says, "Open the medicine cabinet, we'll throw them all in here."

"Why are there so many bottles? They're mostly empty." Sophia reads off some of the names, "Norco, Vicodin, Valium, Percocet." I can just picture the scowl I hear in her voice.

Lucy pulls her head out of the cabinet she was rifling and says, "He figured out all the doctors' systems, and convinced them to prescribe every drug he needed to put off feeling anything. But it's not doctors that are filling them now."

"Do you think the treatment he went through will be effective?"

"That's why we're here, Sophia, to make sure it is."

"I don't know if I'm supposed to force an outcome or wait and see what he chooses?"

Lucy says, "Do you love him?"

I perk my ears to the silence.

Lucy pulls a drawer so hard it crashes to the floor. Sophia startles.

I slide down the wall in the hall as I wait for her answer.

"Do you?" Lucy asks again.

"Yes, I do."

I inhale relief.

"Then fight for him if he's still too weak to fight for himself."

The rifling continues and I use the noise as cover to slink back down the hall, open the front door and slam it noisily. Lucy and Sophia rush into the room with their chins held high. Sophia has the plastic bag tied at the top in one hand.

I eye the bag in her hands and then raise my eyes to hers. Sophia drops her chin and eyes ever so slightly. "I just wanted to help you."

"Is that right?" I say, holding back a smile as I watch her squirm. But as she builds steam to form a frustrated response, I say, "I'm glad you're here," and watch her soften with relief.

But Lucy has no patience for such a scene. She taps my shoulder. "You gonna tell us where you're hiding the rest?"

I head back to the bathroom where I lift the lid from the tank of the toilet and take a Ziploc bag I'd taped there weeks ago with the Vicodin, Valium, and Ambien I was saving for a rainy day. Lucy tries to clutch the bag from my grip the second I've peeled it away from the tank. I hold it out of her reach, and she jumps for it. Sophia in the doorway grimaces and shakes her head.

"Take them, Sophia." I hand them to her at a height beyond Lucy's reach. For a second the look on Sophia's face registers fear, as if I'm asking her to save them for me, from, my sister.

"Do you need them?" Sophia asks. Lucy jumps for them once more.

"No! Are you kidding me? I want you to get of rid of

them."

Lucy jumps again.

"Stop. This means even more to your sister. Give them to her."

I lower my arm and Lucy swipes the bag from me then dumps the pills into the toilet bowl and puts her hand on the lever. She pauses to catch her breath.

"Wait, we'll do it together, Luce. You too, Sophia."

The three of us put our hands together and flush the lever. The pills swirl down and away.

I step back, raise my arms and they both rush into them. "I'm really glad you're both here." They hug me harder. "Don't break me," I say.

Lucy steps to the side. I stroke Sophia's hair and she looks up at me.

"Thank you for being here. It means a lot to me, Sophia."

She presses her cheek to my chest. "I really thought you wanted those stupid pills you'd hidden."

I press her tighter to me. "No, not at all. Thank you for trusting me long enough to get here."

"It's because of your sister."

We both turn to Lucy who is putting the bathroom back together in a pretense of indifference.

"What? Did you honestly think I would ever give up on you? Mom wouldn't let me get away with that."

"Thank you, Luce."

She shrugs, "That's what family is for."

A shadow passes over my joy. Lucy recognizes it. She bites her lip. "How did it go with Dad?"

I hang my head.

"I was so worried about Uncle Carl taking you over

there today, but I thought . . . maybe he's right. Someone has to do something."

Sophia steps aside and hops up on the bathroom counter.

I sit down on the lidded toilet bowl with a heavy exhale. "I tried to talk to him, but he's out of control."

Lucy sits down on the edge of the bathtub. "What happened?"

I rock forward and back as I rehash the scene that unfolded in the closet.

Lucy covers her face with both hands and peers through parted fingers. "It's worse than I feared."

"No, I don't think so. I think it's the best thing that could have happened."

Lucy's face expresses horror at my summary. "How can that be good?"

"You don't know what it felt like to keep actively trying to please him and convince him I'm worthy of the life I see for myself."

Lucy nods in concession. "Okay, I get it."

"And since then, I can hear more of the song too."

Sophia's hand goes to her mouth.

I stand and take both Sophia's hands in mine while she's still seated on the bathroom counter. "Will you help me with the words, Sophia?"

She nods.

"I only have the rest of the day and tomorrow to finish it."

"Is that even possible?" Lucy asks.

I look back at her. "Yeah, Luce, I think it finally is."

Sophia and I settle around the piano. Lucy searches the kitchen for something we can all eat. All she can find is two cans of chicken and rice soup. It will have to do. I feel an intense hunger. The pills had reduced my appetite but now it's back with a vengeance and none of us want to face the horde outside the door.

While she heats the soup, I try to translate what's new for the song and my mind falters. The enthusiasm I felt fades to frustration.

I eat in a hurry and rush back to the piano to try again.

The music is there but the words I'd been certain would work on the way over here no longer make sense.

"I lost it. Why did I lose it?" I hunch over the keys.

Sophia stands behind me and rubs my tense shoulders. Lucy rinses dishes in the kitchen.

Sophia says, "Will you tell me about your mom?"

I pound the keys. "I'm running out of time."

"I think your anxiety blocks you. Maybe you should stop focusing on notes and chords and rhyming words and just remember your mother."

"It hurts too much."

"Isn't the music itself a salve for that pain?"

"Yes, but . . . even though I tried to climb out of the hole in my heart with beautiful notes—" I pause and play the lightest and prettiest of these with my right hand "—the words . . ." I sink my left hand into the heaviest bass notes of the song. "They just hurt."

"What does it feel like?" Sophia persists.

"It's like there's a rat in my chest that never quits gnawing on my broken heart."

She squeezes my trapezius and I exhale into the discomfort of her grip. But when she lets go the tension there is eased. I turn to face her and see that her eyes well with empathy.

"Did the pills ease that pain?"

"Not really, but the high distracted me from it. Now I have to face the pain head on. I just can't do it alone."

"That's why we'll do it together," Lucy says as she walks towards us to stand beside Sophia.

Sophia's face now reflects the confidence of Lucy's. Sophia says, "Sing us the lyric you first played for me on the Steinway that day in the rectory."

I spin back to the keys with the renewed poise our unity provides. They both place a hand on my shoulders. I play the intro, then sing, "Bird of Paradise I long to feel your touch."

With emotion in her voice, Lucy says, "I miss her so much, Santi."

I sing, "And every time I think of you, I'm missing you so much." The words nestle into the musical nest I'd already built for them. Loving energy pulses through their hands on my shoulders and holds me to the task I already want to flee from. I play the melody line over and over until the music becomes a portal that connects me to Mom.

I sing, "Bird of Paradise, you flew away too soon."

Lucy makes a sobbing sound deep in her throat and clenches my shoulder tight. My own throat relaxes as if she's taking on the pain that will leave me free to imagine the next phrase.

I sing, "I see you in my dreams, I feel you in my room."

The words feel too simple to be any good. If I were alone writing them on a page, I'd have crossed them out by now. But when I turn to look over my shoulder at Lucy, she nods to assure me their simplicity is what makes them perfect.

Sophia nods as well.

I keep playing. With Lucy by my side, I remember how

to be playful. I take Sophia's advice and just remember Mom. In the memory that springs to mind, Lucy and I are playing in the backyard pool with mom lounging nearby in the sun, just to be a part of our fun. Mom had the radio on and when songs came on that she loved, she belted them out. These days whenever one of those songs comes on, I hear it in Mom's voice.

I sing: "I hear your voice so sweet and the songs you used to sing,

I feel the breeze across my face, it's like you're touching me."

And then I change the key and sing:

"I know that you are near,

holding my hand,

sunshine in my day, you chase the fear away."

Lucy laughs happily through her tears.

That's been her truth. But it can be mine too.

She wants it to be.

I approach the chorus, music so rich it never felt like there was room for words. When I first intuited the melody after the accident it felt like a miracle to feel Mom through the music. Now I know it's an open invitation to experience her in my life.

I open my mouth and the words rise out.

"Come to me, love me again my angel. Oh,

Come to me, save me again my angel,

You are heaven sent.

How do I live without you?"

Behind me Lucy sniffles softly. "It's a love song for Mom."

"Is that okay?" I ask her with rising concern. "I don't want it to sound romantic."

Lucy says, "Mom's the first person you ever loved."

"She's the one who taught me how to love."

With this approval I sing the chorus once more and understand that just because Mom inspired the song doesn't mean the song has to be entirely about her. That in a way, I may not be able to explain to anyone but Lucy, it is also about the love Mom was leading me towards when she inspired it. The love I discovered in bringing it out. My love for Sophia, and Kitty, and most of all my sister whose love is as unconditional and fierce as Mom's was.

Sophia walks to the couch and leaves me and Lucy to each other. I hadn't expected my sister to be the one I needed to write the words with. But she always was. Even in the church when I'd written the bridge Lucy had been there too. Now, I feel foolish not to have known it sooner.

"Did we take her love for granted, Luce?"

"Just because we never expected to lose it, doesn't mean we took it for granted. Besides, I don't think we have lost it."

"We haven't?"

"When we live in the present, her love can still reach us."

I rethink the words. The line "come to me" is a summons that promises I'll be present to feel Mom's love. And that I'll continue to be open to the love the song has led me to.

I sing it again with more power.

"Come to me, love me again my angel

Oh, oh Come to me, save me again my angel

You are heaven sent.

I don't have to live without you?"

In this iteration of the chorus, instead of, "How can I

live without you?" I understand from Lucy's explanation that I don't have to live without her. Her love is still here for me. It survives even death. The variance in the lyrics of the chorus are a record of that discovery.

I sing a final verse:

"Bird of Paradise I feel you watching me
I hear you call my name
Erase this misery.
Bird of paradise
Though time has passed so long
Angel of my soul
Your love is still so strong."

I play it and sing it through beginning to end, making minor variations and leaning over across the keys to write the words down on sheet music propped up in the music holder. Then I play it again. Lucy takes a seat on the wide bench beside me and listens until she's familiar enough to sing the words with me. We sing it together several times.

When I finally rest my hands, Lucy puts her arm around me and says, "I'm so proud of you."

I hug her back and she leans her head on my shoulder. "I couldn't have done it without you, Luce."

"I didn't do anything."

"You never gave up on me."

"I promised Mom I wouldn't." Lucy stands. She walks to the dining room window and peeks out the wood blinds. "Looks like they're mostly gone. I think I'm going to head out too."

I raise my head from the piano in surprise. "You're leaving?"

"I think I should leave you both alone." She winks at me. I raise my hand in farewell and mouth, *thank you.*

Sophia walks her to the door, and they hug one another goodbye and speak in low voices that I don't hear over the notes of the song that continue to flow through me at the piano.

When Lucy's left, Sophia joins me at the bench. One of the things I love about the piano is that you can share the musical experience by having someone sit beside you while you play. She rests her hand on my leg and I fall back into the artistic trance the song still holds me in, playing it over and over while Sophia runs her hands along my inner thigh and arouses me until I can no longer focus on the song. My fingers fumble. She squeezes my thigh.

I turn to her, and she says, in a low voice, like she's reciting something:

"Your fingers linger on the keys,
 though sometimes they just dance."

She stands between me and the piano and runs her hands through my hair.

I look up at her.

"You pause and then look up at me,
 a deep and thoughtful trance."

I push the bench back from the piano to give her space. It slides easily on felt pads against the wood floor. I tilt my head up to her and she leans down and kisses me with soft pursed lips. Our mouths open, and as I move toward her, kissing her more intensely, she falls back onto the keys, laughing nervously at the sound they make. I coax her up and lower the fall board so that she can rest against it. Then she takes my face in both hands and continues to kiss me with unexpected ardor. I sit back down, take her hands in mine, and tug her towards me. She straddles my lap and when she feels my erection against her, she grinds against it making a soft breathy moan into my mouth.

I stand, and she clings to me, her arms around my neck, her legs locked around my waist, our mouths joined in united desire. I carry her the short distance to the bedroom and ease her down onto my bed.

When we give ourselves to each other it feels like the magic we make together could last forever.

CHAPTER 31

KITTY HOLLADAY

That's Why the Rules are There

MY LEGS ARE tangled with Dirk's and his are heavy on mine with sleep. Golden light peaks around the window shades. It's my second morning waking in my own bed.

Will this finally be enough?

Based on the sustained thrust of my husband's hips, I think not. That thrust could blast a rocket into orbit, or our marriage out of danger, but it hasn't. The atmosphere of betrayal holds it fast.

Our tonic of salvation-sex, alone, cannot atone for the beating heart within my womb.

But that heartbeat drums a new tune my addiction can't dance to. Dirk knows that and it's the reason he's willing to raise the child.

Since our last two sessions together with Dr. Sole we've spoken more honestly with each other than we have in years. That openness is a blessing I hadn't expected. But it also warns me Dirk's forgiveness is still dependent on my behavior in the coming days.

The weight of Dirk's legs becomes unbearable. I wiggle and try to pull mine free. I'm out of breath with the effort.

My full bladder loosens, and a tiny dribble of pee drips down my thigh. I squeeze tight and rub my belly, to soothe baby and me. Nausea roils beneath my palm with the smell of something stronger than the sex we're trying to glue our marriage back together with.

What is it? I wrinkle my nose, and move away from Dirk, but it's still there. I smell my own arm pit; I reek of it.

It's fear.

I'm afraid to face this world sober without him and uncertain his clemency will last given my indiscretion.

I scooch closer to Dirk and put an arm over him. "Dirk, you know I love you, don't you?"

He yawns. "Go back to sleep, Pussy Cat."

"Do you love me, Dirk?"

He wraps an arm around me and pulls me in tight to him. My body softens against his.

"You know I do." He says and kisses my neck.

"Will you love the baby as much as you love me?"

He groans. "If you go along with the plan." He pulls a pillow over his face.

My breath hitches. "I'm not sure I can do it."

Dirk sighs. "I just need you to prove yourself to me."

LATER THAT MORNING, I clench when my phone rings and it's Santiago. Dirk is on a business call at the kitchen table with our breakfast of toast and coffee ignored, while we both pay tribute to our cell phones. I show him the caller ID and he gives me a thumbs up and waves me away to take the call out of ear shot of his own conversation. We've been waiting for Santiago's call. Waiting for his song. Dirk wants to sell it to another artist whose album will be released the same day. An option we have as we own the masters to everything he submits while under contract. A fact Santiago is quite likely unaware of as he had signed the contract in a manic moment with me.

To test my loyalty, Dirk wants me to insure he submits the song tonight by the deadline of 8pm.

I hurry out to the back patio and sit in the bright sun on a cushioned lounge at the side of the pool. My stomach is in knots as I answer the phone. "Hey there." I try and sound natural.

"I did it, Kitty. I finally finished my song."

I can hear the thrill in his voice, it turns my legs to jelly. "Oh?" is all I can manage.

"I quit the pills. You were right. The things we think are giving us power are really taking our power away."

I put my hand over my chest. He may be the only one who's ever taken the things I've said to heart.

"Have you recorded it? You only have until tonight to submit it for the album."

"I know. I want you to record it for me at Barbara's and submit it to Holladay for me. You're the only one I trust with it, Kitty. It means everything to me."

I look around to be sure Dirk hasn't crept up beside me. But I see him through the window and can tell he's still engaged in his phone conversation.

"No, don't entrust me with it. Just leave it be. It

belongs to you, no one else. Remember that Barbara knew your music held a bigger purpose."

"No, this whole time, in interviews, I've been talking about how much it means to me to have a song I wrote on this album. It's the only real expression of who I am in this collection of music."

"I don't think you know yet what it means to give something this special away. Right now, it belongs to you."

Santiago goes on as if he hadn't even heard what I said. "You won't believe what it took to write it. Remember how you said I needed to find my lyricist? Well, it turns out I only needed the assurance of someone that loves me to come up with the words on my own. And that someone was my sister, not Sophia."

I feel a pang of envy at the mention of Sophia and suppress it for the silly notion it is. I make a final attempt to dissuade him while I reason that I can tell Dirk he's called to say the song couldn't be finished on time.

"Save this song for your next album. You may be able to write several on that one."

"No way."

I want to warn him further, but Dirk is approaching, and this is how I strengthen my alliance with my husband. He can't forgive me without some means of blame being placed and punishment being exacted. But is forgiveness real if its dependent on anything else?

Dirk arrives and stands between me and the warm morning sun.

"Just a second, Santiago." I mute the phone. "Dirk he's finished the song."

My husband pumps his fist. "Yes!"

Adrenaline shoots through my limbs.

"Is it professionally recorded?" Dirk asks me.

I shake my head, no, and exhale. "He wants to record it with me at Barbara's."

Dirks arms fly up. "For God's Sake, Pussy Cat, get over there."

I look down. "Don't make me do this."

He rumples my hair. "I trust you. I know you can stay clean, even in the studio." He tucks a strand of hair behind my ear.

I glare up at him. "It's not that. I don't want to be a part of it."

He clicks his tongue several times. "Kitty, I believe we have an understanding."

I unmute the phone. "Santiago, listen, I'm sorry for the hold up, I was just clearing my schedule so I can make it out to Barbara's. I'll be there in a couple hours."

"That's awesome, Kitty. Can my sister and Sophia join us in the studio?"

I want to see him alone. "No, we need to focus to get this done on time."

"Okay," he says. And I know he's agreed so quickly because he wants to see me alone as well.

"But there's a big party you'll want to bring your girlfriend to."

"A party?"

"To celebrate the release of the album. It will be like nothing you've experienced before."

The blood pounds in my ears. I'm so tired I don't know how I'll gather the energy to do this without any coke. I rub my belly and take a deep breath. "I'm leaving soon, so I should be there in just under two hours. I'll call you when I get to Barbara's."

IN THE STUDIO, Santiago is too fired up to sense the space I keep between us. I'm in a dangerous emotional state at the controls of the sound board. Only Dirk's promise to continue to take care of me and the baby hold me to the task. The music keeps me there. Santiago's voice has found its sweet spot in this song.

His sacred song. And I'm here to steal it.

He plays the Yamaha on the studio floor while he sings. The lyrics evoke a new understanding of the love a mother and her child can have for each other. The love I've longed for and want so much for him to be included in. After four takes, one of his vocals alone, two takes of the piano alone, and one with them together, I cut the feed and know any more is pointless. I go down to the studio floor.

He sings the chorus under his breath as I approach him. I sing with him softly because the chorus has done what every good chorus is supposed to do and made the listener sing along. We sing so softly we can barely hear the other, "Love me again my angel," and my heart aches with the sentiment.

And as I sing, "How do I live without you," he sings "I don't have to live without you," in a lower key. The harmony is beautiful. The music we make together is always so beautiful. I wish I had the strength to make the choices that would allow us both to keep making music together. I am getting stronger though, with every passing day of sobriety.

My bottom lip quivers. "Santiago, it's gorgeous. Most people will misunderstand it and think it's a love song."

"It is a love song."

"The best songs always are," I tell him.

We go to the control room and listen back to the song.

I break down in silent tears as the gravity of my actions

becomes apparent. His loss of the song may be detrimental. Will it trigger a relapse into his addiction?

Or worse?

No, he'll have Sophia to protect him from that. I also argue with myself that he will never lose the song writer's credits, or royalties, or the right to perform the song live. As an artist that's an important distinction, though I know it's a flimsy argument on which to stand. My weakness has chosen for me.

He gets out of his chair and sits on the edge of my seat to wrap his arms around me and comfort my sobs. I shake in them. He lifts me onto his lap and rubs my back, shushing me like a mother. I wonder if he learned it from his mother. Or if I'll soothe our child this same way.

"There's some things I want to tell you. But I can't." I press my head into the crook of his neck.

"What happened between us, Kitty? I can't figure it out and it still hurts."

"I know. But you're in love now so it doesn't matter."

"It shouldn't matter, but it still does."

I lift my head from his shoulder. I'm too tall to stay comfortable in the chair with him. My limbs are already going numb. So, I stand, and he stands too.

I cross my arms to keep from embracing him and say, "Just because love is bigger than the rules we've built around it, doesn't mean you won't get hurt when you break them."

He stares past me, then begins to nod slowly. "You're right," he says, "that's why the rules are there."

I want to tell him that the people that break the rules aren't the only ones to get hurt, but he'll understand that more soon, if he doesn't already, and there's something else I need to say.

"Listen, I want to talk about your sobriety."

"I'm good," he says with a naïve wave of his hand.

"Have you thought about if you're going to abstain from all substances?"

His head jerks back. "No, why would I need to do that?"

"You should consider it."

He crosses his arms and looks annoyed. "I don't have a problem with anything else."

I put my hands on his shoulders and try to look him in the eye. But he won't look at me. "Santiago, I want you to keep in mind that the lifestyle ahead of you will keep testing your resolve. Don't roll your eyes at me. I know you've used the drugs to keep your energy up, and deal with the realities of life that way. When your schedule gets tough, trying to write meaningful songs and perform others will be challenging. With the release of the album and the tour that's already being planned your life as you know it is already behind you. I'm telling you; it's going to take all your power to build new habits."

He exhales heavily and meets my eyes. "What do I do?"

"You need a support system of people you trust."

He nods in agreement.

"And we haven't even talked about the party aspect. The shindig to celebrate the album release next weekend will be your first major test. And then they'll just keep coming. As for the party, trust me, Dirk knows how to put on a proper Hollywood celebration, and he won't let anyone down on account of either of us."

"I'll have Sophia with me. That will help."

CHAPTER 32

SANTIAGO DEANGELO

Because I Love You

"SANTIAGO, THE CHAMPAGNE waitresses are all naked." Sophia points discreetly with one hand, the other squeezing mine as we enter the party. I search the hanger that hosts the spectacle and discover she's right, waitresses serving champagne model artistic illusions of clothing created with body paint and sequins.

I look away to scan the interior of the building. It's Dirk's private hangar at Hollywood Burbank Airport. A large open space I'd guess to be about 10,000 square feet. The ceiling is comprised of exposed metal beams and glass sky lights. The fading sun light of early evening reflects off the polished concrete.

Beautiful people in stunning clothes mill about the space eating, drinking, and dancing to songs from my album being pumped in from monstrous size speakers with excellent sound resolution. It's a trip to hear the songs I recorded powering the party. We spend the first ten minutes or so walking slowly and people watching. The bash is part dance party and part red-carpet-chance-to-be-seen. Most people here look like they're dressed for the Academy Awards. But not all.

First, I snicker to Sophia about two girls on the dance floor; one of Indian descent wrapped in a bright pink and orange silk sarong and head scarf who is approached from behind and grinded on by a black girl with gold and black braids wearing platform heals and a red leather mini dress. They both laugh aloud as they continue to dance in a sexually suggestive way. Meanwhile a couple guys in tight black spandex shirts and designer jeans stand aside egging them on. For the hell of it, I surmise that one of them is Greek and the other Syrian. The Greek has biceps the size of my thighs encircled by tattoos.

Another couple traipse by hand in hand, each with the kind of height, bone structure and aloof expressions that seem permanently prepared to be caught on film. Models. My guess, they met on a Polo Ralph Lauren shoot, since that's how they're both attired. He in a seer sucker suit opened to a naked chest and torso that looks like they've been carved from stone. The girl, whose hand he holds, is as tall as he is, and waif thin with golden brown skin and shiny black hair. She wears a white chiffon dress that doesn't hide her brown nipples.

I take in the rainbow of diversity that is my favorite part of LA. So many skin colors, eye colors, hair colors, fabric colors, and so many different colored ways of being unique in the world.

From behind us I hear a horde of girlish giggles and Sophia and I turn as we are swallowed up in a herd of Playboy bunnies. Some are dressed in iconic bunny outfits and others wear a wide variety of party wear that ranges from tasteful lingerie to evening gowns. They're the first to recognize me and greet me as they run their hands over my shoulders and arms. "Santiago, it's you!" they sing.

I'm grateful for their recognition, silly as that sounds. In the city of angels, you never know if people are just pretending not to notice you or really don't.

"Ladies, looking lovely. This is my girlfriend, Sophia."

"Hi Sophia," they croon. Several tug her away from me and coo over her hair and dress, a knee length cocktail gown in bright fuchsia satin designed by Valentino. She looks at me with big eyes, but her own fascination with the dress I arranged for her to borrow for the party has her willing to play along.

A playmate with glowing blue eyes and matching lace lingerie says to me, "You don't have a beverage. Do you want me to call a waitress over?"

I tense beneath my desire to have more than one drink right now so that I can relax into the good time that everyone but me and Sophia seem to be having.

Upon my hesitation she says, "There's a lot more than alcohol if you don't want to drink."

"Like what?" I say over the music.

"Ecstasy, Molly, pills."

"What kind of pills?" I ask automatically, then bite my tongue.

She laughs in concert with a shrug, "You know, the usual; opiates, Valium, Adderall."

"That stuffs not good for you," I tell her.

She titters. "It makes me happy, and happy is good for me."

Sophia escapes the group of models who then spreads

across the party to entertain each guest they overtake.

Sophia and I join hands and walk towards the center of the hangar. I look back at the girl in blue, and my heart goes out to her.

Should I have said something more to her about the pills?

Should I be using the height of (what may only amount to) my fifteen minutes of fame to say more about the things I've learned? She might listen to me under the circumstances. I stop and take a step her way. Sophia drops my hand and continues the direction she was headed. I can still make the girl in blue out in the crowd. But Sophia says, "Wow, check this out." And I instantly follow her, deciding that I'm just here for their entertainment.

Sophia points out an ice sculpture of a life-size grand piano on a table covered in decadent dishes of food.

"Are you hungry?" I ask Sophia. She shakes her head and clutches my arm. Without drugs or alcohol a few plates of this fare could serve as a pleasant distraction. I watch as partygoers move in and away from the banquet with small dishes of delightful options. I have my eye on chilled lobster, shrimp cocktail, and some unique sushi rolls before Sophia tugs me by the hand from the buffet. I follow her lead. Given the fit of her dress, food might not be a good choice.

To the far right several people wait behind red ropes to enter a second hangar through an adjoining door which the invitation explains holds Dirk's exotic car and airplane collection. And is only open to VIP guests.

Sophia leans in and says, "It's more than I bargained for."

"I know, right?"

A beautiful waitress approaches us with hair the color

of champagne swept over one shoulder and across a painted breast. She carries a tray with splits of Moet and Chandon each fitted with a golden sipping spout.

"Refreshments?" she asks.

Sophia and I made a pact to stay completely sober together and we squeeze each other's hand.

"No thanks. But maybe some water." I tell her, looking between the waitress's green eyes and the champagne to keep them from roving over the intricate artistry of her painted form.

She giggles. "Champagne is water here, silly." She hands me a bottle.

I press it back. "No, really, we need some water."

She looks up at the banner of my face hanging across the opposite wall near the ceiling. It's one of the pictures from the shoot with Dara that made the final cut to serve as album art. It trembles from the bass displacing the air.

"Oh my, it's you?" She smiles.

"Guilty. Can you keep a secret?" I gesture her ear to my mouth, and she leans in. "I'm only drinking water today."

This I realize can mean one of two things; I'm either on some of the drugs the playmate mentioned—which tend to make you thirsty—or I'm completely sober. Her darting eyes tell me she's trying to decide which.

"I'll find you some."

The girl returns with two six-ounce bottles of water with a Holladay Music label. She hands them to me. I offer Sophia one and I gulp mine down in record time as we move through the party.

We stop at an exhibition in our direct path where a brunette, painted like a sexy cowgirl, lassos Jamal Reegan. He allows himself to be pulled in by the painted woman who then pours a shot of Don Julio tequila from a holster belt, the shot glass held where the bullets would be. The artistry is mind blowing. She appears to be wearing brown leather chaps and an intricate rodeo vest exposing wide cleavage, but she's completely naked. Her nipples disguised as buttons on the vest. I rub the back of my neck. *Don Julia* ropes another party goer and I greet Jamal, introducing him to Sophia.

"You want a shot, bro?" he asks.

"Nah, man, not today."

He shakes me by the arms. "You can't sit this one out, man. Whose party you think this is?"

"I'm staying sober today."

Jamal narrows his eyes and strokes the coarse black hair of his chin, "Sober? That's no way to party."

"You're telling me! But I just got clean if you know what I mean." I can't decide if I'm proud or embarrassed to admit this fact to him. I think a little of both.

He slaps my back. "Cool, brother. I got you."

I feel myself relax into his support.

The first of the three songs he produced for the album plays and he bobs to the beat. He sings a lyric and his voice cracks. "And that's why we leave the singing to you, man. But seriously," and he opens his arms to the party, "this can't be easy if you're trying to stay sober."

I loosen the bow tie around my neck. "No shit."

Cindy Myers moseys over and unties the bow tie I was fiddling with. She tosses it over her shoulder and pecks me on the lips.

"Cindy, good to see you."

"You too, babe." She smiles sweetly, and I know she means it. Her breath smells of her recent belt of tequila, maybe a double shot.

"This is Sophia." I pull Sophia towards me. Cindy kisses her on the lips too. Sophia's eyes bulge.

Cindy lavishes Sophia in genuine compliments then turns her attention back to me, unbuttoning the top two buttons of my black, silk tuxedo shirt. "That's better. Nice jacket. Armani?"

I nod and take in her ensemble while I scratch my head. Her hair is out of its dreadlocks and piled in a frizzy pastel rainbow explosion at the top of her head. She wears lavender lace pants, and a floral Versace print top with crystal crusted Louboutin heels, a parody of Harper's Bazaar.

"I didn't take you for a fashion nut." I say over the music she too sings along with.

"When in Rome, right?"

I sweep the room. "Rome's got nothing on this place." I rub the back of my neck where the urge for a shot creeps up my collar. "A little liquid courage could go a long way right now."

Sophia, hanging on my arm says, "Maybe we should go, Santi."

Jamal takes a champagne split from a tray offered by another champagne waitress with matching non-dress. "Can't do that," he says. "It's his party. You've got to grit your teeth, honey, and do you what you signed up for. The album's worth it." He sips his drink. "Hey, you ever get that special song recorded?"

A buzz like I downed the champagne hits me. "I did."

Cindy squeezes my shoulder. "Good for you," she says, followed by, "took you long enough though."

I wince dramatically. "I just needed the right people near me to get it done." At this I pull Sophia in and say, "I couldn't have written it without her."

Sophia blushes and says, "He exaggerates."

Cindy beams. "You're sweet," she tells Sophia. Then to me, "Keep her close, DeAngelo." Whether she means to protect her from the jackals of Los Angeles or to keep me writing songs I'm uncertain. I pay the question no further heed when I notice a group of hired actors dressed in pale blue scrubs holding trays of orange prescription bottles and passing their contents out like candy to partygoers. From their shape and color, I recognize my two favorites, Vicodin and Valium on the tray.

I close my eyes and shake my head.

Sophia sees it too and senses my yearning.

"How long until we can leave?" Sophia asks.

I try to unravel her words from the noise that keeps increasing. Half of it outside of me and the other half inside. *You're an outsider at your own party.*

What is it? What is it that's begging me to dive into this ocean of substance abuse? Boredom?

One handful of pills and you wouldn't be a bored outsider anymore.

So, is boredom the cornerstone of addiction?

No, just a recruiter.

I turn away from the temptation. "Let me find out what I've gotta do before we can go."

I take a few steps and turn square into Kitty.

"There you are," she purrs. "What do you think of our little circus?"

I lean in. "I think I need to sit down."

I breathe and take in Kitty's rose-colored, pleated, silk dress that falls mid-calf. Her breasts, at the scooped neckline are more voluptuous than I recall, and her hair is curled in loose spirals around an unusually soft face. As always, her beauty stops me in my tracks. She kisses me once on each cheek.

"How are you?" she asks.

I shrug.

"It's not fair, I know. We shouldn't have to be tested like this. But we're strong enough now. Right?"

I nod, and let her assurance become my own. "You look great," I tell her.

Sophia touches me lightly on the arm and clears her throat. Kitty looks away from me towards Sophia who sways a little on her heels then locks arms with me and gives me a look that says, *who is she?*

I eye the guy handing out pills six feet away.

Kitty extends her hand. "You must be Sophia?"

Sophia shakes her hand warily.

Kitty says, "He tells me he couldn't have written his song without you."

I tilt my head in agreement. But Sophia looks all the more concerned that this incredibly attractive woman knows anything about it.

Kitty seems to sense this. "I'm Katherine Holladay. But you can call me Kitty."

"Oh, you wrote 'New Kind of High'," Sophia says with deepening concern.

"I wrote it," she says while facing Sophia, then turns her gaze on me, "but we brought it to life together, didn't we?"

My heart pounds in my chest at the thought of Sophia recognizing the affinity Kitty and I were bound with while making music together.

Again, I glance at the tray of prescription pills that's now only a few feet away. What I wouldn't give for a Valium right now.

Kitty steps closer to the waiter in scrubs, taps him on the shoulder, and waves him away.

"Listen, Santiago, there's going to be a big announcement soon." Kitty grasps Sophia's hand and pulls her in close. "This gown is gorgeous on you, Sophia."

I watch Sophia's expression change as she decides to let her grievance go for the moment and begins to talk style with Kitty who points out other partygoers and either admires or slams their fashion choices. Sophia goes along with the game which continues as we walk towards the VIP entrance to the second hangar. There we bypass the line and walk straight through.

Dirk is nestled in a small group of suits near a black Ferrari 458 Speciale with a red and white racing stripe. He rests a hand on the roof of the car. He sees us and waves us over. Kitty pulls Sophia away with her and tells me to greet Dirk. I approach the group of men.

"What do you say, DeAngelo, you wanna take this pony for a ride?" Dirk says.

I tilt my head. "You serious?"

"Why not? What do you say if we set up a little obstacle course, maybe some cones in an 'S' shape out on the runway? I'll drive the 458 and you pick any other car here."

I scan the group of exotic cars, a brand-new orange Lamborghini Diablo, an electric blue Bugatti, an older red Ferrari that looks a hell of a lot like the one from Magnum PI and probably is.

"You mean like a race?" I ask him as I decide on the red Ferrari. It's the only one that would have a manual transmission.

"Of course, I mean a race, DeAngelo. You game?"

I scoff and step back. "I don't want to beat a guy in

front of all his friends."

He moves in closer and whispers, "You mean like you did with my wife?"

My mouth goes dry. "Excuse me?"

He clutches my upper arm. "It's just business, right? I mean the kind of music you and Kitty made together doesn't come out of nowhere, right?"

I straighten my spine and hear eight or nine cracks. "I'm not sure what you mean . . . Sir."

"Let's move on to the real show then, shall we?" Dirk says. I follow along with Sophia and Kitty, who have rejoined us.

What were they talking about?

The real show is a Bonanza G-36 airplane. I feel like a kid on Christmas morning. I've missed my plane since I've sold it. Even if I would have been too busy to have flown it since then.

The plane is brand-new. Dirk opens the pilot's door and gestures for me to climb in. He offers the co-pilot's seat to Sophia. She joins me. I thrill as I glide my fingers over the state-of-the-art controls and the leather lined yoke inside the cockpit.

"Can you really fly one like this?" Sophia's voice is cold.

"I trained on one, but I never thought . . ."

From the open door, Dirk stands beside the plane. "You wanna fly her?"

I bite my cheeks to hide a smile. "Yeah, that'd be cool. So, what's the deal?"

"I'll tell you when I tell them," Dirk says.

We exit the plane and Dirk points towards a raised stage erected at the head of the room. We both climb the steps up onto the platform and Dirk takes a microphone in hand.

"Welcome, honored guests. Tony, will you shut the door please."

The entrance to the circus in the other hangar closes, kicking off the private affair I originally imagined.

"I want to thank each one of you for the tremendous effort that this album represents. You've made a piece of art that will really soar. Which is why to launch his debut album, I'm inviting Santiago DeAngelo to pilot this plane from Hollywood to Las Vegas where he'll perform that night when the album is released next Friday."

He pauses for gasps and claps.

"And while the wheels are up the first million people to buy a song will get the entire album for free." Whoops and whistles from the crowd. "We're pushing this hard. To date it will be the biggest marketing campaign the Holladay label has ever launched. We've even got a Russian guy reconfiguring the algorithm at Spotify . . . just kidding. Or am I?" He holds an inverted pinky to his lips, laughs and carries on. "If Sony challenges our marketing, we rise to the challenge." More whoops. "Come on over here, Santiago."

I take in the buoyant applause and recognize a lot of people in the crowd, most of all Vicky in the front row, wearing a baby blue cocktail dress that exposes non-existent cleavage. She smiles and blows me a kiss.

Beyond her are the important people in the music business. I scan their earnest faces, all turned up to me in rapt attention. As is natural in party settings they've assembled into groups. The most elegantly attired are the Holladay Records Execs in black and white evening attire.

I spot Otto amidst the studio techs and studio musicians. He's wearing crisp black jeans and a metallic gold shirt with no tie. His long hair is pulled back. He nods at me and I put out my fist in the gesture of a fist bump.

The group of music lovers he stands with wear colorful clothing as expressive as the music they make. Just like in the studio, they hold nothing back. I recognize a sax player Cindy introduced me to in studio wearing a tux of purple velvet. Then I spot a cellist in a bejeweled gown as grand as her instrument. My smile beams back the elation their preparation for tonight reflects.

I take a moment to recognize the people I connected with while we made this album together. I respect these people. I want to earn their cheers.

I take a second mic in hand. "I can't thank all of you enough for this opportunity. You're the heart and soul of the songs that move the world. I don't know how it's me that ended up on this stage, but I thank you. I had the chance to put an incredibly special song on this album—" The microphone screeches and I flinch from it. The buzz of power to the mic dies in my hand.

"Sorry 'bout that. Technical trouble," "Dirk says into his mic. "So, will you fly this baby to victory?" Dirk hands me his live mic.

"To Vegas!" I pump my fist in the air and gather more applause. I'm pumped by their approval.

I descend the stage and Sophia meets me. "Can we go now?"

I think about the potential grilling Sophia may give me concerning Kitty. About this time getting completely blotto seems like the best bet.

Yet, being with her over this fiasco, still feels like the better choice. "Let's go back to the hotel," I say.

Kitty bars our way. "We're serving a beautiful dinner

in about an hour."

"I made my appearance. Sophia wants to go."

Kitty crosses her arms. "You can't leave before dinner."

"Watch us." I take my cellphone from my pocket and text my driver, Vitali, to pick us up out front.

Vitali pulls up right as we exit the building in a long black stretch Chrysler 300 limousine. He jumps out of the driver seat to open the back door for me and Sophia. We shake hands in the special way we've come up with in the last few months of getting acquainted. "Thanks for getting here so quick," I tell him.

"I got you, Boss," he says with a charming Ukrainian accent.

That accent lets him say just about anything. I love this guy. Vitali is in his mid-thirties. Thin and tall. We're taking 6'5". He has short blonde hair and striking blue eyes that look right at you when he talks. Even if that's through the rear-view mirror. And he's not big on small talk. In the car, together for hours at a time in LA traffic, I found him to be quite the philosopher. The other thing he's big on is giving me a hard time. Sometimes I worry we've gotten too familiar with each other. For example, him calling me Boss is more a playful jest then it is a term of rank. In turn I call him V.

In the car, I ramble on about the party to Vitali through the rolled down partition between the front of the car and the back. I turn the air on full blast.

"It's cold," Sophia says.

I drape my tuxedo jacket over her, and she hugs it on. "Vitali, could you roll the partition up?" she says.

"No, leave it down. I need to see the road ahead to keep my bearings."

She turns a quarter turn to me. "Your bearings?"

"The party, the pills, the plane, the album coming out next week—"

"Kitty." Sophia interrupts my ramble. "Why didn't you ever tell me about Kitty?"

My stomach goes hard. I roll up the partition and start with a stutter. "I-I did. I told you I'd signed a contract for a single with her."

"But you never mentioned her again. She's a knock-out. The kind of woman you totally mention unless there's something you're trying to hide."

My head races through my memories of Kitty at the party. Sophia had to have felt the familiarity between us.

"Did you sleep with her?" Sophia asks me point blank.

"You want to know everyone I've slept with? Cuz if that's the case this is not gonna work out between us."

"Not everyone. Just her. There's something about the way she looks at you."

"She's my boss' wife."

"And the way she said, 'we brought it to life together'." Sophia shudders.

"Look, the only reason I ever signed up for any of this was for the help I thought I'd get writing the one song no one else cared about but you and Lucy."

"You expected Kitty to help you write it. I remember your sister saying that."

"But she didn't help me, did she?"

"But she . . . loves you, I could feel it."

I close my eyes, relieved by even this proof of Kitty's love for me. It bothers me that I still want that. But what I want from Sophia is so much more than the mirage Kitty ever was under the circumstances. Sophia is an oasis in the desert of my life, and I am so fucking thirsty.

She crawls forward on the floor of the long interior of the limo away from me. I un-belt and join her on the carpet beside the bar. She has her back to me, and I place a hand on her stiff shoulder.

"Sophia, I'm with you."

She rolls her shoulder back to shrug my hand off.

"Please turn around," I say.

"I want to go home."

"Please don't leave me now. I need you more than ever."

She turns, and we sit cross legged between the bar and the long bench seat on the carpet of the limo, our knees touch, and I take her hands.

"But am I enough for you?" she asks.

"Yes."

"Even with all of that craziness at the party. You wouldn't have rather been a part of all that?"

"I couldn't wait to leave all of that to be alone with you."

She shakes our joined hands. "Why?"

"Because I love you, Sophia," I tell her for the first time.

Her face contorts with emotion. "You do?" She climbs onto my lap and presses our foreheads together. A tear runs off the end of her nose onto mine. "Did you sleep with Kitty?"

I lick her tear as it slides onto my lip and consider telling her the truth, but it just feels cruel and unnecessary. "No," I tell her.

She rests her forehead on my shoulder and exhales. "I love you too," she says.

CHAPTER 33

SANTIAGO DEANGELO

Namaste

WE BRING THE words, I love you, to life in the marathon of physical love we conduct in our hotel suite that Saturday night and all-day Sunday.

"I don't want you to leave," I tell her as I approach her from behind while she stands at the foot of the bed and packs her weekend bag Sunday evening. Outside the large windows of our hotel suite our view of the sunset is a blaze of orange and pink. I wrap my arms around her and fondle her soft breasts through her lacy bra.

She giggles, turns in my embrace, and kisses me. I grow hard and nuzzle up against her.

"You have to stop," she says between kisses. "You know I have school in the morning."

I unhook her bra, and she removes it herself, followed by my sweatpants. Lying in bed beneath me she says, "Tell me again how much you love me."

"I'll show you," I tell her as I enter her.

Long after the twilight fades, she rises from the bed and says, "I really have to go now."

I concede, texting Vitali that it's time to take Sophia home to Redlands as planned.

I carry her bag out to the waiting Mercedes parked in front of the hotel. (We only take the limo to big events.) Vitali steps forward and takes the bag. "I got that, Boss." He takes Sophia's bag and puts it in the trunk.

"Get her home safe, V."

"What, you think I wouldn't, Boss? She's in good hands with me." He bounces his brows in lascivious jest.

I put my fists up to spar with him playfully. We exchange a few sportive hits and blocks until he purposely leaves himself open and I glance a light blow off his chin. He pretends at pain, stumbling back a few steps and rubbing his chin as he opens the door for Sophia to climb in. "Every time, Boss. You get me every time," he jokes. The comedy of which is multiplied by his accent.

"You guys are too much," Sophia says as she settles herself in the backseat.

I lean into the car and kiss her goodbye one last time. "I'll see you Thursday night. I love you."

"I love you, too. Now go," she says while palming my forehead and pressing me back with a smile so wide I could live inside it forever. Meanwhile, Vitali closes the car door against me. "Oh, sorry, Boss, I had no idea you were still there."

MONDAY MORNING, I jump out of bed the moment light breaks through the open curtains. Today I meet the studio musicians who will vie to form the band I'll be performing with onstage in Vegas. The expectation is a far better high than the Vicodin ever was.

I arrive at 7:28 a.m. at the rehearsal studio near the corner of Hollywood and Vine. There's a line of nine musicians waiting out front when Vitali pulls alongside the curb. These nine were whittled down from a much larger group by a Holladay Records exec last week. I start to open the door on my own, but he says, "No, Boss, let me. You are needing to make right impression."

My fingers, moist with anticipation, slide off the door handle. But as Vitali steps out the driver door of our Mercedes S class sedan, I open my own door and step onto the sidewalk a few feet in front of the line of musicians which have lined up near the studio's double glass doors. The morning sun is behind me and the few that don't wear sunglasses squint at me with their hands over their eyes and straighten their posture. At the back of the pack, a girl—the only girl on the sidewalk— catches my attention with bright purple hair parted down the middle and falling down her back. She wears a studded black leather jacket, black leather pants, and purple Doc Martens that match her hair. She has a guitar case slung over her back. Her oversized black sunglasses make it difficult to see her face. I shake my head ever so slightly wondering what all that is about. Everyone else is dressed down in jeans and shirts, clothing they can be comfortable in in-case the audition lasts longer than expected. Another guitarist with his guitar case on his back catches my eye when he announces to the others that it's me that's arrived. He's a good looking middle eastern guy, with a tight fade and clean-shaven face. I notice right away that the other artists, who'd been busy talking amongst themselves take note when he speaks. "Good morning," he says to me. "I'm Enod. He pats his guitar case, I play bass."

I shake his hand. He is at the front of the line, closest to the doors.

"Good morning, good to meet you, Enod. I look forward to hearing you play today."

From inside the door, a key is turned, and the doors open right at 7:30 a.m. I hold the door for the artists, and they file past me with individual greetings. I sense their nerves. They want this job. Most of them simply say good morning, tell me their names, and the instrument they play after the fashion that Enod introduced. Second to last is a middle-aged Mexican man about 5' 10" with a body that was clearly once made of solid muscle but is now padded with fat. He's got a well-groomed goatee with a little grey in it and wears a Minnesota Vikings t-shirt. He says, "Yo boy, you ready to make some music together?" and puts his fist up so we can bump knuckles as he passes. I chuckle to myself at the joy of that brief link.

The rocker chick tilts her glasses down revealing eyes that slant with Asian influence and a pretty spattering of freckles across the bridge of her nose. She doesn't say anything.

When we're all inside, techs from the studio introduce themselves and show us the raised stage we'll be rehearsing on. The guy in the Vikings shirt hustles up the steps of the platform and looks over the drum kit, nodding his head in satisfaction.

Employees from the facility, led by the label exec who selected this group of nine, do a roll call and let everyone know they'll be auditioning in that order. We get started. The first musician up is a lead guitarist who is asked to play a guitar arrangement that is from one of the songs on the album. He's dark haired and serious, with heavy black brows that shadow his eyes. Albeit solemn, he gives a technically perfect performance.

A second lead guitarist takes the stage as the other descends the steps. He tells his fellow musician, "That was beautiful. Good job man," as he passes. Unlike the first guy, he introduces himself on stage to us all.

"Good morning, I'm Ian." He pushes his straight golden blonde hair back over his tanned face, tunes his guitar, and says, "It's good to be here," like he was addressing a stadium full of fans. He's told to play the same piece, and he too pulls off an impeccable rendition. When the studio tech yells cut, Ian ends the piece but keeps strumming the guitar with a new tune.

"This is something I'm writing," he says, his eyes cast down on the neck of the guitar. The guy in charge says, "Not now."

But I say, "I want to hear it." Ian looks up and our eyes meet. They're grey, and they're eager. He has a little grin that spreads as he sings a lyric to the melody. Without a mic I can't hear the words over the guitar.

There's a murmur from the contenders, and Ian finishes up in less than ten seconds. I give him a nod, and he nods back before leaving the stage. I pay attention to his rival, the third guy in line for lead guitarist. But my mind is already made up. I want Ian in the band. I look over at the guy from Holladay Records and tilt my head subtly at Ian. He nods in the affirmative and approaches the trio of candidates to quietly announce the winner. The other two shake his hand and depart with dignity.

Next, we hear from the three drummers. The drummer is the backbone of the group because he'll maintain the beat the band will depend on to keep a song together. The three artists drum beats so tight I ask to hear all three of them again in a selection of their own choosing. When the guy in the Vikings t-shirt, whose name is Paul Castro, takes the drums back on he points the sticks at me and says, "You ready for this?" Then he goes to town with the freshest jazz drum solo I've ever heard.

"I wasn't expecting that," I tell him.

"I'll never stop surprising you," he says.

He's my guy, and as I look over at the label exec, he gives me a nod that tells me he trusts me to make these decisions on my own. I announce Paul as the official drummer. I can't help but think I knew it the moment we bumped knuckles out front, and I felt our energy connect.

Then we move on to bass guitar. I need someone who's rhythm is second nature and can define each chord played by the rest of the band. The first guy up looks like he's in his forties with sleek, brown, wavy hair that rests just above his shoulders, and eyes so blue I can tell they're still breaking hearts. As is his musical style. I like it. When he's auditioned, I ask if we can hear him alongside Paul on the drums, to see how they vibe together. Their connection will link the main beat.

It's a rough start and I give them a second chance, but the kinship isn't there. I ask Paul to stay seated for the next in line.

Enod takes the stage. I've been eager to hear him play. I liked his vibe from the moment we shook hands. And he was a leader that the others looked to. He rocks the house with a royal blue guitar with custom painted orange flames.

My heart beats faster. I think I've got my guy. I cue Paul. As they play together, I worry they're both trying to outdo the other. But maybe they just need time to fall in sync.

Enod's musical style fits the ensemble I've imagined.

Rocker chick is next. As she ascends the stage, she removes her leather jacket exposing long lean arms that even a ballerina would be envious of. She tosses it carelessly aside and does the same with the purple wig, revealing dark black, glossy hair in a short bob that frames her delicate face. The glasses are also gone. On her own, she cues the drummer with a tilt of her chin. They seem to communicate telepathically, playing first the piece they all auditioned with, followed by a second, which Paul begins with an improvised intro that leads into one of my favorites on my album. A song written by Jamal Reegan that we'll be performing in Vegas.

After about a minute, I slide my hand across my throat and they both cut the music short. Rocker chick looks straight at me with a no-nonsense gaze. I'm thinking about calling Enod back on stage to see if he can muster a connection to the drummer like she has, but her eyes are so engaging and locked into mine, and the way that Paul looks at her with intense respect has my mind made up.

"What's your name?" I ask her. She didn't tell me out front.

"Mimi," she says.

"Mimi, you're in," I tell her.

She puts her hands in prayer position and bows her head ever so slightly. "Namaste," she says.

I return the gesture. She's gonna be good for all of us. I can feel it.

With the selections complete we take an hour break off site. Everyone goes their own way.

When we return, it's just the four of us on stage, and we spend a few hours practicing the three songs, we'll be performing at the Vegas concert. As we play together, there's no doubt I made the right selections.

When we're wrapping up, Ian once again plays the tune he'd broached at the audition.

"What were the words you sang? I couldn't hear them before," I say.

He blushes and shrugs "I only have the one line."

"Sing it for me," I say.

"I don't sing like you, dude."

Mimi says, "Who does? Just sing it."

Ian sings, "Baby we got all day, let's just play."

"That's the hook in the chorus," I tell him.

"You think so?" Ian looks up, smiling guardedly.

"Totally!"

Meanwhile, Paul, still seated at the drums, taps out a crescendo leading to the line which I sing aloud, "Baby we got all day, let's just play," while Ian strums it on his guitar.

Ian laughs with confidence. "Yeah, man."

"Again," I say.

This time, when the drums sound, Mimi plays chords on the bass guitar that give the vamp dimension. I sing the line again.

An energy overtakes the four of us and we all know we could make an entire song out of this together if we wanted to.

We take the attitude of the lyric to heart and spend another couple of hours just jamming, sometimes playing the songs we're preparing for Vegas and sometimes working back to the new song. There's a keyboard on stage and I put it to good use in the process. As we wind down, I play "Bird of Paradise" for them and tell them it's the one song I wrote for the album. They offer sincere praise.

Afterwards, we are all hungry. Mimi asks an employee at the facility to order take out Thai food and when it arrives, we sit and eat together.

"Have you written any other songs?" I ask Ian while slurping yellow curry that's hotter than I expected it to be, both temperature and spice wise.

"Dude, I've written a whole notebook full, but they're all for my wife, and she'd be the first to tell you they're sweet enough to give you a cavity. Not exactly landmark stuff."

"Is your wife going to be okay with you leaving for a big US tour later this summer?" I ask him.

They all look up from their take-out. Chop sticks held aloft.

Mimi says, "I thought this gig was just the Vegas show."

"I have to tour with someone, right?" Vicky has been telling me the tour will be announced soon, so long as the album release goes as planned.

They all nod with controlled enthusiasm.

"So would your wife be okay with that?" I ask Ian again.

"She's a musician so she totally knows the drill."

"What does she play?"

"The cello in the Los Angeles Symphony, but she's sitting this season out because we're expecting a baby in a few months."

Paul raises a Voss water bottle, "Congrats, man."

We all raise our bottles and join the chorus.

"Thanks, actually I wrote that lyric for the baby," Ian tells us.

Mimi crinkles her nose. "I thought the lyric sounded sexual. I'm not so sure about it being for, like, a real baby."

"That's only because you haven't heard the rest of the lyrics," I tell her. "Trust me, it could work."

Paul says, "Dude, kids are the best. They drive you absolutely fucking nuts, trust me, I've got three, but by the end of the day, they make everything worth it."

"I bet," I say to no one as I space out thinking of how my mother adored me, even when I tested her to the fullest. I take another bite and fall further into the daydream of a child that's been with me ever since Kitty sent those texts. What kind of a parent would I even be? I only hope I'd have the capacity for love that my own mother had. But would having a kid, someday, make me feel closer to Mom? Or miss her even more?

Closer, I decide.

"You think you'll ever want kids?" Ian asks me.

The question pulls me out of myself. "Yeah, I think so . . . Is that crazy?"

Paul says, "Yeah bro, it is. You're way too young for that shit, clown. And we've still got a lot of music to make together first."

"For sure," I say.

We all raise our water bottles again.

TUESDAY, WEDNESDAY, AND Thursday race by in a flash. I start each day at the airport familiarizing myself with the plane, and the flight schedule, then meet with the band for a three to four-hour practice session followed by a few interviews each day in which I can't say enough about the band or the upcoming concert I'll fly to. Thursday night, Sophia returns to the Hollywood hotel to fly with me Friday morning to Vegas.

CHAPTER 34

SANTIAGO DEANGELO

Savor It

FRIDAY MORNING, 5:30 A.M. I'm lying beside Sophia, our hands touching when the alarm on my phone sounds. I roll towards her, kiss her neck sleepily, then turn to the nightstand behind me to silence the wake-up call.

"Is it time already?" she yawns.

"It's time," I tell her, then walk to the bathroom while she stretches lazily in the coming dawn light.

I brush my teeth in the hotel suite's bathroom and drop my yellow toothbrush in the glass beside her lavender one.

She hugs me from behind, wearing only my t-shirt.

"I'm nervous for the flight," she says.

I turn inside her embrace. "Were you afraid when we flew to Catalina?" I hop up onto the speckled granite counter beside the sink.

She bites her thumb nail and nods her head. "Flying

doesn't scare you, even a little bit?"

"Sure, it does. But I figured out that, unlike other things I was afraid of, flying was a fear I could manage by increasing my skill. Then it became a thrill I managed."

She knits her brows.

"It gave me a sense of control, when everything else in my life felt out of control."

Her worry deepens. I take her hands. She says, "It's just that . . ."

"What?"

"You said—the day we flew to Catalina—that flying was a way to see how destructive you really were."

I chuckle to ease her fear and hide my thought from her perception.

I'm always afraid of what I might do.

I kiss her knuckles. "With you in my life there's nothing to make me destructive."

"What if it isn't always this good?"

I hop down and lift her chin with my finger. "Why wouldn't it be?" But I can think of countless reasons. Kitty is at the top of the list, followed by the lifestyle my immediate future promises, and the fledgling sobriety I have yet to put to the test.

AS PLANNED, I drive us to the airport in a company car, Vitali having already left for Vegas to meet me when I land. We enter the Hollywood Burbank airport and make our way to Dirk's hangar. I see the Bonanza shining in the morning light, like the continued promise of my good life. Fifty feet away Dirk slams the door to a Cadillac limousine. He motions where to park a few hundred feet further down. Afterwards, I approach the airplane with Sophia's hand in mine. I'm glad we're both comfortable in jeans.

Dirk waits at the pilot-side door to the aircraft. "Santiago, you ready to make Holladay Music history?"

"I just need to perform my usual pre-flight."

He palms my chest. "You're a star now, you don't do pre-flight. That's what the hired help is for. I got a clean bill of health right here." He slaps a clipboard with a schematic of the G36 and the craft's logo in the upper right corner. There are a series of official looking check marks in a neat column down the page.

"I always do pre-flight," I tell him.

The limousine's door open and closes. Kitty advances wearing a long brown-leather trench-coat belted at the waist with wide peach silk slacks that sway with her movements. She stops at Dirk's side, takes his hand, and says good morning to both Sophia and I in an aloof manner.

Dirk checks his submariner Rolex. "Let's get a move on, we've got to stay in sync with the album release. You two, get in the cock pit."

I settle into the pilot's seat. When I put on the headphones, I hear the tower check in. I answer, and they remind me of our scheduled take off in nine minutes on runway 16 B. Through the windshield, I watch Dirk and Kitty climb back into their limousine.

Sophia straps in and puts on her headphones. Her voice reaches me above the static. "Didn't you say once, pre-flight determines everything?"

"Yeah, but he had professionals take care of that already."

"But doesn't it calm your nerves?"

The tower reminds me of the countdown to take off. I

yell, "Clear," look left and right and start the engine. "It's fine Sophia, I got this. I know the flight plan by heart and Dirk had the pre-flight handled ahead of time. I've arrived, that's all."

She bites her thumb nail. "Okay."

I taxi into the compass rose painted on the asphalt to calibrate the compass of my aircraft. I point the nose of the plane North in line with the diagram to set my compass due north.

"Are you going to taxi us to the runway?" I ask.

She shakes her head so hard I get a sense of her nerves and check in with my own. I need to follow my standard routine, the same routine I've followed the last three days before each day's practice flight.

Dirk's limo pulls away, and I turn off the engines. Sophia and I both exit the plane. I walk to the tip of the left wing and run my fingers along its leading edge, followed by the other wing and the tail. The routine of it soothes me.

Sophia stays by my side as I go through the procedure. My cell phone chimes from my Levi's pocket. I ignore it and flip-up the engine cowling to inspect it. Sophia remains by my side. I examine the engine, small and efficient, clean, and new. I run a hand over the fuel lines as I talk myself through the process.

My phone chimes again two times in a row. I reach for it from my pocket, it's an all-caps text from Dirk ordering me to get back on schedule. I slip it back in my pocket and return to my mundane inspection of the engine, feeling pleasantly defiant.

My cell phone rings, and I swipe ignore to a call from Dirk. Seconds later it rings again, this time with Kitty's number. I roll my eyes and hand the phone to Sophia. "Tell them I need three more minutes."

Sophia answers and delivers the brief message while I return to the engine, marveling at the beauty of it.

When I've completed the process, I find Sophia entranced by my phone, a look of increasing alarm overtaking her face. My gut goes cold.

"What is this?" she says, turning the phone towards me to reveal my text messages with Kitty. Messages I couldn't bring myself to erase, and Sophia couldn't help herself but check with the unlocked phone in her hand.

She holds the phone up, just inches from my face. I push it back to a readable distance.

The messages about Kitty leaving her husband and us having a baby together are on the screen.

She hits me with a closed fist on the shoulder.

"You lied to me," Sophia shrieks. "You were in love with her! You wanted to have a baby with her!"

I don't know what to say, where to start, how to make things right. Behind her I see Dirk's limo racing towards us.

"Say something!" Sophia says.

"I-I didn't mean to fall in love with her." Immediately, I regret the words. But what else could I say?

"You didn't mean to?" She shakes her head in disdain, and my regret deepens.

"Sophia, I didn't want to hurt you with the truth of what happened between her and I. It's complicated. I'll tell you all about it on the way."

"I'm not going with you," she says and turns on her heel walking first then skipping into a run towards the faraway exit to the airport. I want to run after her but the limo screeches to a halt a few a few feet away from me. Dirk bolts out of the car. "Get the goddamn plane in the air, DeAngelo."

The central processing unit of my brain shuts down

like a PC with too many programs running at once. I can't think. I can't move. I look over the roof of the car at Sophia getting smaller in the distance.

Again, Dirk orders me back into the plane. "We've got a marketing promotion in play." His face is beat red.

Pain rewires my circuits. *I'm back. You didn't think you could stay happy, did you?*

In a daze I climb back in the cockpit while Dirk moves a safe distance from the craft.

I restart the engines and taxi out to the runway at an unsafe speed bypassing another plane and breaking several rules of the airport. The tower comments but I take off the headphones and toss them on the empty co-pilots seat. I turn onto the runway and bring the plane to speed. I feel the familiar thrill as the dihedral of the wing sucks me into the sky. Everything grows small beneath me, the ground, the airport, the freeways, and then, my purpose, my future, my hope.

By rote I climb to my assigned altitude of 16,000 feet at 500 feet per minute while the weight of my loss settles like a rock in the pit of my stomach.

Just think one good thought, I tell myself, employing a tactic Lucy recently taught me. The one good thought is that, as I took off, the album was released, and I've still got a good signal on my phone. I type my name into Amazon music and the album pops up with a total of 14,688 sold. I scan the list of well-known songs for "Bird of Paradise". I'm anxious to hear the musical arrangement. But the song isn't there.

I return my focus to piloting the plane, checking all the equipment to ensure I'm still on course, then type the name "Bird of Paradise" into the music app.

The song comes up on the roster of an album of a

country music artist I've never heard of before. Her name is Johanna Sotheby. The album art depicts a bleach blonde with cut-off jean short shorts and hot-pink cowgirl boots. I feel sick, click on the song, and listen as my nausea increases ten-fold by the sound of steel guitars accompanying *my* lyrics. When I check the songwriters credits my name is there.

I squeeze my head and claw my scalp. From the right peripheral I see a small drone flying alongside to video my flight as part of the marketing promotion. The entire flight will be tracked on Holladay's website alongside the number of album sales. I flip it the bird as I reach my cruising altitude and level off. The Garmin display shifts from an all-blue screen of sky as I become level with the horizon. Now the display shows half sky, half earth.

But what if there were only the ground in view? That would give the viewers quite the thrill, wouldn't it? And wasn't that the point of learning to fly?

I tally my losses with more cynicism than I've ever steeped on them before.

Mom, *whose death you caused,*

Dad, *who will never be a part of your success.*

Sophia, *whose heartbreak was etched in her face.*

"I never meant to hurt you," I say aloud as I think back on how Sophia ran from me.

My pain multiplies to the sound of the country version of my song still playing on repeat on my phone, just audible over the hum of the engines.

And now to have lost my song.

I rack my brain to understand. Minutes pass in which I stare out the windshield unaware of my surroundings.

There's only one conclusion: I trusted the wrong person with it.

How could Kitty steal it from me, knowing what it meant?

The blow is too much with the force of the rest behind it.

Pain radiates from my heart out. The kind of pain I'm so used to pushing down with pills that I've got no practice managing it on my own. My vision blurs. I switch the transponder off to cover my tracks with air traffic monitoring.

Then in a moment of reckless frenzy, supported by a year's worth of drug-induced daydreams of ending my pain this exact way, I nose the plane down towards the ground.

The rush of speed has a g-force that nails me to the back of the seat. The yoke rattles beneath my grip, and several instruments sound the alarm. High pitched screams that are no match for my own fear.

The pitch of the engine increases, the air speed indicator, which had hovered at 190 miles per hour before I tipped her down, is pinned to the max indication of 280 mph. We're going much faster than that.

The seat of my pants grows warm as I piss myself.

My altimeter indicates 12,000 feet. The ground is coming fast, and I know something that I didn't know before.

I want to live.

Will I die knowing that?

I use all my willpower to avoid my first impulse to yank back on the yoke. That would rip the wings off this diving bird. I concentrate on the training I received for this scenario.

My mind is clear. Pain and fear cowed by something they've never had to face in me before—the desire to live no matter what.

I pull the throttle back to reduce engine RPM while

decreasing the pitch on the propellers. I'm already at 9,000 feet unconsciously begging God, with a chant of, "Jesus, Jesus," that has more sincerity than a curse. I grip the rudder control and slip the plane left and right through the air to create enough drag to bring speed down to 260 mph. Now I can add another ten degrees to the flaps, bleeding more air speed. The precision this requires sharpens my mind and allows me to continue.

I slip back and forth through the air, until I'm at 240 mph and 7500 feet. The weightlessness in my belly makes me laugh aloud like a maniac.

I might make it.

When the air speed indicator reaches 200 miles per hour, a maneuverable speed, I'm at 6000 feet. 10,000 feet lost in mere moments. I inch back on the yoke, engaging my will over my instinctive need to pull it into my chest. The nose tips up and air catches the planes belly. I nose up slowly, I got this, I got this. I edge the throttle forward and add collective pitch until the prop is biting the air again. We're at 4,000 feet and dropping. But the there's a line of blue on the display that calls me to the task. I manage each detail until we're flying level at 2,500 feet above the ground. I throttle up to full power and vomit stomach acids onto the controls.

The bitter taste of life. I savor it.

CHAPTER 35

SANTIAGO DEANGELO

There Are People You Can Connect With

I SWITCH THE transponder back on and contact the tower. When I explain I've had an unknown engine failure that I've corrected, they recommend returning to the airport. "Negative." I ask them for their assistance returning to my original flight plan and they eventually guide me back.

Each button I press and dial I tune is a reminder that I can't temper the tremble in my hands. The jitter that says, the ideas that define us are a fraud. I didn't doubt my disregard for death until it gaped at me with its enormity. The ground would have swallowed me whole, and death's appetite would not be dented.

Suicide was never an option for me, and I'm reduced to shame at the energy I invested in imagining dying that way. I'd let thinking that I was in control of ending my life give me a sense of power. That almost killed me. How many other people, who'd let their fantasies about suicide kill them, experienced the same desire to live in the final moments of their life?

Life, in its mess of suffering, is the gift. And I'll wade into the mess I've made of mine, one footstep at a time.

The first is into the crowd at McCarran International Airport. With jeans that smell like piss, and the reek of vomit still on my hands, there's no way to hide the visceral response to my fear of death. But who says I'm embarrassed?

I'm alive.

Their curled lips and wrinkled noses reflect disgust. But I roll my shoulders back and pump a victory fist. They fix their faces and slap me on the back. News of the engine failure I reported with the tower spread like wildfire long before I landed. I worry that the video shot by the drone flying alongside me won't support the claim. But no one's thinking that . . . yet.

Vicky meets me at the end of the line with a bottle of ice-cold water. It's ridiculously hot outside. Well over a hundred degrees and the heat rising from the asphalt intensifies the calming effect the heat is having on me. The crowd of Holladay employees disperses quickly to seek airconditioned shelter. Vicky's eyebrows bounce along with her voice. She grabs me by the elbow and leads me under an EZ up, where I take a seat in a folding chair that she opens for me. "You did it, superstar!" She holds her iPad up with a chart of online sales wheels up. "You're a platinum artist in one fell swoop."

I take a sip to rinse my mouth then spit some of the water onto the concrete. "One very fell swoop," I say, then drink some more.

"What happened? I mean, we knew you had trouble in the air. But . . ."

I press my knuckles to my lips with a slight shake of the head. I'm not ready to talk about it and have no idea what I'll say yet. But Vicky wants a response. "I don't know," I tell her. "I'm just glad I made it. I almost didn't."

"Thank God you did," she says with a sincere smile.

"I'm not going on stage tonight. You gotta cancel."

She puts her palm in my face like a stop sign. "That's not gonna happen. You're gonna go to the hotel, get cleaned up, get some rest, and sing three songs on stage like your contract says you will." She tilts her head and smiles.

I swallow a gulp of water. "What time do I go on?"

She checks her phone. "In just over ten hours."

I look past the crowd. "When do Dirk and Kitty arrive?"

Another peek at her phone. "They should make it into town in a few more hours. But they'll go straight to their hotel."

I want to confront them both about my song. "Where are they staying?"

She looks at me funny. "Not at the same hotel as you. Don't worry about them." Vicky puts her hands on both of my shoulders and shakes them while she looks down on me from her standing position. "There's going to be a lot of questions about what happened in flight. It created a massive surge of online attention, which along with the campaign is what skyrocketed sales. We're going to have to come up with a statement soon. Thank God we have this part of the airport secured or we'd be surrounded by reporters already."

When she stops shaking my shoulders they continue to shudder involuntarily and I feel the effects of the adrenaline that shot through me in flight evaporate, leaving me shaky and fatigued. I drop my head and perk my ears to the sound of

Vitali searching for me.

"I don't know what to say, Vicky."

"The truth? Maybe?"

"Did you know my song isn't on the album, that they sold it to be released on another album today?"

"What are you talking about?"

"That's what I want to make a statement about."

"Don't do it! I'll look into it. But you can't make anymore reckless moves. I've already seen some very undesirable magazine covers out on shelves today. Published just in time for the album's release."

"About what?" I ask.

She crosses her arms and taps her fingers against one. "Your drug treatment in Loma Linda. And photos of you buying drugs right after you got outta that program."

"Well fuck." I hang my head as I think back on the rustling hedge when I'd paid Zenon for his trouble and said goodbye for good. I look up. "I swear, that's not how it was."

"They have some pretty compelling pictures."

"There you are, Boss." Vitali says when he finds me under the EZ-up. "What happened in plane?" he asks as he pulls me to standing. My legs feel weak, and sensing this, Vitali, who's a good five inches taller than I am supports my weight as he walks me to the car. "I take you to hotel."

In the back seat it's all I can do to keep my head up. As Vitali buckles me in, he chatters on about how the millions of social media viewers who watched the video of me narrowly escaping my own death are framing me a hero in their posts.

But what will the backlash be when they discover you put the plane in the dive in the first place?

I tense as I recall Vicky's insistence that we make a

statement soon. I'm alive with nerves again. The air conditioning in the car is as cold as the feeling inside me.

Wouldn't it be better to admit my mistake now then struggle beneath the discovery later?

My foot taps the footwell. If I had told Sophia the truth about Kitty in the first place, she might be here with me now.

I test the notion of confronting the truth on V. "Can you keep a secret?"

He's already in the driver's seat. I'm seated on the passenger side in the back seat. Before he starts the car, he looks back at me over his shoulder. "Keep your secrets, Boss."

"You're not even a little curious?"

"Are you kidding, I'm dying to know. But I don't think I want to, not really." He watches my face fall. "I mean unless you are insisting."

I'm starting to change my mind. I think he already has his suspicions and doesn't want them confirmed. "I just . . ."

My phone rings. I pull it out of my pocket, it's Lucy.

"I can't talk to her right now." My voice comes out shrill.

"Give it to me, Boss."

I'm shaking as I hand it over. What did I almost do? What would my death have done to Lucy? Or the rest of my family? I shrink with shame. I can't let them know what happened. Oh God, will Sophia have guessed what happened? She wouldn't have watched the video, would she?

Vitali takes the phone. "I'm turning it off. You are not needing to answer any questions right now."

"Wait! Text my sister first. She'll be worried sick if we don't."

He speaks aloud the words he types, "Can't talk right now. Will call you when I can. Good, Boss?"

"Wait, tell her I love her."

"Got it." He types it, sends it, and powers the phone down.

On the way to the hotel, moving at a snail's pace amidst the traffic on Las Vegas Boulevard, I stare out the window at the decadence people's desire to be entertained has built.

A struggle develops.

Your only job is to entertain them.

But that was why Barbara didn't want fame for me. She understood that it comes with responsibility. A responsibility she wasn't sure I could meet. And Dad is certain I can't.

The immensity of my public battle with death—a death I nearly caused—demands an accountable response.

You have a duty to inform people that illusions of suicide are like mythical sirens luring people to unnecessary deaths.

I squeeze my temples. I don't want to think about this anymore. I just need to sleep. It's not my job to save anyone else. They just want me to play the piano and sing for them.

When we arrive Vitali handles everything then walks me up to the suite in a special elevator to avoid being seen. Before he goes, I ask him for one last favor. "You gotta bring me every magazine that mentions me in a negative way. Tabloid stuff."

"I am not thinking this is not such a good idea, Boss."

"Just do it. I need to decide something. Please?"

TEN HOURS LATER I'm backstage with the band as they pump me up for our warmup to Rihanna's Vegas concert.

They congratulate me on the outrageous number of albums sold. There's no mention of my song not making the collection. If the band knows yet, they're not about to bring down the mood before the show with either that or any questions they may have about what happened in flight.

I put it aside myself as I contemplate this gig. Performance nerves are a welcome sensation. Something I've worked well with since the age of seven. We run through the line-up. We'll open with Kitty's hit single, followed by the very groovy track Jamal Reegan produced, introduce the band before I belt out the Vogl's ballad and welcome the headliner. I roll with the heart palpitations and the urge to pee. *I got this*, is my mantra.

We take the stage, and it all unfolds as planned. The surge of raw emotion from the crowd, after we start in on Kitty's song, sucks the breath from my chest and I sing like a motherfucker to appease them. This *is* my new kind of high, and I relish it. We really hit our stride in the next song. As planned, I announce the band starting with Mimi. She takes center stage with her guitar and wows the crowd. Next, it's Paul on drums. The spotlight finds him, and I watch sweat pour off him and bounce off the drum kit as he makes his moment count. When I introduce Ian on lead guitar, he rips a sweet solo that earns him an expansive applause. When it finally fades, I brace myself for the Vogl's song and cue the band. When I meet the stretch of chorus that challenged me, I hold my breath and blow my own mind with the quality of voice that emerges.

I'm grateful for the effort I put in to make those notes possible.

The lights fade to black, time to set the stage for the one they paid to see.

But when we leave the stage, and are behind the scenes, the production manager wants to send me back out. "We need another fifteen minutes," he says. He's a tall, gaunt man with a serious face that wouldn't joke.

"I don't have anything else prepared."

Behind me the crowd is still cheering. The production manager gestures toward the crowd. "They love you, talk to them, sing them something special."

I rock from one foot to the other. "Roll a piano out on stage."

He snaps his fingers. "You heard the man." Stagehands swing into action.

A spotlight follows me onto the stage alone. Hoots and whistles rise above a wall of applause. A wave of warmth comes up from the crowd. I fall to both knees, and hinge at the waste to pay genuine respect to their adoration, my forehead touches the edge of the stage. Hands reach towards me from the crowd standing at its edge, but there is waist-high fencing a few feet away that keeps them at a distance. Their heads are at stage height. Multiple spotlights create a rainbow bubble that I remain in on my knees in to address the crowd.

"I feel your love, Las Vegas." The crowd rallies on. The stadium looks packed. How many of you follow me on social media?" There's a huge response. "And how many of you love your social media?" The crowd roars. "It really connects you, doesn't it? But there's a gap between what you can know about someone there and what they can tell you in person. In fact, there's two . . ." I pause, feel a tremor of anxiety mixed with the incredible high that only performing can provide, "no, *three* things you don't know about me, that I wanna share tonight, because I feel your love. And there's a very special song I want to play for you after I do."

There's a hearty approval: claps, hoots, and whistles.

I sit up on my knees inside my spotlight bubble. "First thing you don't know about me. I lost my mom to a car accident I survived, a little over a year ago."

There's a sympathetic moan that wells up from the mob.

"Number two, I'm recovering from an addiction to opiate pain killers that overtook me after that accident and her death."

Mumbles of confusion ripple through the audience at a dull roar.

"And number three . . ." again, I hesitate. My lips press together in a tight grimace.

From the quiet audience someone in the front row says, "Tell us," in a conversational tone.

"Number three, the reason the plane nearly crashed on my way here, is that for a split second I didn't think I wanted to live with my losses since that accident. Even with the opportunity to be here with you tonight. And that goes to show you how, when we don't understand things, like death, or suicide, we romanticize them in ways we never should."

The crowd is quiet. A feat of its own.

What have I done?

But it's too late to go back.

I stand and continue. "I was lucky, I had a chance to change my mind. But how many people didn't get the same chance? I've experienced so much pain in the last year. But the greatest pain I face, is that I almost lost my life to the belief that suicide was an empowering option. It's not.

"To everyone out there who's ever considered ending their life, there are people you can connect with to help you change your mind."

The crowd is mostly silent. But there are a few isolated woops that emerge with what feels like support.

I go on. "I want to dedicate this song I wrote for my mother, called 'Bird of Paradise', to everyone who's lost someone they love to suicide."

I turn, and the spotlights lead the way to a white concert-grand Yamaha that wasn't there when I walked out. The reflection off the piano glows pink and red.

I play the intro and choke up, extending the instrumental forward until I can catch my breath and sing the heart-felt lyrics. But even then, I don't make it all the way through, my voice cracks and I stop singing to swallow the lump in my throat. The crowd waits in a loaded silence and I croak out the rest of the lyric to their thunderous endorsement. The rendition that follows is a vocal calamity, but the nakedness of it, has the crowd on their feet. I drop my head and wait for the lights to fade to black.

CHAPTER 36

SANTIAGO DEANGELO

I Can Forgive You

BACKSTAGE, THE BAND greets me with a mixed bag of expressions. Paul looks worried, Ian nods his head with understanding, and Mimi bowls me over with a hug. She says, "That was very bold of you."

I look over her shoulder at Paul. He won't make eye contact with me. Mimi continues to squeeze me tight.

Paul finally meets my eyes.

"Did I just fuck up big time?" I ask him.

"I don't know, bro. I really don't know." He shakes his head slowly.

Mimi releases me. "Fuck em'. They just don't know what it feels like to be awake."

Ian says, "You mean, like, spiritually awake?" He looks at her warily.

"Yeah, Ian, that's exactly what I mean."

"I'm sorry you guys. I don't know what came over me. I wasn't planning to go back out there."

On stage there's an explosion of lights and sound as the headliner makes her appearance. We move away from the action down the hall that leads deeper backstage to the dressing rooms.

"What happened when you were flying?" Ian asks as we walk.

"There's nothing I can say that will justify it, but . . ."

Paul slaps my back. "Just spit it out, clown," He says with a jocular laugh to lighten the mood.

Mimi takes my hand as we walk. "It isn't funny."

We make it to my dressing room and the four of us enter together. Inside, I lay it out to a mixture of Paul's incredulous banter, Mimi's support, and Ian's silence.

"I just hope I didn't screw things up for the tour," I tell them.

"Bro, we'll keep making music together no matter what," Paul says.

"Even if we don't get paid?" I ask him.

"Dude, are you kidding me, we're musicians, the music always comes first. If we get paid it's just a bonus."

Mimi adds, "Well, I think we *will* get to tour, because at the end of the day, people are going to respect what you did out there tonight. So, when we do, I think we should all make a pact to stay sober on the road together."

Ian rushes to agree, "That would make my wife really happy."

"You guys can't be serious," Paul says."

Mimi gives him a killer look.

"Alright, alright. I take the music as it comes. Might even be nice for a change of pace."

"Are you guys for real?" I ask them, looking at their committed faces.

We spend the next half hour talking about what it would actually mean to stay sober on the road. Paul lays in plenty of details on the fun we'll miss. But in every story of drunken, drug-induced debauchery he relates from his years of touring with a wide variety of musical acts, there's a hangover he can't help but recall in association to those memories.

Mimi talks about a meditation and yoga practice that would keep us all focused enough to work on a new album while we tour.

Ian decides he's so stoked to tour that he'll go along with anything.

We all join hands to confirm the pledge.

AFTERWARDS, WHEN THEY'VE gone, I find my phone in the dressing room, switch it back on and text V to pick me up and take me straight back home to Redlands. I need to see Sophia face to face. Lucy too.

By the time we're on the 15 South headed home, it's about 10 p.m. Our ETA to Redlands is a little before 2 a.m. I text both Sophia and my sister that I'm headed home.

I know I shouldn't do it, but I start scouring social media for people's reactions to the events of the day.

I fall down the rabbit hole trilling, *we're all mad here*, as I tumble from post to post.

"Friggin, crybaby. Grow some balls. Even my girlfriend was laughing at you."

"I prayed for you while you fell from the clouds. Knew you'd make it. You rock."

"I thought he sounded great live. He's got an amazing voice. I just wish he'd keep to singing and keep his mouth shut about this other stuff."

"I wish he would of just died!"

"I like the country version. Check it out on this link."

"He's another cheap lip-syncing sensation that the man behind the curtain wants to sell. I'm not buying."

"I just think it's a little over the top that this is how he's selling a ton of albums and you guys are buying."

"I couldn't stop crying when you played your Mom's song on stage. I lost my dad three months ago when he shot himself. But why isn't 'Bird of Paradise' on the album??"

"I can't wait to see him live again."

"Thank you for standing up for suicide victims. They need your voice."

As we drive, I share the posts with Vitali from the front seat.

"Boss, stop. You will be making yourself crazy reading that stuff."

"I've gotta face what I've done. No more sleeping through life."

"But look at you. You're like live wire, Boss. You need to chill out before you tweet something stupid."

"Don't worry I'm not responding to anything right now."

A notification pops up on the screen. It's from Holladay Records announcing a thirty-six show US tour that will kick off in July. Tickets go on sale next week.

I send a group text to the band. Their responses have me lit up. But as we near Redlands city limits my focus narrows on Sophia. I give her a call. After five rings it goes to voice mail. "Thank you for calling me. Please leave a message so I'll know why you called." The sound of her voice makes my heart race. It's late, really late, and I know this is a long shot, but I send her a text.

"I need to see you tonight. I came straight home after the concert. I'm only ten minutes away. Please open the gate for me."

Within a few minutes she texts back. "The gates are locked. You're not welcome here."

I tell Vitali how to get to her place and have him pull up on the side street in the one place you can see the house through the trees from the street. There's a break in the wrought iron fence at the bottom of the hill that I'd noticed months before.

"Go get her, Boss," V says as I take a deep breath before opening the car door.

Once I'm through the fence, I text her. "Meet me at the *Boca Della Verita* I want to tell you the truth."

I climb the steps towards the stone carving. My heart skips a beat when I hear the patio door roll open. But then I hear her dog running full force to the command of, "Get him, girl."

I resist the urge to run back to the car, stand straight and walk towards the charging Doberman. "Come here, Ginger. Come here, girl," I coo. The dog slows, walks towards my outstretched hand, and licks it. I take a selfie of me and the pooch and text it to her with a further entreaty to meet me outside.

She responds. "I don't want to see you tonight. I don't want to see you ever again."

Through the sliding door I see a glint of light shine out at me. She's at the sliding door, her phone in her hand. I run up the steps, Ginger follows and soon outpaces me. Sophia opens the door to let her dog back in and slams it before I make it there. I'm panting when I reach the glass and put both my hands on it.

"Sophia, don't go."

She starts to turn away, but she doesn't. Instead, she holds a copy of Star Magazine to the glass. The page is turned to the photo of me handing Zenon a hundred-dollar bill. "I can't trust anything you ever told me."

"Sophia, I love you. Let me explain everything. Just give me that much. I didn't pay him for the drugs. That was right when I knew I never needed the drugs again."

She cuts me off. "I saw what you did tonight." She's standing right against the glass. Her voice, amplified by her emotions, is easy to hear through the barrier. "I don't know if it was incredibly brave or just incredibly stupid—but I know this—I don't want to live like this." She slams the article against the glass. "Everything you do is going to be manipulated to entertain the masses. And then you go and do a thing like that. I don't want to be in love with someone who would pull a stunt like that in the first place. You were going to kill yourself? For what? Because I broke up with you? How was that supposed to make me feel?"

"I know! I just don't have any practice at processing that much pain at one time. I spent too long believing I didn't have to."

"Well, you can't. Okay? Life is pain. And you're going to have to find a way to live with all of it. I'm not going to ease any of it for your convenience."

"That's why I need someone exactly like you, Sophia." I press both palms against the glass in supplication. "Please open the door."

She shakes her head. "You should be at Kitty's door right now."

"Sophia, what happened between me and Kitty was

never in competition with what we have."

"You told her you wanted to have a child with her—more than one—you said. You told her no woman had ever made you feel the way she did. You told her you wanted to be with her because of the music you could make together. You love her still, admit it!"

"I'm here, aren't I? Please just open the door. If this is goodbye, I don't want it to be through the glass."

She crosses her arms. I put a hand against the glass again. Her expression softens and she reaches for the handle saying, "It *is* goodbye, Santiago."

That's when a high-pressure blast of incredibly cold-water assaults me from the side. I tuck into a ball with my hands over my ears to keep water out of them.

Even then I can here Dara screaming as she holds the hose, "You don't deserve her, you fiend."

I untuck, stand, and turn to her with my arms up. She points the hose away. The high-pressure stream of water shoots out across the lawn. She looks at me and moves the blast back in my direction.

"Okay, I'm going." I take a few steps away then chance a last look at Sophia whose face reflects embarrassed shock.

She opens the door. "Mom, stop! What do you think you're doing?"

"I warned him about hurting you."

"Mom, I don't need you to protect me from him. I can do that myself."

Dara looks hurt.

The light breeze in the night air feels chill against my soaked clothing. I shiver involuntarily. Sophia notices, and though she's annoyed, she says, "Hold on, I'll get you a towel." Then to Dara, "Mom, turn the water off right now!"

Dara turns the handle of the garden hose, and the stream of water loses its force and peters out. All the while she stares at me.

Sophia returns with a big, soft, fluffy, pink towel that I press my face into and smell the rose scent her hair always smells of. I hold the towel tight to my face while I get a hold of myself. Then towel off my hair and soak some of the water off my clothes. Then I wrap it around my shoulders to stay warm.

Sophia comes close and looks up at me. "I will always treasure what happened between us. And it will hurt for a long time that we lost it."

"We don't have to—"

"What? Hurt? Of course we do, Santiago. You don't get to love people the way you loved me, then hurt me like you did and not have to suffer."

"So, you're punishing me then? Please forgive me instead."

She shakes her head and maintains eye contact. "No, I'm not punishing you. I'm just refusing to punish myself."

I shake my head slowly in disbelief as the ache sets in. I don't want to get comfortable with the ache she's insisting I accept. How long will it last? I search Sophia's resigned face and recognize the painful path I'm setting off on. I can hear Cher's voice in my head singing:

"Do you believe in life after love? I can feel something inside me say I really don't think I'm strong enough."

I nod resignedly, and she hugs me, pressing her warm body against my cold wet clothes long enough for her pajamas to be soaked through as well.

"Goodbye," she tells me.

I kiss the top of her head and walk away. Her mother who stood at a fair distance joins her in the doorway. When I'm at the top of the hillside staircase, I look over my shoulder at them both and see Sophia crying in her mother's arms.

I make my way down the hill with an increasing sense of the ache I'll have to live with.

ALL'S QUIET BACK at the bungalow. I count that blessing. No one expected me to leave Vegas so soon.

I text Lucy that I'm home.

She texts back. "I'm coming over."

I write. "Can't it wait 'til morning??"

I don't think I have the energy to manage her response to my idiocy tonight. But it's no use. She's on her way.

Inside the bathroom, I strip down and shower while I recognize the old urge for an opiate high to rescue me from my pain.

I know I'm not in danger of surrendering to it, but the loss of it as an option is just one more thing that adds to the ache.

I dress in sweats and head for the piano, certain it's the only cure for the anguish.

I play "Bird of Paradise" several times through without singing. When I try to sing, my throat tightens, and my face swells with emotion. I rest my elbows on the music holder and surrender to the sobs I've held back all day. My body heaves with their force as the ache is released in their torrent.

That's how Lucy finds me when she opens the front door.

She's equal parts exasperation and solace. I choke out

multiple apologies as she walks me to the bedroom and pushes me onto the bed.

"You'd better be sorry. I can't believe you would do that to me, or Dad—"

"Dad doesn't care if I die," I say through my sobs.

"How dare you say that. You had no right to try and punish him that way."

My sobbing takes on new energy as I consider whether she's right.

Were you trying to punish the people that had hurt you?

"Stop it!" she says with force. "I know what they did with your song, and I know what happened with Sophia, she called me. But you have a duty to stay alive. We can't handle another tragic death in this family."

I catch my breath. She hands me a box of Kleenex and I blow my nose multiple times. When I can talk, I tell her, "I know it was selfish and stupid and outrageously reckless, that's why I said what I said onstage." She looks at me apprehensively. "Look, Luce, I spent a lot of time imagining escaping my pain that way. People have to know better than to breathe life into those kinds of fantasies."

"I think I see what you mean."

"Can you forgive me?" I ask.

Lucy drops down on the bed beside me. "You're alive." She puts her hand on my knee. "Of course, I can forgive you."

"What about the rest of the family?" I chew on my lip and stare straight ahead.

"They're probably as angry as I am. But, trust me, we're all just glad you're alive."

"I don't want this to be a new reason to make peace

with Dad. It wasn't about that."

Lucy rubs her face in frustration. "Okay, I get that. And I'm going to let it go with the faith that tells me I'll always be close to you, and I'll always be close to Dad—so if the moment is ever right, I'll be there to help you both."

"Is it genetic?"

She looks at me funny.

"I mean, did you inherit Mom's supreme love and patience in your DNA, or was it more like a transfer that occurred magically when she died?"

Lucy chokes up then laughs it off and shrugs. "I don't know."

I lie down on my side and curl up in my own bed. She remains sitting on the edge and turns her head to me.

"What are you going to do about your song?" Her voice feels just above a whisper, and I don't know if that's because I'm finally fading hard after the events of the day, or if it's because she wants to broach the subject gingerly, afraid of what I might do.

I prop myself up on my elbow, feeling the stiff exhaustion of my body in the motion. "Ya know, I had this whole plan of revenge all cooked up on the way home from Vegas. I could use all of the power they gave me against them to go on a social media campaign and let fans know what Holladay Records was capable of."

Lucy chews her bottom lip nervously.

"But then, Vicky called me and assured me that they own the rights to anything I record under contract." I stop and breathe. "And to be honest . . ."

"Yeah?"

I collapse back onto my back. "Why would I face off with someone who not only has so much more power, but that

I wronged first?"

Lucy tugs on the twisted sheets I'm lying on and tucks my legs beneath them. "You mean with his wife?"

I close my eyes and nod yes while I silently try on the fear Dirk must have felt to think he might have ever lost her. If she were mine, I'd never want to lose her.

"I guess you'd better learn a thing or two about contracts."

I yawn and nod yes.

"Will you still be able to play the song at every concert?"

Another nod yes, as I feel sleep gaining on me.

"That's good. Will you keep dedicating it to people who've lost loved ones to suicide?"

"I might, or I might just dedicate it to everyone who's lost someone they love. I figure I can even re-record it for my next album if there's enough positive response from the song on tour."

Lucy's voice goes up a notch with excitement. "Maybe you could even have Joanna Sotheby come on stage with you, or you could go on stage with her, like a gesture of good will."

I'm surprised the name Joanna Sotheby, the country artist who released "Bird of Paradise" today on her own album, doesn't upset me more. Perhaps I'm too tired to hold it against her, knowing she never knew it was designed to hurt me.

"Maybe, I kind of like that idea," I tell her.

Her responsive smile nurtures the seed she's planted.

I yawn a final time and surrender to the ache that's waiting within. The ache of heartbreak, exhaustion, and loss.

Lucy pulls the sheets up to my chest, a loving gesture that assures me there will be enough love from the people in my life to face the ache.

CHAPTER 37

SANTIAGO DEANGELO

Angelina Mia

T HE TOUR THAT kicks off in July sends me and the band by bus back to Las Vegas for our first show. The ache remains with me, but I make peace with it while I build the relationships with my bandmates that soften its power.

With intention that takes a continual effort, the four of us create a safe space in which kindness and honesty allow creativity to flow in a manner I never knew was possible. The bond we forge makes us a real band. Because of our commitment to stay sober, we end up using the energy we would have partied with, writing music. Over the ten weeks we tour together through the summer we write more than a dozen worthy songs.

Twice, I join Joanna Sotheby to sing "Bird of Paradise" on stage. Once at her own concert in her hometown of Atlanta Georgia, in which we play the country version. I sit at a hot pink grand piano, while she stands on its lid, with her signature matching boots and we both sing the lyrics in a planned duet that harmonizes the line, "I don't want to live without you", with, "I don't have to live without you."

The second time we perform together is at the final show of my tour at the Los Angeles Staples Center.

We perform it as an encore.

Before she comes on stage, I make the announcement that has become standard by now, "I want to dedicate this song to those we've loved and lost."

When Joanna joins me on stage the crowd roars its approval. Then we perform the song to a new arrangement that me and the band have put together which includes us all. Prior to that, I've played it every show alone at the piano.

Tonight, I don't sing the lyrics for the verse in which the key drops. Instead, I hold the microphone to the audience, and they sing the words to me,

"I know that you are near,

holding my hand, sunshine in my day,

you chase the blues away."

Afterwards, saying my final goodnight adds to the ache while also providing relief. The joy of performing will never fade, but I do need to recover from its demands.

TO THE PROTEST of the band, I insist on regaining my natural energy before we dive into recording the songs we've invested so much of our creative forces on.

When I feel ready, we hire out a studio in Burbank and I move to the area to devote myself to the new project in January.

In the studio, we don't rush. We don't have to.

Vicky, who I hire as my manager, believes we should release the album in early December to maximize holiday sales. We all agree. We also agree to split the royalties of each song equally, no matter who contributed more to any individual song.

Vicky challenges me on this aspect. But the unity of our decision is firm.

"Even for 'Bird of Paradise'?" she asks me.

The song will be re-recorded for the album in the version we created together.

"Even 'Bird of Paradise'," I tell her.

"Okay, fine." But I think you should create a video version that is just you and the piano. I'm thinking black and white, very noir."

"That could work," I tell her. "I'll ask them what they think."

"One more thing," Vicky says. "I've got an offer to do a New Year's Eve concert in Vegas at an intimate little venue inside Planet Hollywood."

"New Year's Eve?" I say.

"I know you said you wouldn't perform that night but playing your song New Year's Eve could be good for you." She registers my discomfort at the plan and frowns. "I'm sorry. We don't have to do it. I shouldn't have brought it up."

"No, I think you're right. Let's do it," I tell her.

I WORRY THAT I might cry when I perform mom's song for the cozy little theater of devoted fans who pay way too much for the honor of celebrating the tainted holiday with me and the new collection of songs that mean so much to me and the band.

Just before midnight, on December 31, I play "Bird of Paradise" on a black Steinway piano on stage alone. As I sing, I allow memories of Mom's death to scroll across my mind without causing me to choke up. Because, as the song says, *I don't have to live without her.*

BACKSTAGE, WELL AFTER midnight, when the performance rush has worn off, fatigue sets in beside the ache I've made peace with. I get up from my seat in my dressing room, ready to retire for the night.

There's a knock on the door. A timid knock, unlike any the band members would bother with. Tonight, they've all gone out together to celebrate New Year's Eve, knowing I have no desire to join them. While they returned to their natural settings regarding drugs and alcohol, I've kept my commitment to sobriety because it still feels like the right choice.

The knock comes again, a little bolder this time. I'm too tired to be curious, and I wonder if I can't just stay quiet until whoever it is goes away.

A voice joins the knock, "Santiago, it's me, Kitty."

My heart thrums like I was back on stage, the one place where the ache can never reach me. I reach for the doorknob and hesitate. Why would she show up here, now?

"Please, let me in," she says. "I really need to talk to you." I stand stock still. "Okay, it can wait until tomorrow," she says with resignation.

I unlock the door and open it. Her surprise lights up her face. "You opened the door."

"I couldn't help myself." I stand barring the entrance with my arm, my hand still on the doorknob and look her over.

She's dressed in holiday evening attire. A long, strapless black velvet gown with a sweetheart neckline. Her hair is up in a twist held in place with a jewel covered comb.

"You going out tonight?" I ask her.

"I was at the show, in the back. I didn't want to distract you."

I can't help but ask her what she thought of the show.

"The new songs are incredible. I bought the album the first day it came out, and I've listened to it countless times since then."

"Oh yeah?" I remain noncommittal, still trying to figure out why she's come. I continue to bar the door, assuming that's all this is about. She wanted to let me know she approved of the music. I can appreciate that. I'm about to say, thanks for stopping by, when she says, "Can I come in?" She looks past me into the dressing room, perhaps to see if anyone is with me.

"I'm not sure yet," I tell her as I feel out the dangers of opening more than just the door of my room to her.

"I get that," she says.

"Why tonight? Why would you come to me tonight?"

"There's so much I want to say, I don't know where to start." She looks down at her hands and fidgets with her ring. My eyes watch her twist it on her finger.

"Just pick a place," I tell her.

"I'm not married anymore," she says. I watch her left-hand fidget with the opal ring on her right.

I fight down an urge to comment sarcastically because I can feel how uncomfortable she is.

"Pick something else."

"There's something I need to tell you that I couldn't tell you while I was still married."

I snigger. I don't mean to laugh at her. I can see from the way her face falls that I've hurt her. "I'm sorry," I tell her. "You've just always had a flare for the dramatic that seems a little silly now."

I move away from the door and invite her in with a sweep of my arm. I sit down on a small grey leather loveseat in the corner of the small space. She turns the makeup chair away from the mirror and sits facing me a few feet away.

As she settles into the seat, we both settle into an outward silence while the multitude of things I'd like to say to her rises amidst the thrill her presence has sparked.

"I love the lyrics to your songs. I could feel you in all of them. And I think it's really great that you and the band share credit for music and lyrics for each one equally."

"None of them would have existed without the energy our collaboration made space for."

"I'm so glad you found that. Together you make things like addiction, and suicide, and heartache feel so intimate that people can step inside your pain with you. But what I love most is how every song leaves you hopeful. That's the theme that unites the album. Each song, in its daring to tell private truths, taps into the universality of all those emotions while leaving a trail the listeners can follow out of their pain."

"Thank you. That means a lot to me coming from you. Do you have a favorite song?"

"Yes," she says with a grin. "I love the one about welcoming a child. The fear, and joy and anxiety of becoming a parent. The understanding that all that matters is the time you get to cherish with them."

I sing, "Baby we've got all day, let's just play."

She laughs happily. "That's a beautiful line."

"Ian wrote it for his son."

"I'm glad you've made such good friends."

"Is that what you came to tell me?"

"No. That's something I need to show you."

"Then show me."

"Tomorrow."

I stand up and walk towards her. "Tonight."

She stands over me. "No."

"Why not?"

"I've only been divorced for three months, and I promised myself an entire year of solitude and independence before I did anything . . ." her voice falls off and she fidgets with her ring again.

"Anything what?"

"Intimate," she says.

The way she says it arouses me entirely.

"You came knocking on my door, Kitty."

"I know. I just forgot the way you always made me feel, and that's not what I came for."

"It's not?"

She exhales held breath. "Will you have breakfast with me tomorrow? There's still so much I want to say in the day light to you before I reveal anymore."

"I don't exactly just go out to breakfast anymore," I say, referencing the shadow side of fame.

"I know. We'll meet in my room. I'll order room service. Come to room 32115 at the Bellagio tomorrow at 10 a.m."

"I'll be there. I'm staying at the Bellagio too."

"Perfect," she says with a twinkle in her eye that tells me it's no coincidence.

IN THE MORNING, it's my turn to knock timidly. She answers the door in a white cotton day dress with short cap sleeves. The stylish dress falls just below the knee with a wide red belt at the waist. Her smile is nervous. She ushers me in.

The room is bright with natural light that reflects bright prisms off the chandelier hanging low over the round black glass dining table sitting on an emerald-green rug. The view is of the Bellagio fountains, bursting with a force much like the curiosity I've arrived with.

There are two covered trays of food at the table, but I don't feel like I could eat a bite.

She sits down and pushes them both to the side.

"I want you to know that I'm sorry that I was a part of stealing your song."

"You tried to warn me." This is a feeling I've come to after an intense struggle.

"Don't take this moment away from me by letting me off the hook."

I nod.

"When the plane dropped out of the sky, I knew what I'd done. And when you turned it all around with that confession on stage, I knew I couldn't stay married to a person that would have done a thing like that to a person like you." She stops and breathes, and I want to rush into the open space with assurances that I've forgiven them both. If not for their benefit than for my own. Down below, the fountains cease to erupt. I remain quiet as well.

"When I was trying, from my heart, to work things out with my husband, I kept coming back to that feeling. And after months of saying things to each other that I never thought Dirk and I would get the chance to say, we both realized we didn't need to honor our love for each other by staying together anymore." She breathes again and stares out the window at the blue desert sky dotted with clouds stretched thin like taffy in the winter wind.

My eyes remain on her—*God she's beautiful*—while she stares into the blue, then she turns to me with what feels like gathered courage. "Would you like to record another song together?"

I reach out my hands across the table and she takes them. "I would love that," I tell her.

She exhales pent up breath, pulls her hands away and places them over her heart. "Oh, that's wonderful, I've had so many fantasies of the music we could make together again."

I beam at her.

She composes herself once again from the unabandoned happiness our prospective joint musical ventures stirred. "Okay, I'm ready," she says, "follow me."

She pushes her chair back and stands. In equal parts confusion and curiosity, I follow her into the bedroom of the suite. The curtains are drawn to darkness and there is a soft piano lullaby playing beneath the sound of a beating heart dubbed over the music of the recording.

"Lie down on the bed," Kitty tells me. I surrender to the charade and lie down while she walks to the corner and lifts something from what looks like a tall basket in the corner of the dark room. "Close your eyes," she says.

"Kitty, this is all a bit ridiculous, don't you think?"

"I know, but it will be worth it."

I sit up on the bed. "You better tell me what this is all about."

She's holding a bundle in her the nook of her arm. "I want you to meet your daughter, Santiago."

I jump up.

"Lay down," Kitty says with a laugh, recognizing the absurdity of the whole thing but still committed to her design.

"I'm going to lay her on your chest. That's her favorite way to nap and she's still sleeping," she says in a whisper.

My legs get too weak with surprise to stay standing, so I lie back down as Kitty unwinds the bundle from the blanket. My eyes have adjusted to the little bit of light coming through the place where the curtains meet. Just enough light that I can see the child she lays on my chest is the most beautiful child I've ever laid eyes on because she's mine.

She lays her on her stomach with her cheek pressed into the soft cotton of my t-shirt. I put my hands on her back and feel a love I've never known overtake me.

Kitty cracks the draperies a bit but leaves the bronze sheers closed so that the golden light fills the room. Then she crawls onto the bed and sits in the middle of it beaming at us both. "I don't know that we can be a family, but you deserve the chance to be her father."

"How old is she?" I ask.

"She turned one year on November 15."

"What's her name?"

"Angelina Mia, because she's my little Angel."

My eyes prick with tears. "She's so beautiful."

Kitty nods, her eyes as bright as mine with emotion. "I never knew I could love someone the way that I've loved her. It's changed everything I know about love. And I want both of you to experience that with each other."

"Thank you," I say and kiss the dark black curls on my daughter's sweet head. She rouses and opens her eyes. We stare at each other with wonder, and I can't help but notice that her eyes are eyes are just like my mother's. They reach beyond my face and into my heart, where I experience true love for the first time.

Bird of Paradise

Bird of Paradise
I long to feel your touch
Every time I think of you
I'm missing you so much

Bird of Paradise
you flew away too soon
I see you in my dreams
I feel you in my room

(CHORUS)
Come to me
Love me again my angel
Oh-oh
Come to me
Save me again my angel

You were heaven sent
How can I live without you?

You know I can't survive
I don't want to live without you

I hear your voice so sweet
Songs you used to sing

I feel the breeze across my face
It's like you're touching me

I know that you are here
Holding my hand
Sunshine in my day
You chase my fear away

(CHORUS)

Bird of Paradise
I feel you watching me
I hear you call my name
Erase this misery

Bird of Paradise
Time has passed so long
Angel of my soul
Your love is still so strong

(CHORUS)

(Ghost Chorus)
I don't want to live without you
I don't have to live without you
I don't want to live without you
I don't have to live without you

-Words and Music by
Dominic DeBellis
DeBellis Music ASCAP

Acknowledgements

THANK YOU FOR reading The Music We Make.

The creation of this novel is a testament to the love and patience of my family. My husband Dominic, my son Valentino, and my daughter Angelina. I don't refer merely to the patience they offered in allowing me space to write, but in their tolerance of my obsession with all aspects of this story world and the creation of the physical book you are holding in your hands. It is only through infatuation that anything as intense as the writing of a novel is concluded.

Dominic, thank you for your song, "Bird of Paradise". I fell in love with it the first time I heard it. Its notes nurtured this story idea from its inception into being. I am grateful for the artist in you that could create something so sentimental, and beautiful. But even more importantly, I thank you for the life you've given me in which I could even consider following my art towards the completion of this book. Thank you for building this beautiful life with me.

Mom, you were there for me every time I needed to talk a story detail out or read a new draft. That was essential to the process. I especially appreciate every time you confessed that you didn't like something and why. But more than my gratitude for your contribution to this novel, I thank you for the relationship we've had from the moment God brought us together.

Dad, you've been in my corner from day one and nurtured so much faith in me. There's never been a time where you doubted my ability to do something I had my heart set on. Thank you for that. I love our time together and I promise that I've been paying attention to your wisdom. You are a great man, and it is an honor to have grown up under your tutelage. Also, I know our family name, Cline, isn't on the cover, but this is just one of the ways I'm carrying the Cline banner to victory.

Sara, my beautiful sister, thank you for reading so many drafts and for insisting that Kitty not die in the end. Your hope for her led to the proper ending of this story. I adored reading it aloud to you over the phone so you could treat it like an audible recording. I looked forward to each of those calls and they gave me the courage to voice the audiobook myself.

My character Lucy is based on you, and as my editor once said, she's the only truly good person in this wild story.

Matthew, my genius brother, the dynamic of Lucy and Santiago's relationship is built on the dynamics of our brother-sister relationship. Those scenes were my favorite to write.

Rebecca Rubio, you've always been like a sister to me, and I'm eternally grateful for the love and support provided over the years it took to complete this project. Thank you for your final edits. As always, you're a life saver.

Jessica Bingaman, my dear friend, and head cheer leader of this project. I think you read even more drafts than my mother. (It's not a competition, Mom.) Your support has been legendary. Thank you for letting me talk about the characters like they were real people. Because, I mean, they are right?! Thank you for loving them as much as I do. And thank you for assuring me that I could voice the audiobook and coming with me to record. I will cherish those memories forever.

Speaking of the audiobook, I want to thank Josh Goode for his enthusiasm in its creation. Josh, your passion for the project absolutely kicked up my chi force a couple of notches. You did a remarkable job of editing, mixing, and mastering my voice.

To my developmental editor Stuart Horwitz at Book Architecture, thank you for helping me see the characters in new ways and bringing out writing I didn't know I was capable of before we met.

To all my readers past, present, and future. You are the reason I wrote this story. You were always shimmering at the edge of my imagination calling it into this iteration.

With love for all you've added by reading,

-Michelle Rene